Introduction to Pattern Recognition

Introduction to Pattern Recognition
A MATLAB® Approach

Sergios Theodoridis

Aggelos Pikrakis

Konstantinos Koutroumbas

Dionisis Cavouras

AMSTERDAM • BOSTON • HEIDELBERG • LONDON
NEW YORK • OXFORD • PARIS • SAN DIEGO
SAN FRANCISCO • SINGAPORE • SYDNEY • TOKYO
Academic Press is an imprint of Elsevier

Academic Press is an imprint of Elsevier
30 Corporate Drive, Suite 400
Burlington, MA 01803, USA

The Boulevard, Langford Lane
Kidlington, Oxford, OX5 1GB, UK

Library of Congress Cataloging-in-Publication Data

Introduction to pattern recognition : a MATLAB® approach / Sergios Theodoridis ... [et al.].
p. cm.
"Compliment of the book *Pattern recognition*, 4th edition, by S. Theodoridis and K. Koutroumbas, Academic Press, 2009."
Includes bibliographical references and index.
ISBN 978-0-12-374486-9 (alk. paper)
1. Pattern recognition systems. 2. Pattern recognition systems–Mathematics. 3. Numerical analysis.
4. MATLAB.   I. Theodoridis, Sergios, 1951–. II. Theodoridis, Sergios, Pattern recognition.
TK7882.P3I65 2010
006.4–dc22

2010004354

British Library Cataloguing-in-Publication Data

A catalogue record for this book is available from the British Library.

For information on all Academic Press publications
visit our website at *www.elsevierdirect.com*

Working together to grow
libraries in developing countries

www.elsevier.com | www.bookaid.org | www.sabre.org

ELSEVIER   BOOK AID
International   Sabre Foundation

Transferred to Digital Printing 2012

Contents

Preface

The aim of this book is to serve pedagogic goals as a complement of the book *Pattern Recognition*, 4th Edition, by S. Theodoridis and K. Koutroumbas (Academic Press, 2009). It is the offspring of our experience in teaching pattern recognition for a number of years to different audiences such as students with good enough mathematical background, students who are more practice-oriented, professional engineers, and computer scientists attending short training courses. The book unravels along two directions.

The first is to develop a set of MATLAB-based examples so that students will be able to experiment with methods and algorithms met in the various stages of designing a pattern recognition system—that is, classifier design, feature selection and generation, and system evaluation. To this end, we have made an effort to "design" examples that will help the reader grasp the basics behind each method as well as the respective cons and pros. In pattern recognition, there are no magic recipes that dictate which method or technique to use for a specific problem. Very often, old good and simple (in concept) techniques can compete, from an efficiency point of view, with more modern and elaborate techniques. To this end, that is, selecting the most appropriate technique, it is unfortunate that these days more and more people follow the so-called black-box approach: try different techniques, using a related S/W package to play with a set of parameters, even if the real meaning of these parameters is not really understood.

Such an "unscientific" approach, which really prevents thought and creation, also deprives the "user" of the ability to understand, explain, and interpret the obtained results. For this reason, most of the examples in this book use simulated data. Hence, one can experiment with different parameters and study the behavior of the respective method/algorithm. Having control of the data, readers will be able to "study," "investigate," and get familiar with the pros and cons of a technique. One can create data that can push a technique to its "limits"—that is, where it fails. In addition, most of the real-life problems are solved in high-dimensional spaces, where visualization is impossible; yet, visualizing geometry is one of the most powerful and effective pedagogic tools so that a newcomer to the field will be able to "see" how various methods work. The 3-dimensioanal space is one of the most primitive and deep-rooted experiences in the human brain because everyone is acquainted with and has a good feeling about and understanding of it.

The second direction is to provide a summary of the related theory, without mathematics. We have made an effort, as much as possible, to present the theory using arguments based on physical reasoning, as well as point out the role of the various parameters and how they can influence the performance of a method/algorithm. Nevertheless, for a more thorough understanding, the mathematical formulation cannot be bypassed. It is "there" where the real worthy secrets of a method are, where the deep understanding has its undisputable roots and grounds, where science lies. Theory and practice are interrelated—one cannot be developed without the other. This is the reason that we consider this book a complement of the previously published one. We consider it another branch leaning toward the practical side, the other branch being the more theoretical one. Both branches are necessary to form the pattern-recognition tree, which has its roots in the work of hundreds of researchers who have effortlessly contributed, over a number of decades, both in theory and practice.

All the MATLAB functions used throughout this book can be downloaded from the companion website for this book at *www.elsevierdirect.com/9780123744869*. Note that, when running the MATLAB code in the book, the results may slightly vary among different versions of MATLAB. Moreover, we have made an effort to minimize dependencies on MATLAB toolboxes, as much as possible, and have developed our own code.

Also, in spite of the careful proofreading of the book, it is still possible that some typos may have escaped. The authors would appreciate readers notifying them of any that are found, as well as suggestions related to the MATLAB code.

Introduction to Pattern Recognition

Classifiers Based on Bayes Decision Theory

1.1 INTRODUCTION

In this chapter, we discuss techniques inspired by Bayes decision theory. The theoretical developments of the associated algorithms were given in [Theo 09, Chapter 2]. To the newcomer in the field of pattern recognition the chapter's algorithms and exercises are very important for developing a basic understanding and familiarity with some fundamental notions associated with classification. Most of the algorithms are simple in both structure and physical reasoning.

In a classification task, we are given a *pattern* and the task is to classify it into one out of c classes. The number of classes, c, is assumed to be known a priori. Each pattern is represented by a set of feature values, $x(i)$, $i = 1, 2, \ldots, l$, which make up the l-dimensional *feature vector*[1] $x = [x(1), x(2), \ldots, x(l)]^T \in \mathcal{R}^l$. We assume that each pattern is represented *uniquely* by a single feature vector and that it can belong to only one class.

Given $x \in \mathcal{R}^l$ and a set of c classes, ω_i, $i = 1, 2, \ldots, c$, the Bayes theory states that

$$P(\omega_i|x)p(x) = p(x|\omega_i)P(\omega_i) \tag{1.1}$$

where

$$p(x) = \sum_{i=1}^{c} p(x|\omega_i)P(\omega_i)$$

where $P(\omega_i)$ is the a priori probability of class ω_i; $i = 1, 2, \ldots, c$, $P(\omega_i|x)$ is the a posteriori probability of class ω_i given the value of x; $p(x)$ is the probability density function (pdf) of x; and $p(x|\omega_i)$, $i = 1 = 2, \ldots, c$, is the class conditional pdf of x given ω_i (sometimes called the likelihood of ω_i with respect to x).

1.2 BAYES DECISION THEORY

We are given a pattern whose class label is unknown and we let $x \equiv [x(1), x(2), \ldots, x(l)]^T \in \mathcal{R}^l$ be its corresponding feature vector, which results from some measurements. Also, we let the number of possible classes be equal to c, that is, $\omega_1, \ldots, \omega_c$.

---

[1] In contrast to [Theo 09], vector quantities are not boldfaced here in compliance with MATLAB notation.

According to the Bayes decision theory, x is assigned to the class ω_i if

$$P(\omega_i|x) > P(\omega_j|x), \quad \forall j \neq i \tag{1.2}$$

or, taking into account Eq. (1.1) and given that $p(x)$ is positive and the same for all classes, if

$$p(x|\omega_i)P(\omega_i) > p(x|\omega_j)P(\omega_j), \quad \forall j \neq i \tag{1.3}$$

Remark
- The Bayesian classifier is optimal in the sense that it minimizes the probability of error [Theo 09, Chapter 2].

1.3 THE GAUSSIAN PROBABILITY DENSITY FUNCTION

The *Gaussian* pdf [Theo 09, Section 2.4.1] is extensively used in pattern recognition because of its mathematical tractability as well as because of the central limit theorem. The latter states that the pdf of the sum of a number of statistically independent random variables tends to the Gaussian one as the number of summands tends to infinity. In practice, this is approximately true for a large enough number of summands.

The multidimensional Gaussian pdf has the form

$$p(x) = \frac{1}{(2\pi)^{l/2}|S|^{1/2}} \exp\left(-\frac{1}{2}(x-m)^T S^{-1}(x-m)\right) \tag{1.4}$$

where $m = E[x]$ is the mean vector, S is the covariance matrix defined as $S = E[(x-m)(x-m)^T]$, $|S|$ is the determinant of S.

Often we refer to the Gaussian pdf as the *normal* pdf and we use the notation $\mathcal{N}(m,S)$. For the 1-dimensional case, $x \in \mathcal{R}$, the above becomes

$$p(x) = \frac{1}{\sqrt{2\pi}\sigma} \exp\left(-\frac{(x-m)^2}{2\sigma^2}\right) \tag{1.5}$$

where σ^2 is the variance of the random variable x.

Example 1.3.1. Compute the value of a Gaussian pdf, $\mathcal{N}(m,S)$, at $x_1 = [0.2, 1.3]^T$ and $x_2 = [2.2, -1.3]^T$, where

$$m = [0, 1]^T, \quad S = \begin{bmatrix} 1 & 0 \\ 0 & 1 \end{bmatrix}$$

Solution. Use the function *comp_gauss_dens_val* to compute the value of the Gaussian pdf. Specifically, type

```
m=[0 1]'; S=eye(2);
x1=[0.2 1.3]'; x2=[2.2 -1.3]';
pg1=comp_gauss_dens_val(m,S,x1);
pg2=comp_gauss_dens_val(m,S,x2);
```

The resulting values for *pg*1 and *pg*2 are 0:1491 and 0.001, respectively. ■

Example 1.3.2. Consider a 2-class classification task in the 2-dimensional space, where the data in both classes, ω_1, ω_2, are distributed according to the Gaussian distributions $\mathcal{N}(m_1, S_1)$ and $\mathcal{N}(m_2, S_2)$, respectively. Let

$$m_1 = [1, 1]^T, \quad m_2 = [3, 3]^T, \quad S_1 = S_2 = \begin{bmatrix} 1 & 0 \\ 0 & 1 \end{bmatrix}$$

Assuming that $P(\omega_1) = P(\omega_2) = 1/2$, classify $x = [1.8, 1.8]^T$ into ω_1 or ω_2.

Solution. Utilize the function *comp_ gauss_dens_val* by typing

```
P1=0.5;
P2=0.5;
m1=[1 1]'; m2=[3 3]'; S=eye(2); x=[1.8 1.8]';
p1=P1*comp_gauss_dens_val(m1,S,x);
p2=P2*comp_gauss_dens_val(m2,S,x);
```

The resulting values for *p*1 and *p*2 are 0.042 and 0.0189, respectively, and *x* is classified to ω_1 according to the Bayesian classifier. ■

Exercise 1.3.1
Repeat Example 1.3.2 for $P(\omega_1) = 1/6$ and $P(\omega_2) = 5/6$, and for $P(\omega_1) = 5/6$ and $P(\omega_2) = 1/6$. Observe the dependance of the classification result on the a priori probabilities [Theo 09, Section 2.4.2].

Example 1.3.3. Generate $N = 500$ 2-dimensional data points that are distributed according to the Gaussian distribution $\mathcal{N}(m, S)$, with mean $m = [0, 0]^T$ and covariance matrix $S = \begin{bmatrix} \sigma_1^2 & \sigma_{12} \\ \sigma_{12} & \sigma_2^2 \end{bmatrix}$, for the following cases:

$\sigma_1^2 = \sigma_2^2 = 1, \sigma_{12} = 0$

$\sigma_1^2 = \sigma_2^2 = 0.2, \sigma_{12} = 0$

$\sigma_1^2 = \sigma_2^2 = 2, \sigma_{12} = 0$

$$\sigma_1^2 = 0.2, \sigma_2^2 = 2, \sigma_{12} = 0$$

$$\sigma_1^2 = 2, \sigma_2^2 = 0.2, \sigma_{12} = 0$$

$$\sigma_1^2 = \sigma_2^2 = 1, \sigma_{12} = 0.5$$

$$\sigma_1^2 = 0.3, \sigma_2^2 = 2, \sigma_{12} = 0.5$$

$$\sigma_1^2 = 0.3, \sigma_2^2 = 2, \sigma_{12} = -0.5$$

Plot each data set and comment on the shape of the clusters formed by the data points.

Solution. To generate the first data set, use the built-in MATLAB function *mvnrnd* by typing

```
randn('seed',0) %Initialization of the randn function
m=[0 0]';
S=[1 0;0 1];
N=500;
X = mvnrnd(m,S,N)';
```

where X is the matrix that contains the data vectors in its columns.

To ensure reproducibility of the results, the *randn* MATLAB function, which generates random numbers following the Gaussian distribution, with zero mean and unit variance, is initialized to a specific number via the first command (in the previous code *randn* is called by the *mvnrnd* MATLAB function).

To plot the data set, type

```
figure(1), plot(X(1,:),X(2,:),'.');
figure(1), axis equal
figure(1), axis([-7 7 -7 7])
```

Working similarly for the second data set, type

```
m=[0 0]';
S=[0.2 0;0 0.2];
N=500;
X = mvnrnd(m,S,N)';
figure(2), plot(X(1,:),X(2,:),'.');
figure(2), axis equal
figure(2), axis([-7 7 -7 7])
```

The rest of the data sets are obtained similarly. All of them are depicted in Figure 1.1, from which one can observe the following:

- When the two coordinates of x are uncorrelated ($\sigma_{12} = 0$) and their variances are equal, the data vectors form "spherically shaped" clusters (Figure 1.1(a–c)).
- When the two coordinates of x are uncorrelated ($\sigma_{12} = 0$) and their variances are unequal, the data vectors form "ellipsoidally shaped" clusters. The coordinate with the highest variance corresponds to the "major axis" of the ellipsoidally shaped cluster, while the coordinate with the lowest variance corresponds to its "minor axis." In addition, the major and minor axes of the cluster are parallel to the axes (Figure 1.1(d, e)).

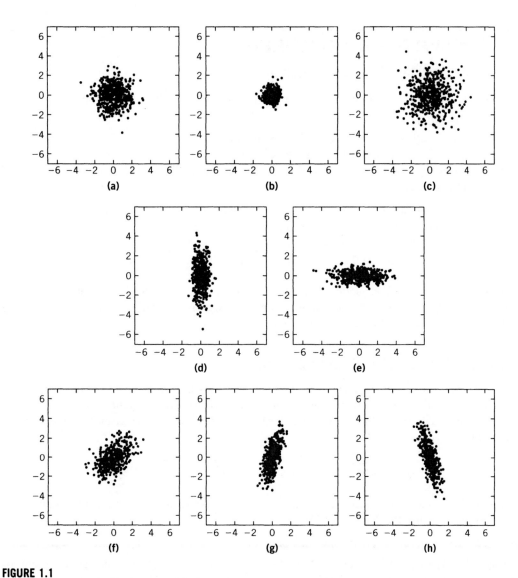

FIGURE 1.1

Eight data sets of Example 1.3.3.

- When the two coordinates of x are correlated ($\sigma_{12} \neq 0$), the major and minor axes of the ellipsoidally shaped cluster are no longer parallel to the axes. The degree of rotation with respect to the axes depends on the value of σ_{12} (Figure 1.1(f–h)). The effect of the value of σ_{12}, whether positive or negative, is demonstrated in Figure 1.1(g, h). Finally, as can be seen by comparing Figure 1.1(a, f), when $\sigma_{12} \neq 0$, the data form ellipsoidally shaped clusters despite the fact that the variances of each coordinate are the same.

1.4 MINIMUM DISTANCE CLASSIFIERS

1.4.1 The Euclidean Distance Classifier

The optimal Bayesian classifier is significantly simplified under the following assumptions:

- The classes are equiprobable.
- The data in *all* classes follow Gaussian distributions.
- The covariance matrix is the *same* for all classes.
- The covariance matrix is diagonal and *all* elements across the diagonal are *equal*. That is, $S = \sigma^2 I$, where I is the identity matrix.

Under these assumptions, it turns out that the optimal Bayesian classifier is equivalent to the minimum Euclidean distance classifier. That is, given an unknown x, assign it to class ω_i if

$$||x - m_i|| \equiv \sqrt{(x - m_i)^T (x - m_i)} < ||x - m_j||, \quad \forall i \neq j$$

It must be stated that the Euclidean classifier is often used, even if we know that the previously stated assumptions are not valid, because of its simplicity. It assigns a pattern to the class whose mean is closest to it with respect to the Euclidean norm.

1.4.2 The Mahalanobis Distance Classifier

If one relaxes the assumptions required by the Euclidean classifier and removes the last one, the one requiring the covariance matrix to be diagonal and with equal elements, the optimal Bayesian classifier becomes equivalent to the minimum Mahalanobis distance classifier. That is, given an unknown x, it is assigned to class ω_i if

$$\sqrt{(x - m_i)^T S^{-1}(x - m_i)} < \sqrt{(x - m_j)^T S^{-1}(x - m_j)}, \quad \forall j \neq i$$

where S is the common covariance matrix. The presence of the covariance matrix accounts for the shape of the Gaussians [Theo 09, Section 2.4.2].

Example 1.4.1. Consider a 2-class classification task in the 3-dimensional space, where the two classes, ω_1 and ω_2, are modeled by Gaussian distributions with means $m_1 = [0, 0, 0]^T$ and $m_2 = [0.5, 0.5, 0.5]^T$, respectively. Assume the two classes to be equiprobable. The covariance matrix for both distributions is

$$S = \begin{bmatrix} 0.8 & 0.01 & 0.01 \\ 0.01 & 0.2 & 0.01 \\ 0.01 & 0.01 & 0.2 \end{bmatrix}$$

Given the point $x = [0.1, 0.5, 0.1]^T$, classify x (1) according to the Euclidean distance classifier and (2) according to the Mahalanobis distance classifier. Comment on the results.

Solution. Take the following steps:

Step 1. Use the function *euclidean_classifier* by typing

```
x=[0.1 0.5 0.1]';
m1=[0 0 0]'; m2=[0.5 0.5 0.5]';
m=[m1 m2];
z=euclidean_classifier(m,x)
```

The answer is $z = 1$; that is, the point is classified to the ω_1 class.

Step 2. Use the function *mahalanobis_classifier* by typing

```
x=[0.1 0.5 0.1]';
m1=[0 0 0]'; m2=[0.5 0.5 0.5]';
m=[m1 m2];
S=[0.8 0.01 0.01;0.01 0.2 0.01; 0.01 0.01 0.2];
z=mahalanobis_classifier(m,S,x);
```

This time, the answer is $z = 2$, meaning the point is classified to the second class. For this case, the optimal Bayesian classifier is realized by the Mahalanobis distance classifier. The point is assigned to class ω_2 in spite of the fact that it lies closer to m_1 according to the Euclidean norm. ∎

1.4.3 Maximum Likelihood Parameter Estimation of Gaussian pdfs

One problem often met in practice is that the pdfs describing the statistical distribution of the data in the classes are not known and must be estimated using the training data set. One approach to this function estimation task is to assume that a pdf has a specific functional form but we do not know the values of the parameters that define it. For example, we may know that the pdf is of Gaussian form but not the mean value and/or the elements of its covariance matrix.

The *maximum likelihood* (ML) technique [Theo 09, Section 2.5.1] is a popular method for such a *parametric estimation* of an unknown pdf. Focusing on Gaussian pdfs and assuming that we are given N points, $x_i \in \mathcal{R}^l$, $i = 1, 2, \ldots, N$, which are known to be normally distributed, the ML estimates of the unknown mean value and the associated covariance matrix are given by

$$m_{ML} = \frac{1}{N} \sum_{i=1}^{N} x_i$$

and

$$S_{ML} = \frac{1}{N} \sum_{i=1}^{N} (x_i - m_{ML})(x_i - m_{ML})^T$$

Often, instead of N, the summation associated with the covariance matrix is divided by $N - 1$ since this provides an unbiased estimate [Theo 09, Section 2.5.1]. The next example focuses on the estimation of the unknown parameters of the Gaussian pdf.

Example 1.4.2. Generate 50 2-dimensional feature vectors from a Gaussian distribution, $\mathcal{N}(m,S)$, where

$$m = [2, -2]^T, \; S = \begin{bmatrix} 0.9 & 0.2 \\ 0.2 & 0.3 \end{bmatrix}$$

Let X be the resulting matrix, having the feature vectors as columns. Compute the ML estimate of the mean value, m, and the covariance matrix, S, of $\mathcal{N}(m,S)$ and comment on the resulting estimates.

Solution. To generate X, type

```
randn('seed',0)
m = [2 -2]; S = [0.9 0.2; 0.2 .3];
X = mvnrnd(m,S,50)';
```

To compute the ML estimates of m and S, type

```
[m_hat, S_hat]=Gaussian_ML_estimate(X);
```

The results are

$$m\_hat = [2.0495, -1.9418]^T, \; S\_hat = \begin{bmatrix} 0.8082 & 0.0885 \\ 0.0885 & 0.2298 \end{bmatrix}$$

It can be observed that the estimates that define the corresponding Gaussian pdf, although close to the true values of the parameters, cannot be trusted as good estimates. This is due to the fact that 50 points are not enough to result in reliable estimates. Note that the returned values depend on the initialization of the random generator (involved in function *mvnrnd*), so there is a slight deviation among experiments. ■

Exercise 1.4.1
Repeat Example 1.4.2 for $N = 500$ points and $N = 5000$ points. Comment on the results.

Example 1.4.3. Generate two data sets, X (training set) and X_1 (test set), each consisting of $N = 1000$ 3-dimensional vectors that stem from three *equiprobable* classes, ω_1, ω_2, and ω_3. The classes are modeled by Gaussian distributions with means $m_1 = [0, 0, 0]^T$, $m_2 = [1, 2, 2]^T$, and $m_3 = [3, 3, 4]^T$, respectively; their covariance matrices are

$$S_1 = S_2 = S_3 = \begin{bmatrix} 0.8 & 0 & 0 \\ 0 & 0.8 & 0 \\ 0 & 0 & 0.8 \end{bmatrix} = \sigma^2 I$$

1. Using X, compute the maximum likelihood estimates of the mean values and the covariance matrices of the distributions of the three classes. Since the covariance matrices are known to be the same, estimate them for each class and compute their average. Use the latter as the estimate of the (common) covariance matrix.

2. Use the Euclidean distance classifier to classify the points of X_1 based on the ML estimates computed before.

3. Use the Mahalanobis distance classifier to classify the points of X_1 based on the ML estimates computed before.

4. Use the Bayesian classifier to classify the points of X_1 based on the ML estimates computed before.

5. For each case, compute the error probability and compare the results (all classifiers should result in almost the same performance. Why?).

Solution. To generate X, use the function *generate_gauss_classes* by typing

```
m=[0 0 0; 1 2 2; 3 3 4]';
S1=0.8*eye(3);
S(:,:,1)=S1;S(:,:,2)=S1;S(:,:,3)=S1;
P=[1/3 1/3 1/3]'; N=1000;
randn('seed',0)
[X,y]=generate_gauss_classes(m,S,P,N);
```

where

 X is the $3 \times N$ matrix that contains the data vectors in its columns,

 y is an N-dimensional vector that contains the class labels of the respective data vectors,

 P is the vector of the respective class a priori probabilities.

The data set X_1 is generated similarly:

```
randn('seed',100);
[X1,y1]=generate_gauss_classes(m,S,P,N);
```

where *randn* is initialized using *seed* = 100.
 Perform the following:

Step 1. To compute the ML estimates of the mean values and covariance matrix (common to all three classes), use *Gaussian_ML_estimate* by typing

```
class1_data=X(:,find(y==1));
[m1_hat, S1_hat]=Gaussian_ML_estimate(class1_data);
class2_data=X(:,find(y==2));
[m2_hat, S2_hat]=Gaussian_ML_estimate(class2_data);
class3_data=X(:,find(y==3));
[m3_hat, S3_hat]=Gaussian_ML_estimate(class3_data);
S_hat=(1/3)*(S1_hat+S2_hat+S3_hat);
m_hat=[m1_hat m2_hat m3_hat];
```

Step 2. For the Euclidean distance classifier, use the ML estimates of the means to classify the data vectors of X_1, typing

```
z_euclidean=euclidean_classifier(m_hat,X1);
```

where *z_euclidean* is an *N*-dimensional vector containing the labels of the classes where the respective data vectors are assigned by the Euclidean classifier.

Step 3. Similarly for the Mahalanobis distance classifier, type

```
z_mahalanobis=mahalanobis_classifier(m_hat,S_hat,X1);
```

Step 4. For the Bayesian classifier, use function *bayes_classifier* and provide as input the matrices *m*, *S, P*, which were used for the data set generation. In other words, use the true values of *m, S*, and *P* and not their estimated values. Type

```
z_bayesian=bayes_classifier(m,S,P,X1);
```

Step 5. To compute the error probability for each classifier, compare the vector y_1 of the true class labels of the vectors of X_1 with vectors *z_euclidean*, *z_mahalanobis*, and *z_bayesian*, respectively. For each comparison, examine the vector elements in pairs and count the number of matches (i.e., correct classifications); divide by the length of y_1. Type

```
err_euclidean = (1-length(find(y1==z_euclidean))/length(y1));
err_mahalanobis = (1-length(find(y1==z_mahalanobis))/length(y1));
err_bayesian = (1-length(find(y1==z_bayesian))/length(y1));
```

The error probabilities for the Euclidean, Mahalanobis, and Bayesian classifiers are 7.61%, 7.71%, and 7.61%, respectively. The results are almost equal since all of the four assumptions in Subsection 1.4.1 are valid, which implies that in the present case the three classifiers are equivalent. ∎

Exercise 1.4.2
Repeat Example 1.4.3 using

$$S_1 = S_2 = S_3 = \begin{bmatrix} 0.8 & 0.2 & 0.1 \\ 0.2 & 0.8 & 0.2 \\ 0.1 & 0.2 & 0.8 \end{bmatrix} \neq \sigma^2 I$$

Comment on the results.

Exercise 1.4.3
Repeat Example 1.4.3 using $P_1 = 1/2$, $P_2 = P_3 = 1/4$ to generate X and X_1. For this case, because the a priori probabilities are not equal, the Bayesian classifier should result in the best performance. Why?

Exercise 1.4.4
Repeat Example 1.4.3 using $P(\omega_1) = P(\omega_2) = P(\omega_3) = 1/3$ and

$$S_1 = \begin{bmatrix} 0.8 & 0.2 & 0.1 \\ 0.2 & 0.8 & 0.2 \\ 0.1 & 0.2 & 0.8 \end{bmatrix}, S_2 = \begin{bmatrix} 0.6 & 0.01 & 0.01 \\ 0.01 & 0.8 & 0.01 \\ 0.01 & 0.01 & 0.6 \end{bmatrix}, S_3 = \begin{bmatrix} 0.6 & 0.1 & 0.1 \\ 0.1 & 0.6 & 0.1 \\ 0.1 & 0.1 & 0.6 \end{bmatrix}$$

Experiment with the mean values (bringing them closer or taking them farther away) and the a priori probabilities. Comment on the results.

1.5 MIXTURE MODELS

When the pdf that describes the data points in a class is not known, it has to be estimated prior to the application of the Bayesian classifier. In this section, we focus on a very popular method to model unknown probability density functions, known as *mixture modeling* [Theo 09, Section 2.5.5].

An arbitrary pdf can be modeled as a linear combination of J pdfs in the form

$$p(x) = \sum_{j=1}^{J} P_j p(x|j) \tag{1.6}$$

where

$$\sum_{j=1}^{J} P_j = 1, \quad \int p(x|j)dx = 1$$

for sufficiently large J. In most cases, $p(x|j)$ are chosen to be Gaussians, $\mathcal{N}(m_j, S_j)$, $j = 1, 2, \ldots, J$.

The expansion in Eq. (1.6) points out a way to generate data from pdfs of a more complex functional form: *multimodal* (many-peaked) pdfs. The meaning of Eq. (1.6) is that the data are generated from each one of the (summand) pdfs, $p(x|j)$, with probability P_j.

Example 1.5.1. Consider the 2-dimensional pdf

$$p(x) = P_1 p(x|1) + P_2 p(x|2) \tag{1.7}$$

where $p(x|j), j = 1, 2$ are normal distributions with means $m_1 = [1, 1]^T$ and $m_2 = [3, 3]^T$ and covariance matrices

$$S_1 = \begin{bmatrix} \sigma_1^2 & \sigma_{12} \\ \sigma_{12} & \sigma_2^2 \end{bmatrix}, \quad S_2 = \begin{bmatrix} \sigma^2 & 0 \\ 0 & \sigma^2 \end{bmatrix}$$

with $\sigma_1^2 = 0.1$, $\sigma_2^2 = 0.2$, $\sigma_{12} = -0.08$, $\sigma^2 = 0.1$.

Generate and plot a set X consisting of $N = 500$ points that stem from $p(x)$ for (i) $P_1 = P_2 = 0.5$, and (ii) for $P_1 = 0.85$, $P_2 = 0.15$; and (iii) experiment by changing the parameters $\sigma_1^2, \sigma_2^2, \sigma_{12}, \sigma^2$ of the covariance matrices and the mixing probabilities P_1 and P_2.

Solution. To generate X, use the function *mixt_model* by typing

```
randn('seed',0); % used for the initialization of MATLAB's randn generator
m1=[1, 1]'; m2=[3, 3]';
m=[m1 m2];
S(:,:,1)=[0.1 -0.08; -0.08 0.2];
S(:,:,2)=[0.1 0; 0 0.1];
P=[1/2 1/2];
N=500;
```

```
sed=0; % used for the initialization of MATLAB's rand generator
[X,y]=mixt_model(m,S,P,N,sed);
plot(X(1,:),X(2,:),'.');
```

where

> *sed* is the "seed" used for the initialization of the built-in MATLAB random generator function *rand*, which generates numbers from the uniform distribution in the interval [0, 1],

> *y* is a vector whose *i*th element contains the label of the distribution that generated the *i*th data vector

The next steps are carried out in a similar manner. From Figure 1.2, one can verify the multimodal nature of the pdf of *x*. That is, *x* is spread over two well-separated regions in space. Comparing Figures 1.2(a, b), observe that in the latter case, since $P_1 \neq P_2$, one of the two high-density regions is sparser in data points.

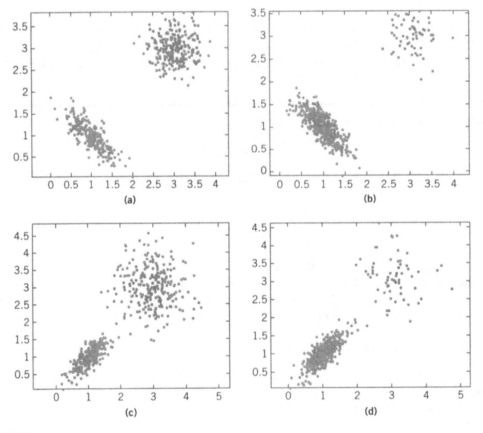

FIGURE 1.2

Example 1.5.1 (a) results obtained for the setup of case (i), (b) setup of case (ii), and (c)–(d) for some values of case (iii).

1.6 THE EXPECTATION-MAXIMIZATION ALGORITHM

Let us assume that we are given a set of N points, $x_i \in \mathcal{R}^l$, $i = 1, 2, \ldots, N$, whose statistical properties are described by a pdf that is expanded as in Eq. (1.6). Adopting a value for J, the task is to use these data points to estimate the parameters that enter in the expansion—that is, the probability parameters P_j, $j = 1, 2, \ldots, J$ and the parameters associated with each one of the terms $p(x|j)$, $j = 1, 2, \ldots, J$. For example, if we assume each one of the summand pdfs to be a Gaussian distribution with $\sigma_j^2 I$ covariance matrix:

$$p(x|j) = \frac{1}{(2\pi)^{l/2}\sigma_j^l} \exp\left(-\frac{(x - m_j)^T (x - m_j)}{2\sigma_j^2}\right), \quad j = 1, 2, \ldots, J$$

then the associated unknown parameters are the mean values m_j, $j = 1, 2, \ldots, J$ (lJ parameters in total) and the J covariances σ_j^2, $j = 1, 2, \ldots, J$ (J parameters in total).

The expectation-maximization (EM) algorithm iteratively computes the corresponding estimates, starting from some user-defined initial values [Theo 09, Section 2.5.5].

Example 1.6.1. Generate a set X of $N = 500$ 2-dimensional points that stem from the following pdf:

$$p(x) = \sum_{j=1}^{3} P_j p(x|j)$$

where the $p(x|j)$'s, $j = 1, 2, 3$ are (2-dimensional) normal distributions with mean values $m_1 = [1, 1]^T$, $m_2 = [3, 3]^T$, $m_3 = [2, 6]^T$ and covariance matrices $S_1 = 0.1I$, $S_2 = 0.2I$, $S_3 = 0.3I$, respectively (I is the 2×2 identity matrix). In addition, $P_1 = 0.4$, $P_2 = 0.4$, and $P_3 = 0.2$.

The idea is to use the previously generated data and pretend that we do not know how they were generated. We assume that the pdf $p(x)$ underlying X is a weighted sum of J (Eq. (1.6)) normal distributions with covariance matrices of the form $S_i = \sigma_i^2 I$, and we employ the EM algorithm to estimate the unknown parameters in the adopted model of $p(x)$. The goal is to demonstrate the dependence of the EM algorithm on the initial conditions and the parameter J. To this end, we use the following sets of initial parameter estimates:

- $J = 3$, $m_{1,ini} = [0, 2]^T$, $m_{2,ini} = [5, 2]^T$, $m_{3,ini} = [5, 5]^T$, $S_{1,ini} = 0.15I$, $S_{2,ini} = 0.27I$, $S_{3,ini} = 0.4I$ and $P_{1,ini} = P_{2,ini} = P_{3,ini} = 1/3$

- $J = 3$, $m_{1,ini} = [1.6, 1.4]^T$, $m_{2,ini} = [1.4, 1.6]^T$, $m_{3,ini} = [1.3, 1.5]^T$, $S_{1,ini} = 0.2I$, $S_{2,ini} = 0.4I$, $S_{3,ini} = 0.3I$ and $P_{1,ini} = 0.2$, $P_{2,ini} = 0.4$, $P_{3,ini} = 0.4$

- $J = 2$, $m_{1,ini} = [1.6, 1.4]^T$, $m_{2,ini} = [1.4, 1.6]^T$, $S_{1,ini} = 0.2I$, $S_{2,ini} = 0.4I$ and $P_{1,ini} = P_{2,ini} = 1/2$

Comment on the results.

Solution. To generate and plot the data set X, type

```
randn('seed',0);
m1=[1, 1]'; m2=[3, 3]';m3=[2, 6]';
m=[m1 m2 m3];
S(:,:,1)=0.1*eye(2);
S(:,:,2)=0.2*eye(2);
S(:,:,3)=0.3*eye(2);
P=[0.4 0.4 0.2];
N=500;
sed=0;
[X,y]=mixt_model(m,S,P,N,sed);
plot_data(X,y,m,1)
```

Then do the following:

Step 1. Use the function *em_alg_function* to estimate the mixture model parameters by typing

```
m1_ini=[0; 2];m2_ini=[5; 2];m3_ini=[5; 5];
m_ini=[m1_ini m2_ini m3_ini];
s_ini=[.15 .27 .4];
Pa_ini=[1/3 1/3 1/3];
e_min=10^(-5);
[m_hat,s_hat,Pa,iter,Q_tot,e_tot]=...
em_alg_function(X,m_ini,s_ini,Pa_ini,e_min);
```

where

> *m_hat* is an $l \times J$ matrix whose jth column is the estimate for the mean of the jth distribution,
>
> *s* is a J-dimensional vector whose jth element is the variance for the jth distribution (it is assumed that the covariance matrices of the distributions are of the form $s(j) * I$, where I is the identity matrix),
>
> *Pa* is a J-dimensional vector with a jth element that is the estimate of the a priori probability of the jth distribution.

The final estimates obtained by the EM algorithm are (rounded to the second decimal):

- $\hat{m}_1 = [1.02, 0.98]^T$, $\hat{m}_2 = [2.94, 3.02]^T$, $\hat{m}_3 = [2.03, 6.00]^T$
- $\hat{S}_1 = 0.10I$, $\hat{S}_2 = 0.22I$, $\hat{S}_3 = 0.30I$
- $\hat{P}_1 = 0.39$, $\hat{P}_2 = 0.43$, $\hat{P}_3 = 0.18$

The algorithm converged after 12 iterations (see Figure 1.3(a)).

Step 2. Working as in step 1, obtain the results

- $\hat{m}_1 = [1.01, 0.84]^T$, $\hat{m}_2 = [2.66, 3.86]^T$, $\hat{m}_3 = [1.02, 1.26]^T$
- $\hat{S}_1 = 0.09I$, $\hat{S}_2 = 1.28I$, $\hat{S}_3 = 0.07I$
- $\hat{P}_1 = 0.26$, $\hat{P}_2 = 0.62$, $\hat{P}_3 = 0.12$

The algorithm converged after 533 iterations (see Figure 1.3(b)).

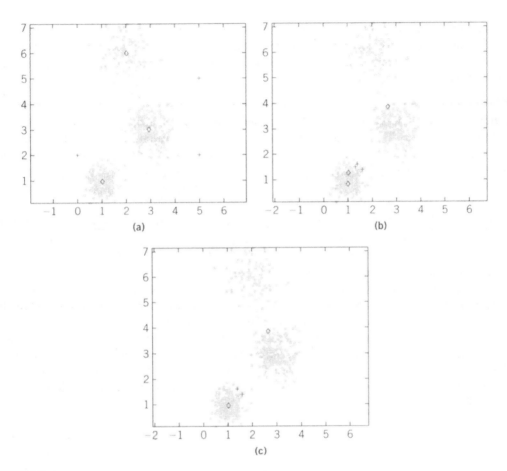

FIGURE 1.3

Example 1.6.1 initial (+) and final (◇) estimates of the mean values of the normal distributions for all three cases.

Step 3. Working as in step 1, obtain the results

- $\hat{m}_1 = [1.01, 0.97]^T, \hat{m}_2 = [2.66, 3.86]^T$
- $\hat{S}_1 = 0.10I, \hat{S}_2 = 1.27I$
- $\hat{P}_1 = 0.38, \hat{P}_2 = 0.62$

The algorithm converged after 10 iterations (see Figure 1.3(c)).

In the first case, the good initialization of the algorithm led to parameter estimates that are very close to the true parameters, which were used for the generation of the data set. In the second case, the bad initialization led to poor parameter estimates. In the third case, the wrong choice of the order of the model (number of involved normal distributions) led to bad estimates. Using the EM algorithm, one has to be cautious about parameter initialization as well as the choice of the value of J.

Some popular methods for estimating the correct order of the problem (in our case J) are based on so-called information-based criteria. For an application of these criteria in the current framework, see [Theo 09, Chapter 16], where such methods are used to identify the number of dense regions (clusters) formed by a set of data vectors.

Example 1.6.2. In this example, the EM algorithm is used in a classification application. A 2-class problem is considered. The data set X consists of $N = 1000$ 2-dimensional vectors. Of these, 500 stem from class ω_1, which is modeled as $p_1(x) = \sum_{j=1}^{3} P_{1j}p_1(x|j)$, where $p_1(x|j)$, $j = 1,2,3$ are normal distributions with mean values $m_{11} = [1.25, 1.25]^T$, $m_{12} = [2.75, 2.75]^T$, $m_{13} = [2, 6]^T$, and covariance matrices $S_{1j} = \sigma_{1j}^2 I$, $j = 1,2,3$, where $\sigma_{11}^2 = 0.1$, $\sigma_{12}^2 = 0.2$, $\sigma_{13}^2 = 0.3$, respectively. The mixing probabilities are $P_{11} = 0.4$, $P_{12} = 0.4$, and $P_{13} = 0.2$.

The other 500 data vectors stem from class ω_2, which is modeled as $p_2(x) = \sum_{j=1}^{3} P_{2j}p_2(x|j)$, where $p_2(x|j)$, $j = 1,2,3$ are also normal distributions with means $m_{21} = [1.25, 2.75]^T$, $m_{22} = [2.75, 1.25]^T$, $m_{23} = [4, 6]^T$, and covariance matrices $S_{2j} = \sigma_{2j}^2 I$, $j = 1,2,3$, where $\sigma_{21}^2 = 0.1$, $\sigma_{22}^2 = 0.2$, $\sigma_{23}^2 = 0.3$, respectively. The mixing probabilities are $P_{21} = 0.2$, $P_{22} = 0.3$, and $P_{23} = 0.5$.

The setup of the problem is shown in Figure 1.4. Each class consists of points that are spread to more than one dense region. Such a setup is a typical scenario where mixture modeling and the EM algorithm are used to estimate the corresponding pdfs for each class.

The data set X is used as the training set, and we pretend that we do not know how it was generated. We assume that, somehow, we have a priori information about the number of dense regions in each class, so we adopt a mixture model with three Gaussian components to model the pdf in each class. The data set X is used by the EM algorithm for estimating the "unknown" parameters involved in the respective model pdf expansions.

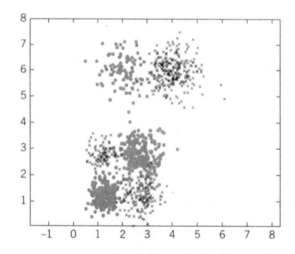

FIGURE 1.4

Data set X of Example 1.6.2.

With the pdf estimates for each class obtained, the Bayesian classifier is mobilized. An additional data set Z of 1000 data vectors is also generated such that the first half stem from $p_1(x)$ and the rest stem from $p_2(x)$. The set Z is used for testing the performance of the resulting classifier.

Use the EM algorithm to estimate $p_1(x)$ and $p_2(x)$ based on the data set X using the following initial parameter estimates:

- For $p_1(x)$: Three normal distributions with initial mean estimates $m_{11,ini} = [0, 2]^T$, $m_{12,ini} = [5, 2]^T$, $m_{13,ini} = [5, 5]^T$; initial variance estimates $\sigma^2_{11,ini} = 0.15$, $\sigma^2_{12,ini} = 0.27$, $\sigma^2_{13,ini} = 0.4$; and mixing probabilities $P_{11,ini} = P_{12,ini} = P_{13,ini} = 1/3$.
- For $p_2(x)$: Three normal distributions with initial mean estimates $m_{21,ini} = [5, 2]^T$, $m_{22,ini} = [3, 4]^T$, $m_{23,ini} = [2, 5]^T$; initial variance estimates $\sigma^2_{21,ini} = 0.15$, $\sigma^2_{22,ini} = 0.27$, $\sigma^2_{23,ini} = 0.35$; and mixing probabilities $P_{21,ini} = P_{22,ini} = P_{23,ini} = 1/3$.

Having obtained the estimates of $p_1(x)$ and $p_2(x)$, employ the Bayes classification rule to classify the vectors in Z and compute the classification error.

Solution. To generate the subset X_1 of X, which contains the data points from class ω_1, type

```
m11=[1.25 1.25]'; m12=[2.75 2.75]';m13=[2 6]';
m1=[m11 m12 m13];
S1(:,:,1)=0.1*eye(2);
S1(:,:,2)=0.2*eye(2);
S1(:,:,3)=0.3*eye(2);
P1=[0.4 0.4 0.2];
N1=500;
sed=0;
[X1,y1]=mixt_model(m1,S1,P1,N1,sed);
```

The subset X_2 of X with the points from class ω_2 is generated similarly (again use *sed* $= 0$). Let *X2* and *y2* be the two MATLAB variables resulting from the *mixt_model* function in this case.

To generate the set Z, we work in a similar manner. Specifically, Z is generated in two steps: First, 500 points are generated from class ω_1 via the following code:

```
mZ11=[1.25 1.25]'; mZ12=[2.75 2.75]';mZ13=[2 6]';
mZ1=[mZ11 mZ12 mZ13];
SZ1(:,:,1)=0.1*eye(2);
SZ1(:,:,2)=0.2*eye(2);
SZ1(:,:,3)=0.3*eye(2);
wZ1=[0.4 0.4 0.2];
NZ1=500;
sed=100;
[Z1,yz1]=mixt_model(mZ1,SZ1,wZ1,NZ1,sed);
```

The remaining 500 points from the second class are generated similarly (with *sed* $= 100$). In this case, let *Z2*, *yz2* be the two corresponding MATLAB variables resulting from the *mixt_model* function.

Finally, type Z = [Z1 Z2]; and do the following:

Step 1. To estimate the Gaussian mixture model of each class, type

```
m11_ini=[0; 2]; m12_ini=[5; 2]; m13_ini=[5; 5];
m1_ini=[m11_ini m12_ini m13_ini];
S1_ini=[0.15 0.27 0.4];
w1_ini=[1/3 1/3 1/3];

m21_ini=[5; 2]; m22_ini=[3; 4]; m23_ini=[2; 5];
m2_ini=[m21_ini m22_ini m23_ini];
S2_ini=[0.15 0.27 0.35];
w2_ini=[1/3 1/3 1/3];

m_ini{1}=m1_ini;
m_ini{2}=m2_ini;
S_ini{1}=S1_ini;
S_ini{2}=S2_ini;
w_ini{1}=w1_ini;
w_ini{2}=w2_ini;
[m_hat,S_hat,w_hat,P_hat]=...
EM_pdf_est([X1 X2],[ones(1,500) 2*ones(1,500)],m_ini,S_ini,w_ini);
```

The estimated values of the remaining parameters involved in $p_1(x)$ and $p_2(x)$ are

- For $p_1(x)$: The mean values are $\hat{m}_{11} = [1.27, 1.22]^T$, $\hat{m}_{12} = [2.69, 2.76]^T$, $\hat{m}_{13} = [2.03, 6.00]^T$; the variances are $\hat{\sigma}_{11} = 0.10$, $\hat{\sigma}_{12} = 0.22$, $\hat{\sigma}_{13} = 0.31$; the mixing probabilities are $\hat{P}_{11} = 0.38$, $\hat{P}_{12} = 0.44$, $\hat{P}_{13} = 0.18$.
- For $p_2(x)$: The mean values are $\hat{m}_{21} = [1.22, 2.77]^T$, $\hat{m}_{22} = [2.75, 1.22]^T$, $\hat{m}_{23} = [4.03, 5.97]^T$; the variances are $\hat{\sigma}_{21} = 0.11$, $\hat{\sigma}_{22} = 0.20$, $\hat{\sigma}_{23} = 0.30$; the mixing probabilities are $\hat{P}_{21} = 0.19$, $\hat{P}_{22} = 0.31$, $\hat{P}_{23} = 0.50$.

The a priori class probability $P(\omega_i)$, $i = 1,2$ for each class is estimated as the number of vectors in the respective class divided by the total number of vectors. In our case, $P(\omega_1) = P(\omega_2) = 0.5$.

Step 2. Use function *mixture_Bayes* to classify the data vectors of Z and function *compute_error* to obtain the classification error. Type

```
for j=1:2
  le=length(S_hat{j});
  te=[];
  for i=1:le
    te(:,:,i)=S_hat{j}(i)*eye(2);
  end
  S{j}=te;
end
```

```
[y_est]=mixture_Bayes(m_hat,S,w_hat,P_hat,Z);
[classification_error]=compute_error([ones(1,500) 2*ones(1,500)],y_est);
```

The computed classification error is equal to 4.20%.

Remark
- In a classification task, when the number of summands in the mixture model is not known, the task is run a number of times with different values of J; the value that results in the lowest classification error over the test set is adopted.

Exercise 1.6.1
Repeat Example 1.6.2 using $X1$, $X2$, $Z1$, $Z2$ with the following initial parameter values:

- For $p_1(x)$: Three normal distributions with initial mean estimates $m_{11,ini} = [5, 5]^T$, $m_{12,ini} = [5.5, 5.5]^T$, $m_{13,ini} = [5, 5]^T$; initial variance estimates $\sigma_{11,ini} = 0.2$, $\sigma_{12,ini} = 0.4$, $\sigma_{13,ini} = 0.3$; and mixing probabilities $P_{11,ini} = 0.2$, $P_{12,ini} = 0.4$, $P_{13,ini} = 0.4$.
  For $p_2(x)$: Three normal distributions with initial mean estimates $m_{21,ini} = [2, 2]^T$, $m_{22,ini} = [1.98, 1.98]^T$, $m_{23,ini} = [2.4, 2.4]^T$; initial variance estimates $\sigma_{21,ini} = 0.06$, $\sigma_{22,ini} = 0.05$, $\sigma_{23,ini} = 0.4$; and mixing probabilities $P_{21,ini} = 0.8$, $P_{22,ini} = 0.1$, $P_{23,ini} = 0.1$.
- For $p_1(x)$: Three normal distributions with initial mean estimates $m_{11,ini} = [1.6, 1.4]^T$, $m_{12,ini} = [1.4, 1.6]^T$, $m_{13,ini} = [1.3, 1.5]^T$; initial variance estimates $\sigma_{11,ini} = 0.2$, $\sigma_{12,ini} = 0.4$, $\sigma_{13,ini} = 0.3$; and mixing probabilities $P_{11,ini} = 0.2$, $P_{12,ini} = 0.4$, $P_{13,ini} = 0.4$.
  For $p_2(x)$: Three normal distributions with initial mean estimates $m_{21,ini} = [1.5, 1.7]^T$, $m_{22,ini} = [1.7, 1.5]^T$, $m_{23,ini} = [1.6, 1.6]^T$; initial variance estimates $\sigma_{21,ini} = 0.6$, $\sigma_{22,ini} = 0.05$, $\sigma_{23,ini} = 0.02$; and mixing probabilities $P_{21,ini} = 0.1$, $P_{22,ini} = 0.8$, $P_{23,ini} = 0.1$.
- For $p_1(x)$: Four normal distributions with initial mean estimates $m_{11,ini} = [0, 2]^T$, $m_{12,ini} = [5, 2]^T$, $m_{13,ini} = [5, 5]^T$, $m_{14,ini} = [3, 4]^T$; initial variance estimates $\sigma_{11,ini} = 0.15$, $\sigma_{12,ini} = 0.27$, $\sigma_{13,ini} = 0.4$, $\sigma_{14,ini} = 0.2$; and mixing probabilities $P_{11,ini} = P_{12,ini} = P_{13,ini} = P_{14,ini} = 1/4$.
  For $p_2(x)$: Four normal distributions with initial mean estimates $m_{21,ini} = [1, 2]^T$, $m_{22,ini} = [3.2, 1.5]^T$, $m_{23,ini} = [1, 4]^T$, $m_{24,ini} = [4, 2]^T$; initial variance estimates $\sigma_{21,ini} = 0.15$, $\sigma_{22,ini} = 0.08$, $\sigma_{23,ini} = 0.27$, $\sigma_{24,ini} = 0.05$; and mixing probabilities $P_{21,ini} = P_{22,ini} = P_{23,ini} = P_{24,ini} = 1/4$.
- For $p_1(x)$: Two normal distributions with initial mean estimates $m_{11,ini} = [0, 2]^T$, $m_{12,ini} = [5, 2]^T$; initial variance estimates $\sigma_{11,ini} = 0.15$, $\sigma_{12,ini} = 0.27$; and mixing probabilities $P_{11,ini} = P_{12,ini} = 1/2$.
  For $p_2(x)$: One normal distribution with initial mean estimate $m_{21,ini} = [1, 2]^T$; initial variance estimate $\sigma_{21,ini} = 0.15$; and mixing probability $P_{21,ini} = 1$.
- For $p_1(x)$: One normal distribution with initial mean estimate $m_{11,ini} = [2, 2]^T$; initial variance estimates $\sigma_{11,ini} = 0.4$; and mixing probability $P_{11,ini} = 1$.
  For $p_2(x)$: One normal distribution with initial mean estimate $m_{21,ini} = [1, 2]^T$; initial variance estimate $\sigma_{21,ini} = 0.15$; and mixing probability $P_{21,ini} = 1$.

For each scenario comment on the EM estimates and find the classification error of the Bayesian classifier.

1.7 PARZEN WINDOWS

This section and the following section deal with *nonparametric* estimation of an unknown pdf associated with a given set of data points. According to the Parzen windows pdf estimation method, if we are given N data points, $x_i \in \mathcal{R}^l$, $i = 1, 2, \ldots, N$, that follow an unknown distribution, their pdf can be estimated using the expansion

$$p(x) \approx \frac{1}{Nh^l} \sum_{i=1}^{N} \phi\left(\frac{x - x_i}{h}\right) \tag{1.8}$$

for sufficiently *large N* and sufficiently *small* values of h, which is a user-defined parameter [Theo 09, Section 2.5.6], $\phi(\cdot)$ is an appropriately defined *kernel* function. A commonly used kernel function is the Gaussian, and in this case the expansion becomes

$$p(x) \approx \frac{1}{N} \sum_{i=1}^{N} \frac{1}{(2\pi)^{l/2} h^l} \exp\left(-\frac{(x - x_i)^T (x - x_i)}{2h^2}\right) \tag{1.9}$$

Example 1.7.1. Generate $N = 1000$ data points lying in the real axis, $x_i \in \mathcal{R}$, $i = 1, 2, \ldots, N$, from the following pdf, and plot $p(x)$:

$$p(x) = \frac{1}{3} \frac{1}{\sqrt{2\pi\sigma_1^2}} \exp\left(-\frac{x^2}{2\sigma_1^2}\right) + \frac{2}{3} \frac{1}{\sqrt{2\pi\sigma_2^2}} \exp\left(-\frac{(x - 2)^2}{2\sigma_2^2}\right)$$

where $\sigma_1^2 = \sigma_2^2 = 0.2$.

Use the Parzen windows approximation of Eq. (1.9), with $h = 0.1$, and plot the obtained estimate.

Solution. The pdf is actually a Gaussian mixture model. Use the function *generate_gauss_classes* to generate the required data set, typing

```
m=[0; 2]';
S(:,:,1)=[0.2];

S(:,:,2)=[0.2];
P=[1/3 2/3];
N=1000;
randn('seed',0);
[X]=generate_gauss_classes(m,S,P,N);
```

Step 1. To plot the pdf, assume $x \in [-5, 5]$ and type

```
x=-5:0.1:5;
pdfx=(1/3)*(1/sqrt(2*pi*0.2))*exp(-(x.^2)/0.4)
      +(2/3)*(1/sqrt(2*pi*0.2))*exp(-((x-2).^2)/0.4);
plot(x,pdfx); hold;
```

Step 2. To compute and plot the approximation of the pdf for $h = 0.1$ and $x \in [-5, 5]$, use function *Parzen_gauss_kernel* as follows:

```
h=0.1;
pdfx_approx=Parzen_gauss_kernel(X,h,-5,5);
plot(-5:h:5,pdfx_approx,'r');
```
■

Exercise 1.7.1

Repeat the experiment in Example 1.7.1 with $h = 0.01$, $N = 1000$ and $h = 0.1$, $N = 10,000$. Comment on the results. The choice of h for a given N needs careful consideration. Tips related to this choice are provided in [Theo 09, Section 2.5.6] and the references therein.

Exercise 1.7.2

Generate $N = 1000$ data points from the following 2-dimensional pdf:

$$p(x) \equiv p(x(1), x(2)) = \frac{1}{3} \frac{1}{2\pi\sigma^2} \exp\left\{-\frac{x^2(1) + x^2(2)}{2\sigma^2}\right\} + \frac{2}{3} \frac{1}{2\pi\sigma^2} \exp\left\{-\frac{x^2(1) + (x(2) - 2)^2}{2\sigma^2}\right\}$$

Repeat the experiment in Example 1.7.1.

Exercise 1.7.3

Use the setup for the classification task in Example 1.4.3. Classify the data points of the set X_1 using the Bayesian classifier, where the estimate of the required values $p(x|\omega_1)$, $p(x|\omega_2)$ for each point in X_1 is obtained via the Parzen window estimation method. Use different values of h and choose the one that results in the best error performance of the classifier.

1.8 *k*-NEAREST NEIGHBOR DENSITY ESTIMATION

Let us consider a set of N points, $x_1, x_2, \ldots, x_N \in \mathcal{R}^l$, that stem from a statistical distribution unknown to us. The goal is to *estimate* the value of the unknown pdf at a given point x. According to the k-nearest neighbor estimation technique, the following steps are performed:

1. Choose a value for k.
2. Find the distance between x and all training points x_i, $i = 1, 2, \ldots, N$. Any distance measure can be used (e.g., Euclidean, Mahalanobis).
3. Find the k-nearest points to x.
4. Compute the volume $V(x)$ in which the k-nearest neighbors lie.
5. Compute the estimate by

$$p(x) \approx \frac{k}{NV(x)}$$

If the Euclidean distance is employed and the distance between the k-furthest neighbor and x is ρ, the volume $V(x)$ is equal to

$$V(x) = 2\rho \quad \text{in the 1-dimensional space}$$

$$V(x) = \pi\rho^2 \quad \text{in the 2-dimensional space}$$

or

$$V(x) = \frac{4}{3}\pi\rho^3 \quad \text{in the 3-dimensional space}$$

For the more general case of l dimensions and/or Mahalanobis distance, see [Theo 09, Section 2.5.6].

Example 1.8.1. Consider the data set generated in Example 1.7.1 and use the k-nearest neighbor density estimator to estimate the required pdf with $k = 21$.

Solution. To generate the set X of the data vectors, work as in Example 1.7.1. Assuming that we are interested in approximating the pdf for $x \in [-5, 5]$ (as in Example 1.7.1), we use the function *knn_density_estimate*, typing

```
pdfx_approx=knn_density_estimate(X,21,-5,5,0.1);
plot(-5:0.1:5,pdfx_approx,'r');
```

Exercise 1.8.1
Repeat Example 1.8.1 for $k = 5,100$. Repeat with $N = 5000$.

Exercise 1.8.2
Use the setup for the classification task in Example 1.4.3. Classify the data points of set X_1 using the Bayesian classifier. Estimate the required values $p(x|\omega_1)$, $p(x|\omega_2)$ for each point in X_1 via the k-nearest neighbor density estimation method. Use different values of k and choose the one that results in the best error performance of the classifier.

1.9 THE NAIVE BAYES CLASSIFIER

In the naive Bayes classification scheme, the required estimate of the pdf at a point $x = [x(1),\ldots,x(l)]^T \in \mathcal{R}^l$ is given as

$$p(x) = \prod_{j=1}^{l} p(x(j))$$

That is, the components (features) of the feature vector x are assumed to be *statistically independent*. This assumption is convenient in high-dimensional spaces, where, because of the curse of dimensionality [Theo 09, Section 2.5.6], a large number of training points should be available to obtain a reliable estimate of the corresponding multidimensional pdf. Instead, with the naive Bayes classifier, although the independence assumption may not be valid, the final performance may still be good since reliable estimates of the 1-dimensional pdfs can be obtained with relatively few data points.

Example 1.9.1. Generate a set X_1 that consists of $N_1 = 50$ 5-dimensional data vectors that stem from two equiprobable classes, ω_1 and ω_2. The classes are modeled by Gaussian distributions with means

$m_1 = [0,0,0,0,0]^T$ and $m_2 = [1,1,1,1,1]^T$ and respective covariance matrices

$$S_1 = \begin{bmatrix} 0.8 & 0.2 & 0.1 & 0.05 & 0.01 \\ 0.2 & 0.7 & 0.1 & 0.03 & 0.02 \\ 0.1 & 0.1 & 0.8 & 0.02 & 0.01 \\ 0.05 & 0.03 & 0.02 & 0.9 & 0.01 \\ 0.01 & 0.02 & 0.01 & 0.01 & 0.8 \end{bmatrix}, \quad S_2 = \begin{bmatrix} 0.9 & 0.1 & 0.05 & 0.02 & 0.01 \\ 0.1 & 0.8 & 0.1 & 0.02 & 0.02 \\ 0.05 & 0.1 & 0.7 & 0.02 & 0.01 \\ 0.02 & 0.02 & 0.02 & 0.6 & 0.02 \\ 0.01 & 0.02 & 0.01 & 0.02 & 0.7 \end{bmatrix}$$

In a similar manner, generate a data set X_2 consisting of $N_2 = 10,000$ data points. X_1 is used for training; X_2, for testing.

In the spirit of the naive Bayes classifier, we assume that for each class the features of the feature vectors are statistically independent (although we know this is not true), and that each follows a 1-dimensional Gaussian distribution. For each of the five dimensions and for each of the two classes, use the training set X_1 to compute the maximum likelihood estimates of the mean values $m_{1j}, m_{2j}, j = 1,2,\ldots,5$ and the variances $\sigma_{1j}^2, \sigma_{2j}^2, j = 1,2,\ldots,5$.

Perform the following steps:

Step 1. Classify the points of the test set X_2 using the naive Bayes classifier, where for a given x, $p(x|\omega_i)$ is estimated as

$$p(x|\omega_i) = \prod_{j=1}^{5} \frac{1}{\sqrt{2\pi\sigma_{ij}^2}} \exp\left(-\frac{(x(j) - m_{ij})^2}{2\sigma_{ij}^2}\right), \quad i = 1,2$$

where $x(j)$ is the jth component of x. Compute the error probability.

Step 2. Compute the ML estimates of m_1, m_2, S_1, and S_2 using X_1. Employ the ML estimates in the Bayesian classifier in the 5-dimensional space. Compute the error probability.

Step 3. Compare the results obtained in steps 1 and 2.

Solution. To generate sets X_1 and X_2, type

```
m=[zeros(5,1) ones(5,1)];
S(:,:,1)=[0.8 0.2 0.1 0.05 0.01;
          0.2 0.7 0.1 0.03 0.02;
          0.1 0.1 0.8 0.02 0.01;
          0.05 0.03 0.02 0.9 0.01;
          0.01 0.02 0.01 0.01 0.8];
S(:,:,2)=[0.9 0.1 0.05 0.02 0.01;
          0.1 0.8 0.1  0.02 0.02;
          0.05 0.1 0.7 0.02 0.01;
          0.02 0.02 0.02 0.6 0.02;
          0.01 0.02 0.01 0.02 0.7];
P=[1/2 1/2]'; N_1=100;
randn('state',0);
[X1,y1]=generate_gauss_classes(m,S,P,N_1);
```

```
N_2=10000;
randn('state',100);
[X2,y2]=generate_gauss_classes(m,S,P,N_2);
```

Assuming that the features are independent, use function *Gaussian_ML_estimate* to compute the ML estimate of the mean and the variance per feature for each class (using set X_1). Type

```
for i=1:5
  [m1_hat(i), S1_hat(i)]=Gaussian_ML_estimate(X1(i,find(y1==1)));
end
m1_hat=m1_hat'; S1_hat=S1_hat';

for i=1:5
  [m2_hat(i), S2_hat(i)]=Gaussian_ML_estimate(X1(i,find(y1==2)));
end
m2_hat=m2_hat'; S2_hat=S2_hat';
```

Then, do the following:

Step 1. To classify each point in X_2 according to the naive Bayes classification scheme, type

```
for i=1:5
  perFeature1(i,:)=normpdf(X2(i,:),m1_hat(i),sqrt(S1_hat(i)));
  perFeature2(i,:)=normpdf(X2(i,:),m2_hat(i),sqrt(S2_hat(i)));
end
naive_probs1=prod(perFeature1);
naive_probs2=prod(perFeature2);
classified=ones(1,length(X2));
classified(find(naive_probs1<naive_probs2))=2;
```

To compute the classification error, type

```
true_labels=y2;
naive_error=sum(true_labels~=classified)/length(classified)
```

Step 2. To compute the maximum likelihood estimates of the "unknown" mean values and covariance matrices m_1, m_2, S_1, and S_2, based on X_1, type

```
[m1_ML, S1_ML]=Gaussian_ML_estimate(X1(:,find(y1==1)));
[m2_ML, S2_ML]=Gaussian_ML_estimate(X1(:,find(y1==2)));
```

To classify the data vectors of X_2 using the Bayesian classifier, which is based on the ML estimates of the respective parameters, type

```
m_ML(:,1)=m1_ML;
m_ML(:,2)=m2_ML;
```

```
S_ML(:,:,1)=S1_ML;
S_ML(:,:,2)=S2_ML;
P=[1/2 1/2];
z=bayes_classifier(m_ML,S_ML,P,X2);
```

To compute the classification error, type

```
true_labels=y2;
Bayes_ML_error=sum(true_labels~=z)/length(z)
```

Step 3. The resulting classification errors—*naive_error* and *Bayes_ML_error*—are 0.1320 and 0.1426, respectively. In other words, the naive classification scheme outperforms the standard ML-based scheme. If the experiment is repeated for the case where X_1 consists of 20 instead of 50 points, the difference between the performance of the two classifiers is even more noticeable in favor of the naive Bayes classifier. ■

Exercise 1.9.1

1. Classify the points of the set X_2 in Example 1.9.1, adopting the optimal Bayesian classifier. That is, use the true values of the means and covariance matrices associated with the 5-dimensional Gaussian pdfs. Compare the results with those obtained in Example 1.9.1.
2. Repeat Example 1.9.1 with X_1 consisting of $N_1 = 1000$ data vectors.

Remark
- The previous example is very important in the sense that it demonstrates that it is often preferable to use *suboptimal* searching techniques if the use of the optimal method results in excessive computations and/or poor estimates due to a limited amount of data. This is often the case in high-dimensional spaces because of the *curse of dimensionality* [Theo 09, Section 2.5.6].

1.10 THE NEAREST NEIGHBOR RULE

Nearest neighbor (NN) is one of the most popular classification rules, although it is an old technique. We are given c classes, ω_i, $i = 1, 2, \ldots, c$, and a point $x \in \mathcal{R}^l$, and N *training* points, x_i, $i = 1, 2, \ldots, N$, in the l-dimensional space, with the corresponding class labels. Given a point, x, whose class label is unknown, the task is to classify x in one of the c classes. The rule consists of the following steps:

1. Among the N training points, search for the k neighbors closest to x using a distance measure (e.g., Euclidean, Mahalanobis). The parameter k is user-defined. Note that it should not be a multiple of c. That is, for two classes k should be an odd number.
2. Out of the k-closest neighbors, identify the number k_i of the points that belong to class ω_i. Obviously, $\sum_{i=1}^{c} k_i = k$.
3. Assign x to class ω_i, for which $k_i > k_j$, $j \neq i$. In other words, x is assigned to the class in which the majority of the k-closest neighbors belong.

For large N (in theory $N \to \infty$), the larger k is the closer the performance of the k-NN classifier to the optimal Bayesian classifier is expected to be [Theo 09, Section 2.6]. However, for small values of N (in theory, for its finite values), a larger k may not result in better performance [Theo 09, Problem 2.34].

A major problem with the k-NN classifier, as well as with its close relative the k-NN density estimator, is the computational complexity associated with searching for the k-nearest neighbors, especially in high-dimensional spaces. This search is repeated every time a new point x is classified, for which a number of suboptimal techniques have been suggested [Theo 09, Section 2.6].

Example 1.10.1

1. Consider a 2-dimensional classification problem where the data vectors stem from two equiprobable classes, ω_1 and ω_2. The classes are modeled by Gaussian distributions with means $m_1 = [0,0]^T$, $m_2 = [1,2]^T$, and respective covariance matrices

$$S_1 = S_2 = \begin{bmatrix} 0.8 & 0.2 \\ 0.2 & 0.8 \end{bmatrix}$$

Generate two data sets X_1 and X_2 consisting of 1000 and 5000 points, respectively.
2. Taking X_1 as the training set, classify the points in X_2 using the k-NN classifier, with $k = 3$ and adopting the squared Euclidean distance. Compute the classification error.

Solution

Step 1. To generate sets X_1 and X_2, type

```
m=[0 0; 1 2]';
S=[0.8 0.2;0.2 0.8];
S(:,:,1)=S;S(:,:,2)=S;
P=[1/2 1/2]'; N_1=1000;
randn('seed',0)
[X1,y1]=generate_gauss_classes(m,S,P,N_1);
N_2=5000;
randn('seed',100)
[X2,y2]=generate_gauss_classes(m,S,P,N_2);
```

Step 2. For the classification task, use function *k_nn_classifier* and type

```
k=3;
z=k_nn_classifier(X1,y1,k,X2);
```

To compute the classification error, type

```
pr_err=sum(z~=y2)/length(y2)
```

The classification error is 15.12%. Note that different seeds for the *randn* function are likely to lead to slightly different results. ■

Exercise 1.10.1
Repeat Example 1.10.1 for $k = 1, 7, 15$. For each case compute the classification error rate. Compare the results with the error rate obtained by the optimal Bayesian classifier, using the true values of the mean and the covariance matrix.

Exercise 1.10.2
Compose your own example of a 2-class classification task in the 5-dimensional space. Assume the data to follow the Gaussian pdf in both classes. Choose the mean values and covariance matrices. Produce two data sets, one for training and one for testing. Use the nearest neighbor classifier. Experiment with different values of the mean values, the covariance matrix, the parameter k, and the length of the training data set. Comment on the obtained results as well as the computational time involved.

Classifiers Based on Cost Function Optimization

2.1 INTRODUCTION

This chapter deals with techniques and algorithms that "emancipate" from the Bayes decision theory rationale. The focus is on the *direct* design of a discriminant function/decision surface that separates the classes in some optimal sense according to an adopted criterion. The techniques that are built around the optimal Bayesian classifier rely on the estimation of the pdf functions describing the data distribution in each class. However, in general this turns out to be a difficult task, especially in high-dimensional spaces. Alternatively, one may focus on designing a decision surface that separates the classes directly from the training data set, without having to deduce it from the pdfs. This is an easier problem, and although the solution may not correspond to the optimal (Bayesian) classifier, in practice, where the size of the available training data set is *limited*, it most often turns out to result in better performance compared to that of the Bayes classifier when the latter employs *estimates* of the involved pdfs. The interested reader can find a few more related comments in [Theo 09, Section 10.5.2].

We begin with the simple case of designing a linear classifier, described by the equation

$$w^T x + w_0 = 0$$

which can also be written as

$$w'^T x' \equiv [w^T, w_0] \begin{bmatrix} x \\ 1 \end{bmatrix} = 0$$

That is, instead of working with hyperplanes in the $\mathcal{R}^l$ space, we work with hyperplanes in the $\mathcal{R}^{l+1}$ space, which pass through the *origin*. This is only for notational simplification.

Once a w' is estimated, an x is classified to class $\omega_1 (\omega_2)$ if

$$w'^T x' = w^T x + w_0 > (<)0$$

for the 2-class classification task. In other words, this classifier generates a hyperplane decision surface; points lying on one side of it are classified to ω_1 and points lying on the other side are classified to ω_2. For notational simplicity, we drop out the prime and adhere to the notation w, x; the vectors are assumed to be augmented with w_0 and 1, respectively, and they reside in the $\mathcal{R}^{l+1}$ space.

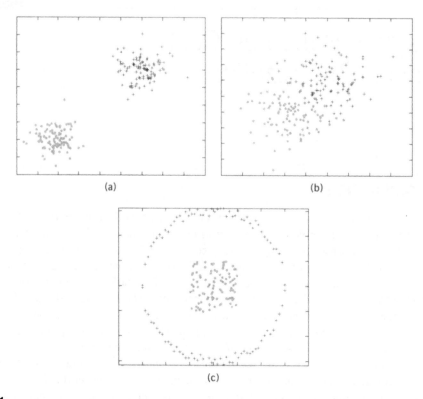

FIGURE 2.1

(a) Linearly separable 2-class classification problem; (b)–(c) 2-class classification problems that are not linearly separable.

2.2 THE PERCEPTRON ALGORITHM

The perceptron algorithm is appropriate for the 2-class problem and for classes that are *linearly separable*. Figure 2.1(a) shows an example of linearly separable classes, and Figure 2.1(b,c) shows two cases of classes that are not linearly separable. The perceptron algorithm computes the values of the weights w of a linear classifier, which separates the two classes.

The algorithm is iterative. It starts with an initial estimate in the extended $(l + 1)$-dimensional space and converges to a solution in a *finite* number of iteration steps. The solution w correctly classifies all the training points (assuming, of course, that they stem from linearly separable classes). Note that the perceptron algorithm converges to one out of *infinite* possible solutions. Starting from different initial conditions, different hyperplanes result. The update at the tth iteration step has the simple form

$$w(t + 1) = w(t) - \rho_t \sum_{x \in Y} \delta_x x$$

where w is the augmented-by-w_0 vector, Y is the set of wrongly classified samples by the current estimate $w(t)$, δ_x is -1 if $x \in \omega_1$ and $+1$ if $x \in \omega_2$, and ρ_t is a user-defined parameter that controls the convergence speed and must obey certain requirements to guarantee convergence (for example, ρ_t can be chosen to be constant, $\rho_t = \rho$). The algorithm converges when Y becomes empty.

Once the classifier has been computed, a point, x, is classified to either of the two classes depending on the outcome of the following operation:

$$f(w^T x) = f(w_1 x(1) + w_2 x(2) + \cdots + w_l x(l) + w_0) \tag{2.1}$$

The function $f(\cdot)$ in its simplest form is the step or sign function ($f(z) = 1$ if $z > 0$; $f(z) = -1$ if $z < 0$). However, it may have other forms; for example, the output may be either 1 or 0 for $z > 0$ and $z < 0$, respectively. In general, it is known as the *activation* function.

The basic network model, known as *perceptron* or *neuron*, that implements the classification operation implied by the operation in Eq. (2.1), is shown in Figure 2.2. For a more theoretical treatment of the perceptron algorithm see [Theo 09, Section 3.3].

To run the perceptron algorithm, type

$$[w, iter, mis\_clas] = perce(X, y, w\_ini, rho)$$

where

X is the $(l+1) \times N$ matrix that contains the (augmented-by-1) training vectors as columns,

y is the N-dimensional vector, whose ith component is the class label of the respective feature vector (-1 or $+1$),

w_ini is the initial estimate of w,

rho is the (constant) learning rate,

w is the vector computed by the algorithm,

$iter$ is the number of performed iterations,

mis_clas is the number of misclassified vectors (it is nonzero if the iterations reach 20000, which indicates that the algorithm has not converged and the problem is likely not to be linearly separable; otherwise it is 0).

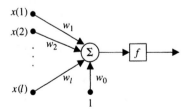

FIGURE 2.2

Perceptron structure.

Example 2.2.1. Generate four 2-dimensional data sets X_i, $i = 1,\ldots,4$, each containing data vectors from two classes. In all X_i's the first class (denoted -1) contains 100 vectors uniformly distributed in the square $[0, 2] \times [0, 2]$. The second class (denoted $+1$) contains another 100 vectors uniformly distributed in the squares $[3, 5] \times [3, 5]$, $[2, 4] \times [2, 4]$, $[0, 2] \times [2, 4]$, and $[1, 3] \times [1, 3]$ for X_1, X_2, X_3, and X_4, respectively. Each data vector is augmented with a third coordinate that equals 1.

Perform the following steps:

1. Plot the four data sets and notice that as we move from X_1 to X_3 the classes approach each other but remain linearly separable. In X_4 the two classes overlap.
2. Run the perceptron algorithm for each X_i, $i = 1,\ldots,4$, with learning rate parameters 0.01 and 0.05 and initial estimate for the parameter vector $[1, 1, -0.5]^T$.
3. Run the perceptron algorithm for X_3 with learning rate 0.05 using as initial estimates for w $[1, 1, -0.5]^T$ and $[1, 1, 0.5]^T$.
4. Comment on the results.

Solution. To retain the reproducibility of the results, the MATLAB random number generator for the uniform distribution is initialized using as seed the value of 0. This is achieved by typing

```
rand('seed',0)
```

To generate the data set X_1 as well as the vector containing the class labels of the points in it, type

```
N=[100 100]; % Number of vectors in each class
l=2;  % Dimensionality of the input space
x=[3 3]';
X1=[2*rand(l,N(1)) 2*rand(l,N(2))+x*ones(1,N(2))];
X1=[X1; ones(1,sum(N))];
y1=[-ones(1,N(1)) ones(1,N(2))];
```

The remaining data sets may be generated by repeating the preceding code where the third line is replaced by

```
x=[2 2]'; for X2
x=[0 2]'; for X3
x=[1 1]'; for X4
```

Then, do the following:

Step 1. To plot X_1, where points of different classes are denoted by different colors, type

```
figure(1), plot(X1(1,y1==1),X1(2,y1==1),'bo',...
X1(1,y1==-1),X1(2,y1==-1),'r.')
figure(1), axis equal
```

Table 2.1 Number of Iterations Performed by the Perceptron Algorithm in Example 2.2.1

	X_1	X_2	X_3	X_4
rho$=0.01$	134	134	5441	No convergence
rho$=0.05$	5	5	252	No convergence

Step 2. To run the perceptron algorithm for X_1 with learning parameter 0.01, type

```
rho=0.01;          % Learning rate
w_ini=[1 1 -0.5]';
[w,iter,mis_clas]=perce(X1,y1,w_ini,rho)
```

By altering the previous code, the perceptron algorithm may be performed on the remaining data sets using different learning parameter values. Table 2.1 contains the results obtained by performing the previous experiments.

Step 3. Working as in step 2, compute the w's using the perceptron algorithm for initial estimates $[1, 1, -0.5]^T$ and $[1, 1, 0.5]^T$. The results are $[-0.0002, 0.5364, -1.0725]^T$ and $[-0.0103, 0.3839, -0.7525]^T$, respectively.

Step 4. Based on the previous results, three general conclusions may be drawn: First, for a fixed learning parameter, the number of iterations (in general) increases as the classes move closer to each other (i.e., as the problem becomes more difficult). Second, the algorithm fails to converge for the data set X_4, where the classes are not linearly separable (it runs for the maximum allowable number of iterations that we have set). Third, different initial estimates for w may lead to different final estimates for it (although all of them are optimal in the sense that they separate the training data of the two classes). ∎

2.2.1 The Online Form of the Perceptron Algorithm

The form of the perceptron algorithm just described is known as the *batch* form; at each iteration step, all of the data points are considered and an update is performed after *all* of the data have been processed by the current estimate. In the online version, data are considered sequentially, several times, and an update may be performed after the consideration of *each* point. Every set of N successive iterations, where all data points have been considered, is known as an *epoch*. The algorithmic update is performed according to the following scheme:

$$w(t+1) = w(t) + \rho y_{(t)} x_{(t)}, \quad \text{if } y_{(t)}(w^T(t)x_{(t)}) \leq 0$$

$$w(t+1) = w(t) \quad \text{otherwise}$$

where ρ is the parameter controlling convergence, and $x_{(t)}$ denotes the point considered in the tth iteration.

The class labels $y_{(t)}$ are equal to -1 and $+1$ for the two classes ω_2 and ω_1, respectively. A pseudocode for this scheme is given as:

1. Choose $w(0)$; usually $w(0) = 0$
2. Choose ρ
3. Choose *max_iter* (maximum number of iterations)
4. $t = 0$
5. Repeat
   - $count\_miscl = 0$
   - For $i = 1$ to N
     - If $y_i(w(t)^T x_i) \leq 0$, then
       $$w(t+1) = w(t) + \rho y_i x_i$$
       $$count\_miscl = count\_miscl + 1$$
     - Else
       $$w(t+1) = w(t)$$
     - End {If}
     - $t = t + 1$
   - End {For}
6. Until $count\_miscl = 0$ or $(t >= max\_iter)$

Example 2.2.2. Run the online version of the perceptron algorithm on the data sets of Example 2.2.1, with learning parameter values 0.01 and 0.05 and an initial estimate for the parameter vector $[1, 1, -0.5]^T$. Comment on the results.

Solution. Repeat the code given in Example 2.2.1, where now the *perce* function is replaced by the *perce_online* function. (The maximum number of iterations was set to 10^7. This large number is required when classes are very close together.) The results obtained after performing the experiments are given in Table 2.2. Once more, the closer the classes, the more iterations required for convergence. In addition, no convergence occurs for data sets containing classes that are not linearly separable.

Table 2.2 Number of Iterations Performed by Online Perceptron Algorithm in Example 2.2.2

	X_1	X_2	X_3	X_4
rho=0.01	600	600	6589400	No convergence
rho=0.05	400	400	7729200	No convergence

Note: *The number of iterations required for convergence increases by 1 when the next vector is considered. In contrast, in the batch mode of the algorithm the number of iterations increases by 1 after the whole data set has been considered once.*

2.3 THE SUM OF ERROR SQUARES CLASSIFIER

The goal in this section remains the same: to estimate the vector of parameters, w, in the extended $\mathcal{R}^{l+1}$ space of a linear classifier (hyperplane),

$$w^T x = 0$$

where x is the (augmented-by-1) feature vector. However, in this section the assumption of linear separability is *not required*. The method, also known as least squares (LS), estimates the best linear classifier, where the term "best" corresponds to the w that minimizes the cost:

$$J(w) = \sum_{i=1}^{N} (y_i - w^T x_i)^2 \tag{2.2}$$

where y_i is the known class label of x_i, $i = 1, 2, \ldots, N$; and N is the number of training points.

Define

$$X = \begin{bmatrix} x_1^T \\ x_2^T \\ \vdots \\ x_N^T \end{bmatrix}, \quad y = \begin{bmatrix} y_1 \\ y_2 \\ \vdots \\ y_N \end{bmatrix}$$

It can be shown that the LS estimate is given by

$$\hat{w} = (X^T X)^{-1} X^T y \tag{2.3}$$

The matrix $(X^T X)^{-1} X^T$ is also known as the *pseudoinverse* of X and is denoted as $X^{\#}$ [Theo 09, Section 3.4.3].

A significant advantage of the LS method is that it has a *single* solution (corresponding to the single minimum of $J(w)$). In addition, this is obtained by solving a *linear* system of equations (Eq. (2.3)).

In practice, the inversion of the $(l+1) \times (l+1)$ matrix, $X^T X$, may pose some numerical difficulties, especially in high-dimensional spaces. Besides being computationally complex, it is not uncommon for the matrix to be nearly singular. In such cases, one may add a small positive constant along the main diagonal and solve the system:

$$\hat{w} = (X^T X + CI)^{-1} X^T y \tag{2.4}$$

where I is the $(l+1) \times (l+1)$ identity matrix, and C is a user-defined small positive constant. It can be shown [Theo 09, Section 4.19.2] that Eq. (2.4) is the minimizer of the *regularized* version of the cost in Eq. (2.2), or

$$J(w) = \sum_{i=1}^{N} (y_i - w^T x_i)^2 + Cw^T w \tag{2.5}$$

To obtain the LS solution use the function

$$function\ [w] = SSErr(X,\ y, C)$$

where

X, y are defined as in the *perce* function,

C is the parameter included in Eq. (2.4),

w is the LS estimator returned by the function.

Note that the original (nonregularized) version of the LS classifier is obtained for $C = 0$.

Example 2.3.1

1. Generate a set X_1 of $N_1 = 200$ data vectors, such that the first 100 vectors stem from class ω_1, which is modeled by the Gaussian distribution with mean $m_1 = [0, 0, 0, 0, 0]^T$. The rest stem from class ω_2, which is modeled by the Gaussian distribution with mean $m_2 = [1, 1, 1, 1, 1]^T$. Both distributions share the following covariance matrix:

$$S = \begin{bmatrix} 0.9 & 0.3 & 0.2 & 0.05 & 0.02 \\ 0.3 & 0.8 & 0.1 & 0.2 & 0.05 \\ 0.2 & 0.1 & 0.7 & 0.015 & 0.07 \\ 0.05 & 0.2 & 0.015 & 0.8 & 0.01 \\ 0.02 & 0.05 & 0.07 & 0.01 & 0.75 \end{bmatrix}$$

Generate an additional data set X_2 of $N_2 = 200$ data vectors, following the prescription used for X_1. Apply the optimal Bayes classifier on X_2 and compute the classification error.

2. Augment each feature vector in X_1 and X_2 by adding a 1 as the last coordinate. Define the class labels as -1 and $+1$ for the two classes, respectively. Using X_1 as the training set, apply the *SSErr* MATLAB function (with $C = 0$) to obtain the LS estimate $\hat{w}$. Use this estimate to classify the vectors of X_2 according to the inequality

$$\hat{w}^T x > (<)0$$

Compute the probability of error. Compare the results with those obtained in step 1.

3. Repeat the previous steps, first with X_2 replaced by a set X_3 containing $N_3 = 10,000$ data vectors and then with a set X_4 containing $N_4 = 100,000$ data vectors. Both X_3 and X_4 are generated using the prescription adopted for X_1. Comment on the results.

Solution. Do the following:

Step 1. To ensure reproducibility of the results, set $seed = 0$ for the *randn* MATLAB function for the generation of X_1; for the generation of X_2, X_3, and X_4 set $seed = 100$. Set the parameters of the Gaussians that model the two classes by typing

```
m(:,1)=[0 0 0 0 0]';
m(:,2)=[1 1 1 1 1]';
S=[.9 .3 .2 .05 .02; .3 .8 .1 .2 .05;
```

```
.2 .1 .7 .015 .07; .05 .2 .015 .8 .01; .02 .05 .07 .01 .75];
P=[1/2 1/2];
```

To generate X_1 and the required class labels (1 for ω_1, 2 for ω_2), type

```
N1=200;
randn('seed',0)
X1=[mvnrnd(m(:,1),S,fix(N1/2)); mvnrnd(m(:,2),S,N1-fix(N1/2))]';
z1=[ones(1,fix(N1/2)) 2*ones(1,N1-fix(N1/2))];
```

X_2 is generated in a similar fashion. To compute the Bayesian classification error based on X_2, type

```
S_true(:,:,1)=S;
S_true(:,:,2)=S;
[z]=bayes_classifier(m,S_true,P,X2);
err_Bayes_true=sum(z~=z2)/sum(N2)
```

This error is 14%.

Step 2. To augment the data vectors of X_1 by an additional coordinate that equals $+1$, and to change the class labels from 1, 2 (used before) to $-1, +1$, respectively, type

```
X1=[X1; ones(1,sum(N1))];
y1=2*z1-3;
```

The set X_2 is treated similarly. To compute the classification error of the LS classifier based on X_2, type

```
[w]=SSErr(X1,y1,0);
SSE_out=2*(w'*X2>0)-1;
err_SSE=sum(SSE_out.*y2<0)/sum(N2)
```

This error is 15%.

Step 3. By replacing X_2 with X_3 and X_4, and applying the code given in steps 1 and 2, the results shown in Table 2.3 are obtained. From this table one can easily see that the classification error of the LS

Table 2.3 Classification Error Estimates for the Bayesian and LS Classifiers as Test Points Increase, in Example 2.3.1

	Bayesian Classifier	LS Classifier
N = 200	14.00%	15.00%
N = 10,000	14.68%	14.98%
N = 100,000	14.67%	14.75%

classifier is very close to that of the Bayesian classifier. This is justified by the fact that the optimal decision classifier for our problem is linear [Theo 09, Section 2.4.2]. Note that as the classification errors of the two classifiers are computed with more accuracy (i.e., as the number of vectors in the test set increases), they get closer to each other. This shows the importance of having large data sets not only for training but for testing as well. ∎

Example 2.3.2. Generate a set of $N_1 = 1000$ data vectors such that the first 500 stem from class ω_1 modeled by the Gaussian distribution with mean $m_1 = [0, 0, 0, 0, 0]^T$ and the rest stem from class ω_2 modeled by the Gaussian distribution with mean $m_2 = [2, 2, 0, 2, 2]^T$. Both distributions have the following covariance matrix:

$$S = \begin{bmatrix} 1 & 0 & 0 & 0 & 0 \\ 0 & 1 & 0 & 0 & 0 \\ 0 & 0 & 10^{-350} & 0 & 0 \\ 0 & 0 & 0 & 1 & 0 \\ 0 & 0 & 0 & 0 & 1 \end{bmatrix}$$

Each data vector is augmented by a sixth coordinate, which equals $+1$ for all vectors. Let X_1 be the $(l+1) \times N$ matrix whose columns are the vectors of the data set (for reproducibility of the results, set $seed = 0$ for the $randn$ MATLAB function).

In addition, generate a set X_2 that contains 10,000 points, using the prescription followed for X_1 (for reproducibility of the results, set $seed = 100$ for the $randn$ MATLAB function).

1. Compute the condition number of the matrix $X_1 X_1^T$ (the larger the condition number, the closer the matrix is to singularity). Run the original (nonregularized) version of the LS classifier (Eq. (2.3)) to estimate w.

2. Repeat step 1 for the regularized version (Eq. (2.4)) of the LS classifier for $C = 0.1$.

3. Comment on the results obtained in steps 1 and 2.

4. Estimate the classification error associated with the w's resulting from steps 1 and 2 based on the data set X_2.

Solution. To generate the matrix X_1, type

```
m=[0 0 0 0 0; 2 2 0 2 2]';
S=[1 0 0 0 0; 0 1 0 0 0; 0 0 10^(-350) 0 0; 0 0 0 1 0; 0 0 0 0 1];
[l,l]=size(S);
N1=1000;
randn('seed',0)
X1=[mvnrnd(m(:,1),S,fix(N1/2)); mvnrnd(m(:,2),S,N1-fix(N1/2))]';
X1=[X1; ones(1,N1)];
y1=[ones(1,fix(N1/2)) -ones(1,N1-fix(N1/2))];
```

In a similar manner, produce X_2. Take the following steps:

Step 1. To compute the condition number of $X_1 X_1^T$ and the solution vector w for the original version of the LS classifier, type

```
cond_num=cond(X1*X1')
w=SSErr(X1,y1,0)
```

Step 2. To repeat step 1 for the regularized version of the LS classifier, type

```
C=0.1;
cond_num=cond(X1*X1'+C*eye(l+1))
w=SSErr(X1,y1,C)
```

Step 3. Observe that the condition number of $X_1 X_1^T$ (1.4767×10^{17}) is orders of magnitude greater than that of $X_1 X_1^T + CI$ (9.3791×10^4), where I is the $(l+1) \times (l+1)$ identity matrix. In the original version ($C = 0$), and for the current MATLAB working precision, $X_1 X_1^T$ is singular and no estimates of w are provided, since the linear system (Eq. (2.3)) cannot be solved. In contrast, the regularized version $X_1 X_1^T + CI$ is invertible and an estimate for w is obtained, namely $[-0.2158, -0.1888, 0, -0.2178, -0.1851, 0.8012]^T$.

Step 4. Compute the classification error on X_2 for a given w by typing

```
SSE_out=2*(w'*X2>0)-1;
err_SSE=sum(SSE_out.*y2<0)/N2
```

For the regularized version of the LS classifier, the classification error rate equals 2.67%.   ◼

2.3.1 The Multiclass LS Classifier

Assume that we are given a set of N training data points, $x_i \in \mathcal{R}^l$, $i = 1, 2, \ldots, N$, and assume that these originate from $c > 2$ classes. The task is to design a classifier that consists of c linear discriminant functions (one for each class):

$$g_j(x) \equiv w_j^T x + w_{j0}, \quad j = 1, 2, \ldots, c$$

The design is based on the LS criterion.

The classification rule is now as follows: Given x, classify it to class ω_i if

$$g_i(x) > g_j(x), \quad \forall j \neq i$$

Following the rationale exposed in [Theo 09, Section 3.4.1], we design the c linear functions as follows: For each x_i, define the c-dimensional class label vector

$$y_i = [y_{i1}, y_{i2}, \ldots, y_{ic}]^T, \quad i = 1, 2, \ldots, N$$

whose jth element, y_{ij}, is 1 if $x_i \in \omega_j$, and 0 otherwise. Estimate w_j and w_{j0} to minimize the cost

$$\sum_{i=1}^{N}(y_{ij} - w_j^T x_i - w_{j0})^2, \quad j = 1, 2, \ldots, c$$

That is, one has to solve c LS problems, one for each class. It has to be emphasized that *the class labels associated with each training point are different for each one of the c problems depending on whether the point belongs to the respective class or not.* More specifically, in the jth LS problem, the class label is 1 for each point of the jth class and 0 for the points from all the other classes. Note that each hyperplane, w_j, is trained so that ideally all the points from class ω_j lie on one of its sides and all the other points lie on the other side.

To solve each one of the c LS problems, we follow exactly the same procedure followed for Eq. (2.2). As before, the thresholds w_{j0} are embedded in the respective w_j's by extending the dimensionality of the feature space by one.

Example 2.3.3

1. Consider a 3-class classification problem that involves three equiprobable classes ω_1, ω_2, and ω_3. The classes are modeled by Gaussian distributions with means $m_1 = [1, 1, 1]^T$, $m_2 = [5, 3, 2]^T$, and $m_3 = [3, 3, 4]^T$, respectively. All distributions share the same covariance matrix:

$$S = \begin{bmatrix} 0.8 & 0.2 & 0.1 \\ 0.2 & 0.8 & 0.2 \\ 0.1 & 0.2 & 0.8 \end{bmatrix}$$

Generate and plot two data sets, X_1 (training set) and X_2 (test set), which respectively consist of 1000 and 10,000 data vectors. Apply the *SSErr* MATLAB function on X_1 to estimate the parameter vectors w_1, w_2, w_3 of the three linear discriminant functions in the extended 4-dimensional space. Use the set X_2 to compute the error probability.

2. From the theory [Theo 09, Section 3.5.2], it is known that the LS criterion, when used with 0, 1 as desired response values (class labels), provides the LS estimates of the posterior probabilities; that is, if w_j is the LS estimate of the parameter vector of the jth linear discriminant function, then

$$g_j(x) \equiv w_j^T x \approx P(\omega_j | x)$$

To verify this, compute the true a posteriori probabilities $P(\omega_j | x_i)$ and their LS estimates, $g_j(x_i)$, $j = 1, \ldots, c$, $i = 1, \ldots, N_2$, on the vectors of X_2 (N_2 is the number of vectors in X_2). Then compute the average square error of the estimate of the $P(\omega_j | x_i)$'s using the $g_j(x_i)$'s.

3. Compute the classification error of the (optimal) Bayesian classifier on X_2 and compare it with that resulting from the LS classifier in step 1.

Hint
Recall that

$$P(\omega_j | x) = \frac{p(x | \omega_j)P(\omega_j)}{p(x)}, \quad j = 1, 2, 3$$

where

$$p(x) = P(\omega_1)p(x|\omega_1) + P(\omega_2)p(x|\omega_2) + P(\omega_3)p(x|\omega_3)$$

with $P(\omega_i)$ being the a priori probability of class ω_i.

Solution. Take the following steps:

Step 1. To ensure reproducibility of the results, initialize the *randn* MATLAB function using as seed the values 0 for X_1 and 100 for X_2. To generate X_1, type

```
% Definition of the parameters
m=[1 1 1; 5 3 2; 3 3 4]';
[l,c]=size(m);
S1=[0.8 0.2 0.1; 0.2 0.8 0.2; 0.1 0.2 0.8];
S(:,:,1)=S1;
S(:,:,2)=S1;
S(:,:,3)=S1;
P=[1/3 1/3 1/3];
% Generation of the data set X1
N1=1000;
randn('seed',0)
[X1,y1]=generate_gauss_classes(m,S,P,N1);
[l,N1]=size(X1);
X1=[X1; ones(1,N1)];
```

To plot the data set X_1, using different colors for points of different classes, type

```
figure(1), plot3(X1(1,y1==1),X1(2,y1==1),X1(3,y1==1),'r.',...
X1(1,y1==2),X1(2,y1==2),X1(3,y1==2),'g.',...
X1(1,y1==3),X1(2,y1==3),X1(3,y1==3),'b.')
```

Use the Rotate 3D button to view the data set from different angles.

Next, define the $c \times N_1$ dimensional matrix z_1, each column of which corresponds to a training point. Specifically, its ith column elements equal zero except one, which equals unity. The position of the latter indicates the class where the corresponding vector x_i of X_1 belongs.

```
z1=zeros(c,N1);
for i=1:N1
    z1(y1(i),i)=1;
end
```

In a similar manner, generate X_2 and z_2. To estimate the parameter vectors of the three discriminant functions, type

```
w_all=[];
for i=1:c
    w=SSErr(X1,z1(i,:),0);
    w_all=[w_all w];
end
```

In the $(l+1) \times c$ matrix w_all, the ith column corresponds to the parameter vector of the ith discriminant function.

To compute the classification error using the set X_2, type

```
[vali,class_est]=max(w_all'*X2);
err=sum(class_est~=y2)/N2
```

The classification error in this case is 5.11% (estimated based on X_2).

Step 2. To compute the estimates of the a posteriori probabilities as they result in the framework of the LS classifier, type

```
aposte_est=w_all'*X2;
```

To compute the true a posteriori probabilities, type the following block of statements

```
aposte=[];
for i=1:N2
    t=zeros(c,1);
    for j=1:c
        t(j)=comp_gauss_dens_val(m(:,j),S(:,:,j),X2(1:1,i))*P(j);
    end
    tot_t=sum(t);
    aposte=[aposte t/tot_t];
end
```

To compute the average square error in the estimation of the $P(\omega_j|x_i)$'s by using the $g_j(x_i)$'s, type

```
approx_err=sum(sum((aposte-aposte_est).^2))/(N2*c)
```

The error is 0.0397. Note that this is very low, indicating a good estimate.

Step 3. To compute the optimal Bayesian classification error, and since the true a posteriori probabilities are known, type

```
[vali,class]=max(aposte);
err_ba=sum(class~=y2)/N2
```

Alternatively, use the *bayes_classifier* MATLAB function. The classification error for this case is 4.82% (estimated based on X_2).

Some comments are in order. First, it is easy to check that the probability estimates may be greater than 1 or less than 0. Although this contradicts the physical meaning of the probability, it can happen since the method that estimates the parameter vector w of the LS classifier does not *impose* any restrictions affecting the values of the a posteriori probabilities (i.e., nonnegativity and sum to 1). However, the sum of the estimates of the a posteriori probabilities for a given vector is very close to 1. ■

Exercise 2.3.1

1. Consider the setup of Example 2.3.3 where now the means of the three classes ω_1, ω_2, and ω_3 are $m_1 = [0, 0, 0]^T$, $m_2 = [1, 2, 2]^T$, and $m_3 = [3, 3, 4]^T$, respectively. Apply the *SSErr* MATLAB function on the data set X_1 to estimate the parameter vectors w_1, w_2, and w_3 of the three linear discriminant functions, in the extended 4-dimensional space. Use the set X_2 to compute the error probability.
2. Compute the classification error of the (optimal) Bayesian classifier on X_2 and compare it with that resulting from the LS classifier in step 1.

Hint

It turns out that the classification errors for the LS and Bayesian classifiers are 18.36% and 9.90%, respectively. In contrast to Example 2.3.3, the difference between these errors is large. (Why? Observe the plot of X_1 and think how w_1, w_2, and w_3 are placed in the feature space.)

2.4 SUPPORT VECTOR MACHINES: THE LINEAR CASE

Analytic treatment and derivation of the associated formulas for the SVM classifiers can be found in [Theo 09, Section 3.7]. Here, besides the MATLAB functions, we provide a few hints related to the physical understanding behind the SVM rationale.

At the heart of SVM classifier design is the notion of the *margin*. Consider the linear classifier

$$w^T x + w_0 = 0 \tag{2.6}$$

The margin is the region between the two *parallel* hyperplanes

$$w^T x + w_0 = 1, \quad w^T x + w_0 = -1 \tag{2.7}$$

It can easily be shown [Theo 09, Section 3.2] that the Euclidean distance of any point that lies on either of the two hyperplanes in Eq. (2.7) from the classifier hyperplane given by Eq. (2.6) is equal to $\frac{1}{||w||}$, where $|| \cdot ||$ denotes the Euclidean norm.

A question sometimes raised by a newcomer in the field is why the margin is defined by these two "magic" numbers, $+1$ and -1. The answer is that this is not an issue. Let us consider a hyperplane in space—for example, Eq. (2.6), as shown in Figure 2.3 by the full line and two parallel to it hyperplanes (*dotted lines*) $w^T x + w_0 = \pm d$. The parameter d can take any value, which means that the two planes can be close to or far away from each other. Fixing the value of d and dividing both sides of the previous equation by d, we obtain ± 1 on the right side. However, the direction and the position in space of the two

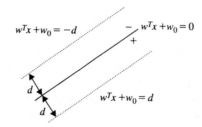

FIGURE 2.3

Line and its margin of size $2d$.

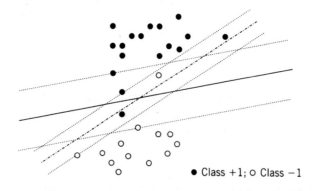

FIGURE 2.4

Two linear classifiers and the associated margin lines for a 2-class classification problem (*filled circles* correspond to class +1; *empty circles* correspond to class −1).

hyperplanes do not change. The same applies to the hyperplane described by Eq. (2.6). Normalization by a constant value d has no effect on the points that lie on (and define) a hyperplane.

So far, we have considered that an error is "committed" by a point if it is on the wrong side of the decision surface formed by the respective classifier. Now we are going to be more demanding. It is not only the points on the wrong side of the classifier that contribute to an error-counting function; it is also any point that lies *inside* the margin, even if it is on the correct side of the classifier. Only points that lie *outside* the margin and on the correct side of the classifier make no contribution to the error-counting cost. Figure 2.4 shows two overlapping classes and two linear classifiers denoted by a dash-dotted and a solid line, respectively. For both cases, the margins have been chosen to include five points. Observe that for the case of the "dash-dotted" classifier, in order to include five points the margin had to be made narrow.

Imagine that the open and filled circles in Figure 2.4 are houses in two nearby villages and that a road must be constructed in between the two villages. One has to decide where to construct the road so that it will be as wide as possible and incur the least cost (in the sense of demolishing the smallest number of houses). No sensible engineer would choose the "dash-dotted" option.

The idea is similar with designing a classifier. *It should be "placed" between the highly populated (high probability density) areas of the two classes and in a region that is sparse in data, leaving the largest possible margin.* This is dictated by the requirement for good *generalization performance* that any classifier has to exhibit. That is, the classifier must exhibit good error performance when it is faced with data outside the training set. Any classifier "knows" the training set very well, since it has been trained on it. Thus, we can construct a classifier that results in a very low error rate on the training set but behaves poorly when faced with "unknown" data. Loosely speaking, this is because the classifier has adjusted itself to learn the "idiosyncrasies" of the specific training set—its specific details—and so it cannot behave well in a slightly different set [Theo 09, Sections 3.7.1, 4.9, 5.1]. Elaborate on this reasoning and explain why the "dash-dotted" classifier is expected to result in inferior generalization performance compared to the "solid" classifier, even though both have similar performance with respect to the number of margin errors on the training set.

This discussion leads to the following mathematical formulation. Given a set of training points, x_i, with respective class labels, $y_i \in \{-1, 1\}$, $i = 1, 2, \ldots, N$, for a 2-class classification task, compute a hyperplane (Eq. (2.6)) so as to

$$\text{Minimize} \quad J(w, w_0, \xi) = \frac{1}{2}||w||^2 + C \sum_{i=1}^{N} \xi_i \tag{2.8}$$

$$\text{Subject to} \quad w^T x_i + w_0 \geq 1 - \xi_i, \quad \text{if } x_i \in \omega_1 \tag{2.9}$$

$$w^T x_i + w_0 \leq -1 + \xi_i, \quad \text{if } x_i \in \omega_2 \tag{2.10}$$

$$\xi_i \geq 0 \tag{2.11}$$

The margin width is equal to $2/||w||$. The margin errors, ξ_i, are nonnegative; they are zero for points outside the margin and on the correct side of the classifier and positive for points inside or outside the margin and on the wrong side of the classifier (This can be verified by a close inspection of the constraints in Eqs. (2.9) and (2.10). C is a user-defined constant. Minimizing the cost is a trade-off between a large margin and a small number of margin errors (for more details see [Theo 09, Section 3.7]). It turns out that the solution is given as a weighted average of the training points:

$$w = \sum_{i=1}^{N} \lambda_i y_i x_i \tag{2.12}$$

The coefficients λ_i are the Lagrange multipliers of the optimization task and they are zero for all points outside the margin and on the correct side of the classifier. These points therefore do not contribute to the formation of the direction of the classifier. The rest of the points, with nonzero λ_i's, which contribute to the buildup of w, are called *support vectors*.

To generate a linear SVM classifier, the *SMO2* MATLAB function can be used. Specifically, *SMO2* is called by typing

```
[alpha, w0, w, evals, stp, glob] = ...
SMO2(X', y', kernel, kpar1, kpar2, C, tol, steps, eps, method)
```

where its inputs are

a matrix X' containing the points of the data set (each row is a point),

the class labels of the data points (y'),

the type of kernel function to be used (in our case *'linear'*),

two kernel parameters *kpar1* and *kpar2* (in the linear case both are set to 0),

the parameter C,

the parameter *tol*,

the maximum number of iteration steps of the algorithm,

a threshold *eps* (a very small number, typically on the order of 10^{-10}) used in the comparison of two numbers (if their difference is less than this threshold, they are considered equal to each other),

the optimization method to be used ($0 \rightarrow$ Platt, $1 \rightarrow$ Keerthi modification 1, $2 \rightarrow$ Keerthi modification 2),[1]

and its outputs are

alpha is a vector containing the Lagrange multipliers corresponding to the training points,

w0 is the threshold value,

w is the vector containing the hyperplane parameters, returned by the algorithm.

The parameter *tol* is a scalar that controls the accuracy of the obtained solution [Theo 09, Section 3.7.2]. The larger the value of *tol* is, the farther from the solution the algorithm may stop. A typical value for *tol* is 0.001.

Example 2.4.1. In the 2-dimensional space, we are given two equiprobable classes, which follow Gaussian distributions with means $m_1 = [0, 0]^T$ and $m_2 = [1.2, 1.2]^T$ and covariance matrices $S_1 = S_2 = 0.2I$, where I is the 2×2 identity matrix.

1. Generate and plot a data set X_1 containing 200 points from each class (400 points total), to be used for training (use the value of 50 as seed for the built-in MATLAB *randn* function). Generate another data set X_2 containing 200 points from each class, to be used for testing (use the value of 100 as seed for the built-in MATLAB *randn* function).
2. Based on X_1, run Platt's algorithm to generate six SVM classifiers that separate the two classes, using $C = 0.1, 0.2, 0.5, 1, 2, 20$. Set $tol = 0.001$.
    (a) Compute the classification error on the training and test sets.
    (b) Count the support vectors.
    (c) Compute the margin $(2/\|w\|)$.
    (d) Plot the classifier as well as the margin lines.

Solution. Do the following:

Step 1. To generate the data set X_1, type

---

[1]More details can be found in the comments of the function.

```
randn('seed',50)
m=[0 0; 1.2 1.2]'; % mean vectors
S=0.2*eye(2); % covariance matrix
points_per_class=[200 200];
X1=mvnrnd(m(:,1),S,points_per_class(1))';
X1=[X1 mvnrnd(m(:,2),S,points_per_class(2))'];
y1=[ones(1,points_per_class(1))...
    -ones(1,points_per_class(2))];
```

To plot the data set X_1, type

```
figure(1), plot(X1(1,y1==1),X1(2,y1==1),'r.',...
X1(1,y1==-1),X1(2,y1==-1),'bo')
```

Notice that the classes overlap.

To generate X_2 repeat the code, replacing the first line with

```
randn('seed',100)
```

Step 2. To generate the required SVM classifier for $C = 0.1$, use the SMO2 function, typing

```
kernel='linear';
kpar1=0;
kpar2=0;
C=0.1;
tol=0.001;
steps=100000;
eps=10^(-10);
method=0;
[alpha, w0, w, evals, stp, glob] = SMO2(X1', y1',...
  kernel, kpar1, kpar2, C, tol, steps, eps, method)
```

The other classifiers are generated similarly.

(a) To compute the classification error on the training set, X_1, type

```
Pe_tr=sum((2*(w*X1-w0>0)-1).*y1<0)/length(y1)
```

The classification error on the test set, X_2, is computed similarly.

(b) To plot the classifier hyperplane as well as the margin lines, use the function *svcplot_book* by typing[2] the following:

---

[2] To plot the results of more than one experiment, change the value of *figt4*, which is the number of the figure where the plot will take place.

Table 2.4 Results for Various Values of C in Example 2.4.1

	$C = 0.1$	$C = 0.2$	$C = 0.5$	$C = 1$	$C = 2$	$C = 20$
No. support vectors	82	61	44	37	31	25
Training error	2.25%	2.00%	2.00%	2.25%	3.25%	2.50%
Test error	3.25%	3.00%	3.25%	3.25%	3.50%	3.50%
Margin	0.9410	0.8219	0.7085	0.6319	0.6047	0.3573

```
global figt4
figt4=2;
svcplot_book(X1',y1',kernel,kpar1,kpar2,alpha,-w0)
```

(c) To count the support vectors, type

```
sup_vec=sum(alpha>0)
```

(d) To compute the margin, type

```
marg=2/sqrt(sum(w.^2))
```

The results of these experiments are shown in Table 2.4. It is readily seen that the margin of the solution increases as C decreases. This is natural because decreasing C makes the "margin term" in Eq. (2.8) more significant. For the problem at hand, the best performance (minimum test error) is obtained for $C = 0.2$. ∎

Exercise 2.4.1
Repeat Example 2.4.1, now with the covariance matrices of the Gaussian distributions $S_1 = S_2 = 0.3I$. Comment on the results.

2.4.1 Multiclass Generalizations

In the previous section, we dealt with the SVM for the 2-class case. Although mathematical generalizations for the multiclass case are available, the task tends to become rather complex. When more than two classes are present, there are several different approaches that evolve around the 2-class case. In this section, we focus on one of these methods, known as *one-against-all* (for more details on the multiclass problem see [Theo 09, Section 3.7.3]). These techniques are not tailored to the SVM. They are general and can be used with any classifier developed for the 2-class problem. Moreover, they are not just pedagogical toys, but are actually widely used.

According to the one-against-all method, c classifiers have to be designed. Each one of them is designed to separate one class from the rest (recall that this was the problem solved in Section 2.3.1, based on the LS criterion). For the SVM paradigm, we have to design c linear classifiers:

$$w_j^T x + w_{j0}, \quad j = 1, 2, \ldots, c$$

For example, to design classifier w_1, we consider the training data of all classes other than ω_i to form the second class. Obviously, unless an error is committed we expect all points from class ω_1 to result in

$$w_1^T x + w_{10} > 0$$

and the data from the rest of the classes to result in negative outcomes. A x is classified in ω_i if

$$w_i^T x + w_{i0} > w_j^T x + w_{j0}, \quad \forall i \neq j$$

Remark

- A drawback of one-against-all is that after the training there are regions in the space, where no training data lie, for which more than one hyperplane gives a positive value or all of them result in negative values [Theo 09, Section 3.7.3, Problem 3.15].

Example 2.4.2

1. Generate and plot two data sets X_1 (training) and X_2 (test) using the prescription of Example 2.3.3, except that now each set consists of 120 data points.
2. Based on X_1, estimate the parameter vectors w_1, w_2, w_3 of the three linear discriminant functions using the first modification of Platt's algorithm [Keer 01] (SVM classifiers). Estimate the classification error rate based on X_2.

Solution. Proceed as follows:

Step 1. To generate X_1 and X_2, work as in Example 2.3.3. To plot X_1, type

```
figure(1), plot3(X1(1,z1(1,:)==1),X1(2,z1(1,:)==1),...
X1(3,z1(1,:)==1),'r.',X1(1,z1(2,:)==1),X1(2,z1(2,:)==1),...
X1(3,z1(2,:)==1),'gx',X1(1,z1(3,:)==1),X1(2,z1(3,:)==1),...
X1(3,z1(3,:)==1),'bo')
```

Step 2. In this case, matrices z_1 and z_2 are created in the same spirit as in Example 2.3.3, but now the 0 elements are replaced by -1. Specifically, type

```
z1=-ones(c,N1);
for i=1:N1
    z1(y1(i),i)=1;
end
```

where c is the number of classes and N_1 is the number of training vectors. Similarly obtain z_2.

To compute the SVM classifiers, type

```
kernel='linear';   %SVM parameter defintion
kpar1=0;
kpar2=0;
C=20;
```

```
tol=0.001;
steps=100000;
eps=10^(-10);
method=1;
for i=1:c
    [alpha(:,i), w0(i), w(i,:), evals, stp, glob] =...
    SMO2(X1', z1(i,:)', kernel, kpar1, kpar2, C,...
    tol, steps, eps, method)
    marg(i)=2/sqrt(sum(w(i,:).^2))  % Margin
    %Counting the number of support vectors
    sup_vec(i)=sum(alpha(:,i)>0)
end
```

To estimate the classification error rate based on X_2, type

```
[vali,class_est]=max(w*X2-w0'*ones(1,N2));
err_svm=sum(class_est~=y2)/N2
```

The classification error in this case turns out to be 5.00%. For comparison, we mention that the Bayesian classification error is 3.33%. (Explain why the latter value is different from that extracted in Example 2.3.3.) ∎

2.5 SVM: THE NONLINEAR CASE

To employ the SVM technique for solving a nonlinear classification task, we adopt the philosophy of mapping the feature vectors in a higher-dimensional space, where we expect, with high probability, the classes to be linearly separable. This is guaranteed by the celebrated Cover's theorem [Theo 09, Section 4.13]. The mapping is as follows:

$$x \mapsto \phi(x) \in H$$

where the dimension of H is higher than $\mathcal{R}^l$ and, depending on the choice of the (nonlinear) $\phi(\cdot)$, can even be infinite. Moreover, if the mapping function is carefully chosen from a known family of functions that have specific desirable properties, the inner product between the images $(\phi(x_1), \phi(x_2))$ of two points x_1, x_2 can be written as

$$< \phi(x_1), \phi(x_2) >= k(x_1, x_2)$$

where $< \cdot, \cdot >$ denotes the inner product operation in H and $k(\cdot, \cdot)$ is a function known as *kernel* function. That is, inner products in the high-dimensional space can be performed in terms of the associated kernel function acting in the original low-dimensional space. The space H associated with $k(\cdot, \cdot)$ is known as a reproducing kernel Hilbert space (RKHS) (for more formal definitions see [Theo 09, Section 4.18] and references therein).

A notable characteristic of the SVM optimization is that all operations can be cast in terms of inner products. Thus, to solve a linear problem in the high-dimensional space (after the mapping), all we have to do is replace the inner products with the corresponding kernel evaluations. Typical examples of kernel functions are (a) the *radial basis function* (RBF), defined as

$$k(x,y) = \exp\left(-\frac{||x-y||^2}{\sigma^2}\right)$$

where σ is a user-defined parameter that specifies the rate of decay of $k(x,y)$ toward zero, as y moves away from x and (b) the *polynomial function*, defined as

$$k(x,y) = (x^T y + \beta)^n$$

where β and n are user-defined parameters.

Note that solving a linear problem in the high-dimensional space is equivalent to solving a nonlinear problem in the original space. This is easily verified. As in Eq. (2.12), the hyperplane computed by the SVM method in the high-dimensional space H is

$$w = \sum_{i=1}^{N} \lambda_i y_i \phi(x_i) \tag{2.13}$$

Given a x, we first map it to $\phi(x)$ and then test whether the following is less than or greater than zero:

$$g(x) \equiv < w, \phi(x) > +w_0 = \sum_{i=1}^{N} \lambda_i y_i < \phi(x), \phi(x_i) > +w_0$$

$$= \sum_{i=1}^{N} \lambda_i y_i k(x,x_i) + w_0 \tag{2.14}$$

From the previous relation, it becomes clear that the explicit form of the mapping function $\phi(\cdot)$ is not required; all we have to know is the kernel function since data appear only in inner products. Observe that the resulting discriminant function, $g(x)$, is nonlinear because of the nonlinearity of the kernel function.

To generate a nonlinear SVM classifier, the *SMO2* MATLAB function, discussed in Section 2.4, may be used. The input argument *kernel* takes the values *'poly'* for the polynomial kernel or *'rbf'* for the RBF kernel. In the former case, *kpar*1 and *kpar*2 correspond to the β and n parameters, respectively; in the latter case, *kpar*1 corresponds to the σ parameter.

■——————————————————————————

Example 2.5.1

1. Generate a 2-dimensional data set X_1 (training set) as follows. Select $N=150$ data points in the 2-dimensional $[-5, 5] \times [-5, 5]$ region according to the uniform distribution (set the seed for the *rand* function equal to 0). Assign a point $x = [x(1), x(2)]^T$ to the class $+1$ (-1) according to the rule $0.05(x^3(1) + x^2(1) + x(1) + 1) > (<)x(2)$. (Clearly, the two classes are nonlinearly separable;

in fact, they are separated by the curve associated with the equation $0.05(x^3(1) + x^2(1) + x(1) + 1) = x(2)$.) Plot the points in X_1. Generate an additional data set X_2 (test set) using the same prescription as for X_1 (set the seed for the *rand* function equal to 100).

2. Design a linear SVM classifier using the first modification of Platt's algorithm with parameters $C = 2$ and *tol* $= 0.001$. Compute the training and test errors and count the number of support vectors.

3. Generate a nonlinear SVM classifier using the radial basis kernel functions for $\sigma = 0.1$ and 2. Use the first modification of Platt's algorithm, with $C = 2$ and *tol* $= 0.001$. Compute the training and test error rates and count the number of support vectors. Plot the decision regions defined by the classifier.

4. Repeat step 3 using the polynomial kernel functions $(x^T y + \beta)^n$ for $(n, \beta) = (5, 0)$ and $(3, 1)$. Draw conclusions.

5. Design the SVM classifiers using the radial basis kernel function with $\sigma = 1.5$ and using the polynomial kernel function with $n = 3$ and $\beta = 1$. Use the first modification of Platt's algorithm with *tol* $= 0.001$ for $C = 0.2, 20, 200$.

Solution. Take the following steps:

Step 1. To generate the data set X_1 and the vector y_1 containing the class labels for the vectors in X_1, type

```
l=2;    % Dimensionality
N=150;  % Number of vectors
% Generating the training set
rand('seed',0)
X1=10*rand(l,N)-5;
for i=1:N
    t=0.05*(X1(1,i)^3+X1(1,i)^2+X1(1,i)+1);
    if(t>X1(2,i))
        y1(i)=1;
    else
        y1(i)=-1;
    end
end
```

To plot the data set X_1 (see Figure 2.5(a)), type

```
figure(1), plot(X1(1,y1==1),X1(2,y1==1),'r+',...
X1(1,y1==-1),X1(2,y1==-1),'bo')
figure(1), axis equal
```

To generate X_2 work as in the case of X_1.

Step 2. To generate a linear SVM classifier based on X_1 with $C = 2$ and *tol* $= 0.001$, type

```
kernel='linear';
kparl=0;
```

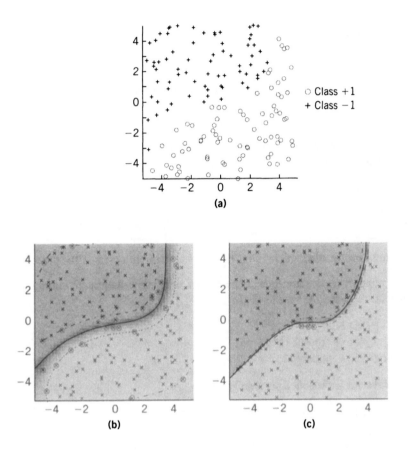

FIGURE 2.5

(a) Training set for Example 2.5.1. (b) Decision curve associated with the classifier using the radial basis kernel function ($\sigma = 2$) and $C = 2$. (c) Decision curve realized by the classifier using the polynomial kernel function ($\beta = 1$, $n = 3$) and $C = 2$. Observe that different kernels result in different decision surfaces. Support vectors are encircled. Dotted lines indicate the margin.

```
kpar2=0;
C=2;
tol=0.001;
steps=100000;
eps=10^(-10);
method=1;
[alpha, w0, w, evals, stp, glob] = SMO2(X1', y1', ...
kernel, kpar1, kpar2, C, tol, steps, eps, method)
```

To compute the training error, type

```
Pe1=sum((2*(w*X1-w0>0)-1).*y1<0)/length(y1)
```

Similarly compute the test error. To count the number of support vectors, type

```
sup_vec=sum(alpha>0)
```

Step 3. To generate a nonlinear SVM classifier employing the radial basis kernel function with $\sigma = 0.1$, work as in step 2 but now set

```
kernel='rbf';
kpar1=0.1;
kpar2=0;
```

Work similarly for the other value of σ. To compute the training error, the process is as follows:

- The support vectors are stacked in a matrix, while their Lagrange multipliers and their class labels are stacked to vectors. Type

```
X_sup=X1(:,alpha'~=0);
alpha_sup=alpha(alpha~=0)';
y_sup=y1(alpha~=0);
```

- Each vector is classified separately. Type

```
for i=1:N
    t=sum((alpha_sup.*y_sup).*...
    CalcKernel(X_sup',X1(:,i)',kernel,kpar1,kpar2)')-w0;
    if(t>0)
        out_train(i)=1;
    else
        out_train(i)=-1;
    end
end
```

- Compute the training error as

```
Pe1=sum(out_train.*y1<0)/length(y1)
```

The test error is computed in a similar manner. To count the number of support vectors, type

```
sup_vec=sum(alpha>0)
```

To plot the decision regions formed by the classifier (see Figure 2.5(b)), type

```
global figt4=3;
svcplot_book(X1',y1',kernel,kpar1,kpar2,alpha,-w0)
```

Table 2.5 Results for the SVM Classifiers Designed in Steps 2, 3, and 4 of Example 2.5.1

	Training Error	Testing Error	No. Support Vectors
Linear	7.33%	7.33%	26
RBF (0.1)	0.00%	32.67%	150
RBF (2)	1.33%	3.33%	30
poly (5,0)	—	—	----
poly (3,1)	0.00%	2.67%	8

Note: *RBF(a) denotes the SVM classifier corresponding to the radial basis kernel function with $\sigma = a$; poly (n,β) denotes the SVM classifer with the polynomial kernel function of the form $(x^T y + \beta)^n$. The algorithm does not converge for the case poly(5,0).*

Step 4. To generate a nonlinear SVM classifier with the polynomial kernel function using $n = 3$ and $\beta = 1$, work as before but now set

```
kernel='poly';
kpar1=1;
kpar2=3;
```

The training and test errors as well as the number of support vectors are computed as in the previous step (see also Figure 2.5(c)). Work similarly for the other combinations of β and n. The results obtained by the different SVM classifiers are summarized in Table 2.5. From this table, the following conclusions can be drawn.

First, the linear classifier performs worse than the nonlinear SVM classifiers. This is expected since the involved classes in the problem at hand are nonlinearly separable. Second, the choice of parameters for the kernel functions used in the nonlinear SVM classifiers significantly affect the performance of the classifier; parameters should be chosen carefully, after extensive experimentation (see, for example, *RBF*(0.1) and try *RBF*(5)). Finally, low training error does not necessarily guarantee low test error; note that the latter should be considered in evaluating performance.

Step 5. To generate the corresponding SVM classifiers, work as before but set C to $0.2, 20, 200$. ■

Example 2.5.2

1. Generate a 2-dimensional data set X_1 (training set) as follows. Consider the nine squares $[i, i + 1] \times [j, j + 1]$, $i = 0, 1, 2, j = 0, 1, 2$ and draw randomly from each one 30 uniformly distributed points. The points that stem from squares for which $i + j$ is even (odd) are assigned to class $+1$ (-1) (reminiscent of the white and black squares on a chessboard). Plot the data set and generate an additional data set X_2 (test set) following the prescription used for X_1 (as in Example 2.5.1, set the seed for *rand* at 0 for X_1 and 100 for X_2).

2. **(a)** Design a linear SVM classifier, using the first modification of Platt's algorithm, with $C = 200$ and $tol = 0.001$. Compute the training and test errors and count the number of support vectors.

(b) Employ the previous algorithm to design nonlinear SVM classifiers, with radial basis kernel functions, for $C = 0.2, 2, 20, 200, 2000, 20, 000$. Use $\sigma = 1, 1.5, 2, 5$. Compute the training and test errors and count the number of support vectors.

(c) Repeat for polynomial kernel functions, using $n = 3, 5$ and $\beta = 1$.

3. Draw conclusions.

Solution. Do the following:

Step 1. To generate the data set X_1, type

```
l=2; %Dimensionality
poi_per_square=30; %Points per square
N=9*poi_per_square; %Total no. of points
%Generating the training set
rand('seed',0)
X1=[];
y1=[];
for i=0:2
    for j=0:2
        X1=[X1 rand(l,poi_per_square)+...
        [i j]'*ones(1,poi_per_square)];
        if(mod(i+j,2)==0)
            y1=[y1 ones(1,poi_per_square)];
        else
            y1=[y1 -ones(1,poi_per_square)];
        end
    end
end
```

To plot X_1 work as in Example 2.5.1 (see Figure 2.6(a)). To generate X_2, work as in the case of X_1.

Step 2. For all these experiments, work as in Example 2.5.1 (see also Figure 2.6(b)).

Step 3. From the results obtained, the following conclusions can be drawn.

- First, as expected, the linear classifier is inadequate to handle this problem (the resulting training and test errors are greater than 40%). The same holds true for the SVMs with polynomial kernels ($> 20\%$ test error for all combinations of parameters). This has to do with the specific nature of this example.
- Second, the SVM classifiers with radial basis kernel functions give very good results for specific choices of the parameter σ. In Table 2.6, the best results for the radial basis kernel SVM classifiers are presented (all of them have been obtained for $C = 2000$). From this table, once more it can be verified that very low values of σ lead to very poor generalization (k training error, high test error). An intuitive explanation is that very small σ's cause the

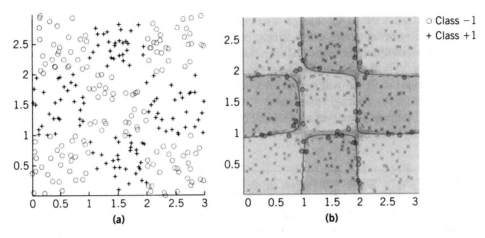

FIGURE 2.6

(a) Training set for Example 2.5.2. (b) Decision curve of the SVM classifier, with radial basis kernel functions ($\sigma = 1$) and $C = 2000$. Support vectors are encircled; dotted lines indicate the margin.

Table 2.6 Results for the SVM Classifiers Obtained for $\sigma = 0.1, 1, 1.5, 2, 5$ in Example 2.5.2

	Training Error	Test Error	No. Support Vectors
RBF(0.1)	0.00%	10.00%	216
RBF(1)	1.85%	3.70%	36
RBF(1.5)	5.56%	7.04%	74
RBF(2)	8.15%	8.52%	128
RBF(5)	35.56%	31.48%	216

Note: *RBF(α) denotes the SVM classifier with radial basis kernel functions with $\sigma = a$.*

$k(x, x_i)$'s to drop rapidly toward zero around each $x_i \in X_1$, which leads to an increase in the number of support vectors (since many points are required to "cover" the space where the data lie). For each training point, x_i, the summation in the classification rule in Eq. (2.14) is mostly affected by the corresponding term $\lambda_i y_i k(x_i, x_i)$. This explains the low training error. In contrast, since the $k(x, x_i)$'s do not sufficiently "cover" the space away from the training points, the summation in Eq. (2.14) may be almost zero for several test points (from both classes) and the respective labels cannot be accurately predicted.

On the other hand, large values of σ (in our example $\sigma = 5$ is considered as such) lead to poor results for both the training and test sets. An intuitive explanation for this is that, when σ is large, all $k(x, x_i)$'s remain almost constant in the area where the data points lie. This also leads to an increase in support vectors (since almost all points are of equal importance) with almost equal values for the λ_i's. Thus, the summation in the classification rule in Eq. (2.14) exhibits low variation for the various x's (from both the training and the test set), which leads to reduced discrimination capability. Values between these two ends lead to more acceptable results, with the best performance being achieved for $\sigma = 1$ in the present example. The previous discussion makes clear the importance of choosing, for each problem, the right values for the involved parameters.

- Third, for fixed kernel parameters and C varying from 0.2 to 20,000, the number of SVs (in general) decreases, as expected. ■

2.6 THE KERNEL PERCEPTRON ALGORITHM

As stated before, all operations in obtaining the SVM classifier can be cast in the form of inner products. This is also possible with a number of other algorithms; the perceptron algorithm is a notable example. The "inner product formulation" can be exploited by following the so-called kernel trick.

Kernel trick: Substitute each inner product $x^T y$ with the kernel function $k(x,y)$. This is equivalent to solving the problem in some high-dimensional space where the inner product is defined in terms of the respective kernel function. Adopting this trick, a linear task in the high-dimensional space is equivalent to a nonlinear task in the original feature space, where the training data lie. More on this issue may be found in [Theo 09, Section 4.19].

To call the kernel perceptron algorithm, type

$$[a, iter, count\_misclas] = kernel\_perce(X, y, kernel, kpar1, kpar2, max\_iter)$$

where

X is the matrix whose columns are the data vectors,

y is a vector containing the class labels of the data points,

kernel, *kpar*1, and *kpar*2 are defined as in the *SMO2* function,

max_iter is the maximum allowable number of iterations that the algorithm can perform,

a is a vector, whose ith coordinate contains the number of times the ith point was misclassified,

iter is the number of iterations performed by the algorithm,

count_misclas is the number of misclassified points.

A given vector x is classified to class $+1$ or class -1 according to whether the following is positive or negative:

$$g(x) = \sum_{i=1}^{N} a_i y_i k(x, x_i) + \sum_{i=1}^{N} a_i y_i$$

Example 2.6.1

1. Consider the data sets X_1 (training set) and X_2 (test set) from Example 2.5.1. Run the kernel perceptron algorithm using X_1 as the training set where the kernel functions are (a) linear, (b) radial basis functions with $\sigma = 0.1, 1, 1.5, 2, 5, 10, 15, 20$, and (c) polynomials of the form $(x^T y + \beta)^n$

for $(n, \beta) = (3, 1), (5, 1), (15, 1), (3, 0), (5, 0)$. For all these cases compute the training error and the test error rates and count the training vectors x_i with $a_i > 0$ as well as the iterations the algorithm runs. Use 30,000 as the maximum number of allowable iterations.

2. For each one of the previous cases, plot in the same figure the training set X_1 (use different colors and symbols for each class) and the decision boundary between the classes.

Solution. Take the following steps:

Step 1. To run the kernel perceptron algorithm for the linear kernel, type

```
kernel='linear';
kpar1=0;
kpar2=0;
max_iter=30000;
[a,iter,count_misclas]=kernel_perce(X1,y1,kernel,...
kpar1,kpar2,max_iter);
```

where *kpar*1 and *kpar*2 are defined as in the *SMO2* MATLAB function depending on the type of kernel function considered.

To run the algorithm using the radial basis kernel function with $\sigma = 0.1$, type

```
kernel='rbf';
kpar1=0.1;
kpar2=0;
max_iter=30000;
[a,iter,count_misclas]=kernel_perce(X1,y1,kernel,...
kpar1,kpar2,max_iter);
```

To run the algorithm using the polynomial kernel function with $(n, \beta) = (3, 1)$, type

```
kernel='poly'; kpar1=1; kpar2=3;
max_iter=30000;
[a,iter,count_misclas]=kernel_perce(X1,y1,kernel,...
kpar1,kpar2,max_iter);
```

Other cases with different parameters are treated similarly.

To compute the training error, type

```
for i=1:N
    K=CalcKernel(X1',X1(:,i)',kernel,kpar1,kpar2)';
    out_train(i)=sum((a.*y1).*K)+sum(a.*y1);
end
err_train=sum(out_train.*y1<0)/length(y1)
```

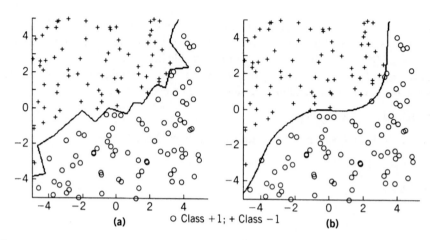

FIGURE 2.7

Training set for Example 2.6.1 and resulting decision curves associated with the kernel perceptron algorithm, using the radial basis kernel function with (a) $\sigma = 0.1$ and (b) $\sigma = 1.5$.

where N is the number of training vectors. To compute the test error, type

```
for i=1:N
    K=CalcKernel(X1',X2(:,i)',kernel,kpar1,kpar2)';
    out_test(i)=sum((a.*y1).*K)+sum(a.*y1);
end
err_test=sum(out_test.*y2<0)/length(y2)
```

To count the total number of misclassifications during training, type

```
sum_pos_a=sum(a>0)
```

Step 2. To plot the training set (see Figures 2.7 and 2.8), type

```
figure(1), hold on
figure(1), plot(X1(1,y1==1),X1(2,y1==1),'ro',...
X1(1,y1==-1),X1(2,y1==-1),'b+')
figure(1), axis equal
```

Note that the vectors of the training set from class $+1$ (-1) are marked by circles (pluses). Finally, to plot the decision boundary in the same figure, type

```
bou_x=[-5 5];
bou_y=[-5 5];
resolu=.05;
fig_num=1;
plot_kernel_perce_reg(X1,y1,a,kernel,kpar1,kpar2,...
bou_x,bou_y, resolu,fig_num)
```

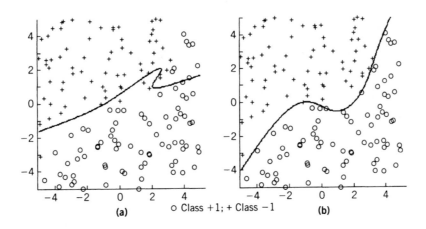

FIGURE 2.8

(a) Training set for Example 2.6.1 and resulting decision curves associated with the kernel perceptron algorithm using polynomial kernel functions with (a) $(n, \beta) = (3, 0)$ and (b) $(n, \beta) = (3, 1)$.

where

    bou_x and *bou_y* are 2-dimensional vectors that define the (rectangular) region of space over which the boundary will be drawn; specifically, $(bou\_x(1), bou\_y(1))$ defines the lower left corner of the region while $(bou\_x(2), bou\_y(2))$ defines the upper right corner of the region,

    resolu is the resolution with which the decision boundary is determined (the lower the resolution, the finer the drawing of the decision boundary),

    fig_num is the number of the MATLAB figure where the plot of the decision boundary takes place.

The results of the experiments for the linear and radial basis kernel functions are summarized in Table 2.7. The results of the experiments for the polynomial kernel functions are summarized in Table 2.8. From the tables three conclusions can be drawn.

- First, for the linear kernel, the kernel perceptron algorithm does not converge because the problem is not linearly separable (it terminates after 30,000 iterations).
- Second, for the radial basis kernel functions, the kernel perceptron algorithm converges for a wide range of σ values. However, as the value of σ increases, the algorithm needs more iterations to converge and when σ becomes very large, the algorithm fails to converge. Moreover, the decision line obtained for the case where $\sigma = 0.1$ is rather "rough," indicating a classifier with poor generalization performance (why?). The best values for σ seem to be around 1. Finally, the number of vectors with nonzero a_i's generally increases as σ increases (why?).
- Third, for the polynomial kernel functions, the kernel perceptron algorithm does not converge when the β parameter equals 0, but does converge when β is set to 1. For $\beta = 0$ the high-dimensional space (in which the "implicit" mapping is performed) is of lower dimensionality compared to that corresponding to $\beta = 1$; thus it follows that the problem is not linearly separable in the 4-dimensional

Table 2.7 Results of Linear and RBF Kernel Functions in Example 2.6.1

	Training Error	Test Error	Vectors x_i with Positive a	No. Iterations
Linear	6.00%	5.33%	29	30000
RBF(0.1)	0.00%	1.33%	32	4
RBF(1)	0.00%	2.00%	33	6
RBF(1.5)	0.00%	2.00%	29	18
RBF(2)	0.00%	3.33%	27	5
RBF(5)	0.00%	1.33%	42	52
RBF(10)	0.00%	3.33%	55	409
RBF(15)	0.00%	5.33%	65	7747
RBF(20)	11.33%	16.00%	65	30000

30000 means no convergence.
Note: *RBF(a) denotes the radial basis kernel functions with $\sigma = a$.*

Table 2.8 Results of Polynomial Kernel Functions in Example 2.6.1

	Training Error	Test Error	Vectors x_i with Positive a	No. Iterations
poly(3,0)	8.00%	8.67%	40	30000
poly(5,0)	6.00%	7.33%	34	30000
poly(3,1)	0.00%	3.33%	39	256
poly(5,1)	0.00%	3.33%	37	474
poly(15,1)	0.00%	5.33%	31	4977

30000 means no convergence.
Note: *poly(n, β) denotes the polynomial kernel functions of the form $(x^T y + \beta)^n$.*

space defined by $poly(3,0)$, but is linearly separable in the 9-dimensional space defined by $poly(3,1)$.[3]

Remark

- As with SVMs, we observe that the right choice of kernel function, as well as the choice of respective parameters, comes with experimentation. It depends on the specific data set and there are yet no magic recipes (see Exercise 2.6.1). ■

Exercise 2.6.1

1. Consider the data sets X_1 (training set) and X_2 (test set) from Example 2.5.2. Run the kernel perceptron algorithm using X_1 as the training set where the kernel functions are (a) linear, (b) radial basis with $\sigma = 0.1, 0.5, 1, 1.5, 2, 5$, and (c) polynomial of the form $(x^T y + 1)^n$ for $n = 3, 5, 15, 18, 20, 22$. For all three

---

[3]The choice $n = 3, \beta = 0$ implies the mapping $[x(1), x(2)]^T \rightarrow [x^3(1), x^3(2), \sqrt{3}x^2(1)x(2), \sqrt{3}x(1)x^2(2)]^T$ (4-dimensional space); the choice $n = 3$, $\beta = 1$ implies the mapping $[x(1), x(2)]^T \rightarrow [x^3(1), x^3(2), \sqrt{3}x^2(1)x(2), \sqrt{3}x(1)x^2(2), \sqrt{3}x^2(1), \sqrt{3}x^2(2), \sqrt{6}x(1)x(2), \sqrt{3}x(1), \sqrt{3}x(2)]^T$ (9-dimensional space).

cases, count the training and test errors, the number of misclassifications during training and the number of iterations the algorithm runs. Use 30,000 as the maximum number of allowable iterations.
2. For each case plot in the same figure the training set X_1, the test set X_2, and the decision boundary between the two classes. Use different colors and symbols for each class.

Hint
To perform the required experiments, work as in the previous example, now defining the *bou_x* and *bou_y* parameters as

```
bou_x=[0 3];
bou_y=[0 3];
```

This problem is more difficult than the one considered in Example 2.6.1. The results show that both the linear and the polynomial kernels are unable to solve it (with the specific values for the parameters). The radial basis function kernel can solve the problem for a rather narrow range of values for parameter σ.

2.7 THE ADABOOST ALGORITHM

The AdaBoost algorithm implements a very interesting idea. To start with, a very simple classifier, known as *base* or *weak*, is adopted. By simple we mean a classifier that does slightly better than a random guess; that is, it results in an error rate slightly less than 0.5 (for the 2-class case). AdaBoost is an iterative algorithm that generates (final) classifier that is based on a number of base classifiers designed in a sequential manner, one after the other.

The secret of the algorithm is that during the training of the tth base classifier (at the tth iteration), each training vector x_i is appropriately weighted by a weight w_i, whose value depends on whether x_i was incorrectly classified by the $(t-1)$ base classifier (w_i is increased) or not (w_i is decreased). Thus vectors that keep failing receive more and more attention (weight). The final classifier (defined after the termination of the algorithm) is given as a weighted average of all the base classifiers designed before.

It turns out that such a scheme converges to a *zero error on the training set*. The error rate on the test set converges to a certain level. This is very interesting. Usually, training a classifier until zero error over the training set is obtained results in overfitting [Theo 09, Section 4.9]. This is because as was stated before, the classifier learns much about the "specificities" of the *particular* training set and tends to result in high error rates when facing a test data set, which is "unknown" to it. This is not the case with the AdaBoost algorithm and has been an issue of discussion among experts [Theo 09, Section 4.22; Meas 08].

The choice of a base classifier that achieves a classification error rate of less than 0.5 is not always obvious. Several base classifiers have been proposed, a popular class of which is the so-called "stumps." Stumps may be represented as single-node classification trees. That is, the two classes in the classification problem are separated according to a single rule. Such a classifier is discussed next.

Assume the dimensionality of the feature space to be equal to l. First, a dimension, say $j \leq l$, is chosen and the minimum and maximum values of the N (l-dimensional) vectors of the training set X along the jth dimension are computed. A number θ, which serves as a threshold, is randomly chosen between these two extreme values and the data vectors are separated into two classes depending on the position of their jth coordinates, $x_i(j)$, $i = 1, \ldots, N$ with respect to θ.

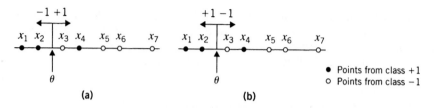

FIGURE 2.9

First scenario (a) and second scenario (b) of the base classifier applied to a 7-point data set.

More specifically, the following two scenarios are considered: (a) the vectors whose jth coordinate is less than θ are assigned to class -1; (b) the vectors whose jth coordinate is less than θ are assigned to class $+1$ (obviously, this is opposite to the first scenario). For both, the error classification rates e_a and e_b are computed (as the summation of the weights of all vectors that are misclassified). The scenario that results in a lower classification rate is adopted to define the classifier.

To better understand this idea, consider the setup of Figure 2.9, which shows projections of the seven points of a training data set to a given dimension. The scenarios (a) and (b) are illustrated in Figures 2.9(a) and 2.9(b), respectively. In Figure 2.9(a) we observe that six vectors (all except x_4) are misclassified. Assuming that the weights for all of the data points are equal, $e_a = 6/7$. The opposite holds in Figure 2.9(b), where $e_b = 1/7$.

The previously described base classifier is completely specified by

- The dimension along which the classification takes place
- The value of the threshold θ
- An index that takes the values $+1$ or -1 according to whether scenario (a) or (b) has been selected

It turns out that the resulting classifier generally satisfies the requirement for the classification error to be less than 0.5.

Example 2.7.1. Consider the 2-class 2-dimensional classification problem where the classes are described by the pdfs given in Example 1.6.2, where now $m_{11} = [1.25, 1.25]^T$, $m_{12} = [2.75, 4.5]^T$, $m_{13} = [2, 11]^T$, $m_{21} = [2.75, 0]^T$, $m_{22} = [1.25, 2.75]^T$ and $m_{23} = [4, 8]^T$. Generate a data set X consisting of $N = 100$ data points, such that 50 stem from the first class and 50 stem from the second class.

1. Run the AdaBoost algorithm on the data set X to generate a "strong" classifier as a sequence of simple stump classifiers having the structure described before. Use $T\_max = 3000$, the maximum number of base classifiers (i.e., iterations).
2. Classify the vectors of the training set X using the previous classifier. Compute the classification error P when only the first t base classifiers are taken into account, $t = 1, \ldots, T\_max$. Plot P versus the number of base classifiers.
3. Generate a test data set Z using the specifications of set X. Classify the vectors of set Z using the classifier that results from the previous step. Compute the classification error P when only the

first t base classifiers are taken into account, $t = 1, \ldots, T\_max$. Plot P versus the number of base classifiers.

4. Observe the plots generated in steps 2 and 3 and draw conlusions.

Solution. To generate the data sets X and Z, work as in Example 1.6.2, as follows:

Step 1. Use the *boost_clas_coord* MATLAB function by typing

$$[pos\_tot, thres\_tot, sleft\_tot, a\_tot, P\_tot, K] = boost\_clas\_coord(X, y, T\_max)$$

where

    X is an $l \times N$ matrix, each column of which is a feature vector,

    y is an N-dimensional vector whose ith coordinate is the class label ($+1$ or -1) of the class in which the ith data vector belongs,

    T_max is the maximum allowable number of base classifiers,

    pos_tot is a vector whose tth coordinate is the integer indicating the chosen dimension for the tth base classifier,

    thres_tot is a vector whose tth coordinate is the threshold on the chosen dimension for the tth base classifier,

    sleft_tot is a vector whose tth coordinate is a variable taking the value $+1$ or -1 according to whether scenario (a) or (b) has been selected in the tth base classifier,

    a_tot is a vector whose tth coordinate is the weight for the tth base classifier,

    P_tot is a vector whose tth coordinate is the (weighted) probability of classification error for the tth base classifier,

    K is the number of base classifiers generated by the algorithm.

Step 2. Use the *boost_clas_coord_out* MATLAB function by typing

$$[y\_out, P\_error] = boost\_clas\_coord\_out(pos\_tot, thres\_tot, sleft\_tot, a\_tot, P\_tot, K, X, y)$$

where

    pos_tot, *thres_tot*, *sleft_tot*, *a_tot*, *P_tot*, K, X, y are defined as in the *boost_clas_coord* MATLAB function,

    y_out is an N-dimensional vector whose ith coordinate is the class label ($+1$ or -1) of the class in which the ith data vector has been assigned by the classifier,

    P_error is a K-dimensional vector whose tth coordinate gives the (unweighted) classification error for the current data set when only the tth first base classifiers are taken into account.

To plot the classification error on X versus the number of base classifiers (see Figure 2.10(a)), type

```
figure(3), plot(P_error)
```

Step 3. Work as in step 2, replacing X with Z (see Figure 2.10(b)).

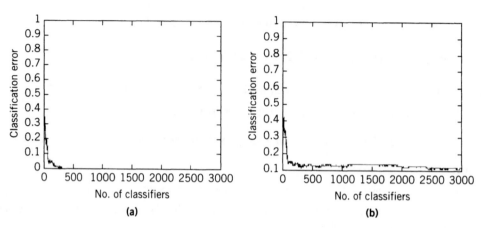

FIGURE 2.10

Results from Example 2.7.1: (a) classification error for the training set versus the number of base classifiers; (b) classification error for the test set versus the number of base classifiers.

Step 4. For the training set X, the classification error tends to 0 as the number of base classifiers increases (see Figure 2.10(a)). For the test set Z, the classification error tends to a positive limit as the number of base classifiers increases (see Figure 2.10(b)).[4]   ∎

Exercise 2.7.1

Consider a 2-class 2-dimensional classification task, where the classes are described by normal distributions with means $[1, 1]^T$ (class $+1$) and $[s, s]^T$ (class -1) and identity covariance matrices. Set $s = 2$. Generate a data set X consisting of 50 points from the first class and 50 points from the second class.

1. Repeat steps 1, 2, and 3 of Example 2.7.1 and draw conclusions.
2. Repeat step 1 for $s = 3, 4, 6$.

2.8 MULTILAYER PERCEPTRONS

The perceptron algorithm and the associated "architecture" of the basic perceptron element were discussed in Section 2.2. The perceptron can be considered an attempt to model the basic building element, the *neuron*, of the human brain. Each neuron is excited by receiving input signals $x(1), x(2), \ldots, x(l)$. Each is subsequently weighted by the weights $w_1, w_2, \ldots, w_l$, which are also known as *synaptic* weights, in analogy to the terminology used in neuroscience. The weighted sum then goes through the activation function, and if its value is higher than a *threshold* value $(-w_0)$ the neuron "fires." That is, it gives an output value; otherwise, it remains inactive.

In a multilayer perceptron, many basic perceptron elements (neurons) are connected in a network topology. Figure 2.11 illustrates such a multilayer perceptron or neural network. The neurons are placed

---

[4]The plots may be slightly different if different initial conditions are used for the functions *rand* and *randn*.

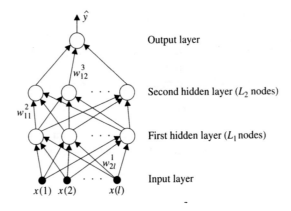

Output layer

Second hidden layer (L_2 nodes)

First hidden layer (L_1 nodes)

Input layer

FIGURE 2.11

Multilayer perceptron with two hidden-layers and a single node in the output layer. The input is applied to the input-layer nodes. The weight that connects the ith node of the $k-1$ layer with the jth node of the k layer is denoted w_{ji}^k. Each node has the perceptron structure depicted in Figure 2.2. To keep the figure simple, the activation function and the threshold value w_0 for all nodes are not shown.

in successive layers and connections are allowed only between nodes of successive layers. In Figure 2.11 there are three layers of neurons: two hidden layers and one output layer consisting of a single neuron. Sometimes the nodes, where the inputs (the feature values in our case) are applied, are said to form the input layer. However, no processing takes place in the input nodes.

It is not difficult to see that the output of a neural network, denoted $\hat{y}$, is a highly nonlinear function of the input (feature) values $x(i)$, $i = 1, 2, \ldots, l$. This is because, in each neuron of the network, the result of the corresponding linear combination is "pushed" through the associated nonlinear activation function and the outcome is subsequently passed over to the neurons of the next layer.

The goal of training a multilayer perceptron is to estimate the weights, as well as the threshold values, of all neurons involved in the network. To this end, a cost function is chosen. The most popular choice is the least squares loss function. Assume that we are given a set of training data points, (y_i, x_i), $i = 1, 2 \ldots, N$, where y_i is the true class label of $x_i \in \mathcal{R}^l$. The labels are usually either 1, for class ω_1 or 0 for class ω_2 in a 2-class classification task. Other choices are possible. If $\hat{y}_i$ denotes the output of the network when its input is fed with x_i, the goal is to compute the unknown weights so that

$$J = \sum_{i=1}^{N} (y_i - \hat{y}_i)^2 \tag{2.15}$$

is minimum. Note that each $\hat{y}_i$ is a function of all the weights and thresholds of all neurons.

The algorithmic scheme for performing the previous minimization is iterative and is widely known as the *backpropagation* (BP) *algorithm*. The algorithm starts from some arbitrary initial values for all the unknown parameters, and converges to a *local* minimum of the cost function in Eq. (2.15). In general, the cost function has a number of local minima. Thus, the choice of initial values influences the solution obtained by the algorithm. In practice, the algorithm runs several times, starting from different initial values; the weights corresponding to the best solution are chosen. (More on the properties of multilayer perceptrons and backpropagation can be found in [Theo 09, Chapter 4].)

For an understanding of the meaning of the parameters involved in the associated MATLAB code, let us briefly comment on the basic structure of the backpropagation algorithm. It belongs to the gradient descent family of algorithms, and its basic iteration step is of the form

$$w(new) = w(old) + \Delta w \tag{2.16}$$

where *old* and *new* refer to the estimates at the previous and current iteration steps, respectively. The correction term is related to the gradient of the cost, computed at $w(old)$:

$$\Delta w = -\mu \frac{\partial J}{\partial w} \tag{2.17}$$

and w refers to the weight parameters (including the threshold) of a network neuron.[5]

Because of the highly nonlinear dependence of the cost function on the unknown parameters, the convergence of the algorithm presents difficulties and can be very slow and nonsmooth with an oscillatory behavior with respect to the successive values of the cost function. The behavior of the algorithm largely depends on the value of the learning rate μ. This should be small enough to guarantee convergence of the algorithm, but not too small, since such a choice may lead to very slow convergence rates. One would like larger μ values when the algorithm moves to regions of the landscape, defined by $J(w)$, that exhibit broad minima in order to speed up convergence. On the other hand, smaller μ values are desirable when the algorithm moves to regions that exhibit steep or narrow minima, in order to avoid overshooting the minimum. Figure 2.12 shows the landscape of a 2-dimensional cost function, which contains two minima, one broad and one narrow.

A better-behaved and popular version of the algorithm is the so-called backpropagation with momentum term. This version needs an extra parameter, α, known as the *momentum term* (usually between 0.1 and 0.8), that controls the correction, which now becomes

$$\Delta w(new) = \alpha \Delta w(old) - \mu \frac{\partial J}{\partial w}$$

It can be shown that the momentum term effectively increases the learning rate when the algorithm moves to regions of the landscape of $J(w)$ that exhibit broad local minima [Theo 09, Section 4.7].

Another variant of the BP algorithm, called *adaptive BP*, adapts the value of μ at each iteration based on the current ($J(t)$) as well as the previous ($J(t-1)$) values of the cost function. It works as follows: If $\frac{J(t)}{J(t-1)} < 1$, μ increases by a factor of r_i (typically 1.05); if $\frac{J(t)}{J(t-1)} > c$ (typically 1.04), μ decreases by a factor of r_d (typically 0.7).

To generate a multilayer perceptron one may use the *NN_training* function by typing

$$[net, tr] = NN\_training(X, y, k, code, iter, par\_vec)$$

---

[5]To make possible the computation of $\frac{\partial J}{\partial w}$, the activation function must be smoothed out to become differentiable. A popular smoothed activation function that takes values in the interval $[-1, 1]$ is the *hyperbolic tangent* defined as $\tanh(z) = \frac{1-exp(-z)}{1+exp(-z)}$, $z \in \mathcal{R}$. Other choices are possible.

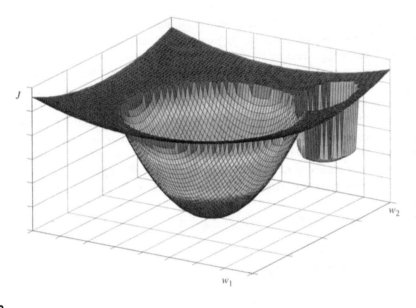

FIGURE 2.12

Landscape of a 2-dimensional function containing a broad and a narrow minima.

where

  X contains the training vectors in its columns,

  y is a vector containing the class labels for the data vectors,

  code specifies the training algorithm to be used (1 for standard BP, 2 for BP with momentum term, and 3 for BP with adaptive learning rate),

  iter is the maximum number of iterations to be performed by the algorithm,

  par_vec is a 5-dimensional vector containing the values of (a) the learning rate used in the standard BP algorithm, (b) the momentum term used in the BP with momentum term, and (c) the three values involved in the BP with adaptive learning rate,

  net is the network structure returned, which follows the programming structure used by MATLAB,

  tr is a structure which contains, among other quantities, the performance of the network during training with respect to the number of epochs.[6]

Example 2.8.1. Consider a 2-class 2-dimensional classification problem. The points of the first (second) class, denoted $+1$ (-1), stem from three (four) Gaussian distributions with means $[-5, 5]^T$, $[5, -5]^T$, $[10, 0]^T$ $([-5, -5]^T, [0, 0]^T, [5, 5]^T, [15, -5]^T)$, with equal probability. The covariance matrix for each distribution is $\sigma^2 I$, where $\sigma^2 = 1$ and I is the 2×2 identity matrix.

[6]See the MATLAB help tool for more details.

1. Generate and plot a data set X_1 (training set) containing 60 points from class $+1$ (approximately 20 from each distribution) and 80 points from class -1 (again approximately 20 points from each distribution). Use the same prescription to generate a set X_2 (test set).
2. Based on X_1, train two 2-layer feedforward neural networks (FNNs) with two and four nodes in the hidden layer.[7] All hidden-layer nodes use the hyperbolic tangent (*tanh*) as the activation function, while the output node uses the linear activation function.[8] Run the standard backpropagation (BP) algorithm for 9000 iterations with a learning rate of 0.01. Compute the training and test errors (based on X_1 and X_2, respectively) and plot the training points as well as the decision regions formed by each network. Also plot the training error versus the number of iterations.
3. Repeat step 2 using a learning rate of 0.0001 in the standard BP algorithm.
4. Repeat step 2, employing the adaptive BP algorithm for 6000 iterations, with a learning rate of 0.0001 and $r_i = 1.05$, $r_d = 0.7$, and $c = 1.04$.
5. Comment on the results obtained in steps 2, 3, and 4.

Solution. Take the following steps:

Step 1. To generate the data set X_1, type

```
randn('seed',0)
%Parameter definition
l=2; % Dimensionality
m1=[-5 5; 5 -5; 10 0]';   %Means of Gaussians
m2=[-5 -5; 0 0; 5 5; 15 -5]';
[l,c1]=size(m1);   %no of gaussians per class
[l,c2]=size(m2);
P1=ones(1,c1)/c1; %Probabilities of the gaussians per class
P2=ones(1,c2)/c2;
s=1;      %variance
%%%%%%%%%%%%%%%%%%%%
% Generation of training data from the first class
N1=60;   %Number of first class data points
for i=1:c1
    S1(:,:,i)=s*eye(l);
end
sed=0; %Random generator seed
[X1,y1]=mixt_model(m1,S1,P1,N1,sed);
%%%%%%%%%%%%%%%%%%%%
```

---

[7]The number of input nodes is equal to the dimensionality of the input space (two in our case); the number of output nodes is equal to the number of classes minus 1 (one in our case).
[8]Note that the latter can also be of the tanh type. However, one can generally use different activation functions in the various layers; this is the philosophy adopted here.

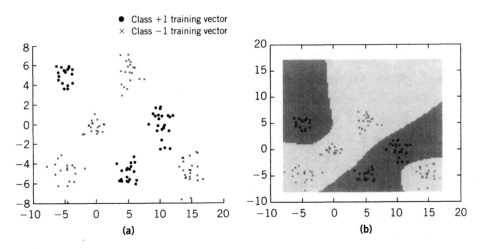

FIGURE 2.13

(a) Training set for Example 2.8.1. (b) Decision regions formed by the two-layer FNN with four hidden-layer nodes, trained with the standard BP algorithm with learning rate 0.01 and 9000 iterations.

```
% Generation of training data from the second class
N2=80; %Number of second class data points
for i=1:c2
     S2(:,:,i)=s*eye(1);
end
sed=0; %Random generator seed
[X2,y2]=mixt_model(m2,S2,P2,N2,sed);
%%%%%%%%%%%%%%%%%
%Production of the unified data set
X1=[X1 X2];   %Data vectors
y1=[ones(1,N1) -ones(1,N2)];   %Class labels
```

To plot the data set X_1 (see Figure 2.13(a)), type

```
figure(10), hold on
figure(10), plot(X1(1,y1==1),X1(2,y1==1),'r.',...
X1(1,y1==-1),X1(2,y1==-1),'bx')
```

In a similar manner, X_2 can be generated (to maintain reproducibility of the results, use $sed = 100$ where the previous code used $sed = 0$).

Step 2. To train a two-layer FNN with two nodes in the hidden layer, using the standard BP algorithm with a learning rate of 0.01 and a maximum of 9000 iterations, type the following:

```
rand('seed',100)  %Random generators initialization
randn('seed',100)
iter=9000; %Number of iterations
code=1; %Code for the chosen training algorithm
k=2; %number of hidden layer nodes
lr=.01; %learning rate
par_vec=[lr 0 0 0 0];
[net,tr]=NN_training(X1,y1,k,code,iter,par_vec);
```

To compute the training and test error rates, type

```
pe_train=NN_evaluation(net,X1,y1)
pe_test=NN_evaluation(net,X2,y2)
```

To plot the data points as well as the decision regions formed by the resulting FNN, type

```
maxi=max(max([X1'; X2']));
mini=min(min([X1'; X2']));
bou=[mini maxi];
fig_num=1;  %Number of figure
resolu=(bou(2)-bou(1))/100; %Resolution of figure
plot_NN_reg(net,bou,resolu,fig_num) %Decision region plot
figure(fig_num), hold on %Plotting training set
figure(fig_num), plot(X1(1,y1==1),X1(2,y1==1),'r.',...
X1(1,y1==-1),X1(2,y1==-1),'bx')
```

To plot the training error versus the number of iterations (see Figure 2.14), type

```
figure(11), plot(tr.perf)
```

The FNN with four hidden-layer nodes can be designed similarly. The only change is in the parameter *k*, which indicates the number of nodes. The decision regions are shown in Figure 2.13(b). The results are summarized in Table 2.9.

Step 3. Working as in step 2, design the required FNNs. The only change in this case is in the learning rate parameter *lr*.

Step 4. In this case, work as in step 2 with the following changes

```
iter=6000; %Number of iterations
code=3; %Code for the chosen training algorithm
k=2; %number of hidden layer nodes
lr=.0001; %learning rate
par_vec=[lr 0 1.05 0.7 1.04]; %Parameter vector
```

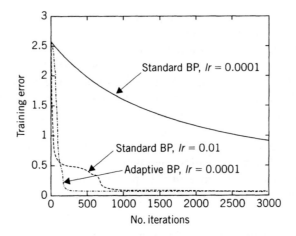

FIGURE 2.14

Plot of the training error versus the number of iterations for standard BP with $lr = 0.01$ (dashed line), standard BP with $lr = 0.0001$ (solid line), and adaptive BP with $lr = 0.0001$ (dash-dotted line), for Example 2.8.1.

Table 2.9 Results for the FNNs Trained by the Standard BP Algorithm, with Learning Rate 0.01 and 9000 Iterations, from Example 2.8.1

	Two Nodes	Four Nodes
Training error	29.29%	0
Test error	30.71%	0

Note: *When fewer than the minimum required hidden-layer nodes are employed, the resulting FNN is unable to solve the problem.*

Table 2.10 Results for the FNNs Trained by the Adaptive BP Algorithm, with Learning Rate 0.0001 and 6000 Iterations, from Example 2.8.1

	Two Nodes	Four Nodes
Training error	29.29%	0
Test error	32.14%	0

As in the previous cases, the value of k should be changed to 4 in order to design a two-layer FNN with four hidden-layer nodes. The results are summarized in Table 2.10.

Step 5. Note that the classes involved in the current classification problem can be perfectly separated using three lines.

From the previous experiments the following conclusions can be drawn. First, the number of hidden nodes directly affects the learning ability of the neural network. The experiments indicate that an FNN with two hidden-layer nodes is unable to learn the classification problem considered in this example. In contrast, an FNN with four hidden-layer nodes has enough nodes to realize the required decision curves (see Tables 2.9 and 2.10 as well as the decision regions formed by each FNN).

Second, the learning rate affects the speed of the convergence of the backpropagation algorithm. Small learning rate values may slow down the convergence speed of the BP algorithm (see Figure 2.14).

Third, even when it starts with a small learning rate value, the adaptive BP algorithm exhibits very fast convergence compared to the standard BP algorithm because it adjusts the value at each iteration to "match" the landscape terrain (see Figure 2.14). The price for this desirable behavior is some additional checks during the execution of the algorithm to adjust the learning rate.

Remark

• When the dimensionality of the data is higher than 3 (which is often the case), no visualization of the data is possible. In such cases, the number of hidden-layer nodes chosen is usually the result of extensive experimentation. ∎

Exercise 2.8.1

Repeat Example 2.8.1, now with the covariance matrix of the involved Gaussian distributions being $\sigma^2 I$, where $\sigma^2 = 4$.

In this case, the points from each class are more spreadout and the classes are not so clearly separated as in Example 2.8.1. Thus, a degradation of the resulting networks' performance is expected (see Figure 2.15). The training and test errors are (slightly) increased compared with those given in the previous example. However, the results support the conclusions drawn in Example 2.8.1.

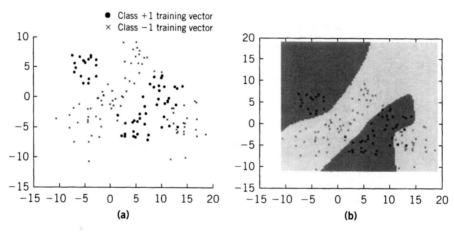

FIGURE 2.15

(a) Training set for Exercise 2.8.1. (b) Decision regions produced by the two-layer FNN with four hidden-layer nodes, trained with the standard BP algorithm with learning rate 0.01 and 9000 iterations.

Example 2.8.2. Consider a 2-class 2-dimensional classification problem. The points of the first (second) class, denoted $+1$ (-1), stem from one out of four (five) Gaussian distributions with means $[-10, 0]^T, [0, -10]^T, [10, 0]^T, [0, 10]^T$ $([-10, -10]^T, [0, 0]^T, [10, -10]^T, [-10, 10]^T, [10, 10]^T)$ with equal probability. The covariance matrix for each distribution is $\sigma^2 I$, where $\sigma^2 = 4$ and I is the 2×2 identity matrix.

1. Generate and plot a data set X_1 (training set) containing 80 points from class $+1$ (20 from each distribution) and 100 points from class -1 (20 points from each distribution). Use the same prescription to generate a data set X_2 (test set).
2. Based on X_1, train three 2-layer feedforward neural networks (FNNs) with three, four, and ten nodes in the hidden layer. The activation function of the hidden-layer nodes is the hyperbolic tangent (*tanh*); the output node has a linear activation function. Use the adaptive BP algorithm for 10,000 iterations with a learning rate of 0.01 (for the rest of the parameters of the algorithm, use the values given in Example 2.8.1). Compute the training and test errors (based on X_1 and X_2, respectively) and plot the data points as well as the decision regions formed by each network. Draw conclusions.
3. Design a two-layer FNN with 10 hidden-layer nodes and use the adaptive BP algorithm to train it, based on X_1. Compute the training and test error rates after 300, 400, 1000, 2000, 3000, 4000, 5000, and 10,000 iterations. Set the learning rate parameter to 0.01 and the other parameters to the same values used in Example 2.8.1. Draw conclusions.

Solution. Take the following steps:

Step 1. Generate X_1 and X_2 as in Example 2.8.1.

Step 2. The required experiments can be carried out working as in step 2 of Example 2.8.1. The data set and the decision regions formed by the previous three FNNs are given in Figure 2.16. The classification results are shown in Table 2.11.

　　The minimum number of required nodes for this example is four (why?). The decision regions defined by the FNN with four hidden-layer nodes capture well the data distribution of each class. However, they lead to greater classification error compared with that obtained by the FNN with ten hidden-layer nodes. The latter offers enhanced capabilities in solving the current classification problem because it has more free parameters (the weights) to adjust in order to fit the problem. However, care must be taken when training large networks, as discussed next.

Step 3. From the results given in Table 2.12, observe that in the (approximate) range of 500 to 3000 iterations the test error (which is indicative of the generalization capability of the network) remains 3.89%. For more iterations, the training error is further decreased while the test error is increased to values higher than 3.89%. This suggests that, in this case, more than (approximately) 3000 iterations leads to network *overtraining*. That is, the network starts to focus on the "specificities" of the training set X_1, which leads to degraded generalization performance. This is an important issue in the training of FNNs. One way to detect overtraining is to adopt a set of data (a *validation set*) which is different from X_1, and periodically measure on it the performance of the FNN that is obtained during training. If the error resulting from this data set starts to increase, while the training error decreases, the training stops.

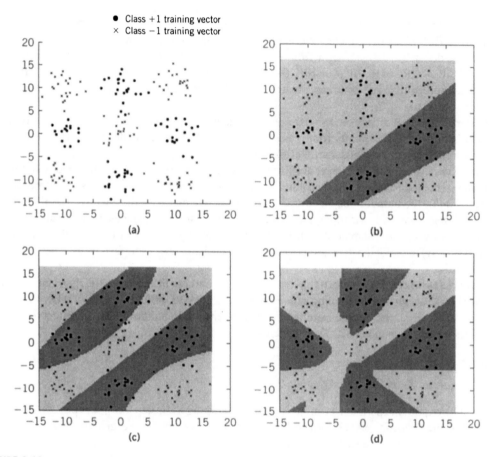

FIGURE 2.16

(a) Training set for Example 2.8.2. (b)–(d) Decision regions formed by the 2-layer FNN with three, four, and ten hidden-layer nodes, respectively, trained with the adaptive BP algorithm with learning rate 0.01 and 10,000 iterations.

Table 2.11 Results for the FNNs Trained by the Adaptive BP Algorithm, with Learning Rate 0.01 and 10,000 Iterations from Example 2.8.2

	Three Nodes	Four Nodes	Ten Nodes
Training error	25.56%	6.67%	1.67%
Test error	30.00%	8.33%	7.22%

Note: *The other parameters of the algorithm are specified as in Example 2.8.1.*

Table 2.12 Results for a Two-Layer FNN with 10 Hidden-Layer Nodes Trained by the Adaptive BP Algorithm, with Learning Rate 0.01 and for Various Numbers of Iterations from Example 2.8.2

	No. Iterations							
	300	500	1000	2000	3000	4000	5000	10,000
Training error	3.89%	2.22%	2.22%	2.22%	2.22%	1.67%	1.67%	1.67%
Test error	4.44%	3.89%	3.89%	3.89%	3.89%	5.56%	6.11%	7.22%

Exercise 2.8.2

Consider a 2-class 2-dimensional classification problem. The points of the first (second) class, denoted $+1$ (-1), stem from one out of eight Gaussian distributions with means $[-10, 0]^T$, $[0, -10]^T$, $[10, 0]^T$, $[0, 10]^T$, $[-10, 20]^T$, $[10, 20]^T$, $[20, 10]^T$, $[20, -10]^T$ ($[-10, -10]^T$, $[0, 0]^T$, $[10, -10]^T$, $[-10, 10]^T$, $[10, 10]^T$, $[20, 20]^T$, $[20, 0]^T$, $[0, 20]^T$) with equal probability. The covariance matrix for each distribution is $\sigma^2 I$, where $\sigma^2 = 1$ and I is the 2×2 identity matrix.

Take the following steps:

1. Generate and plot a data set X_1 (training set) containing 160 points from class $+1$ (20 from each distribution) and another 160 points from class -1 (20 points from each distribution). Use the same prescription to generate a data set X_2 (test set).

2. Run the adaptive BP algorithm with learning rate 0.01 and for 10,000 iterations, to train 2-layer FNNs with 7, 8, 10, 14, 16, 20, 32, and 40 hidden-layer nodes (the values of the rest of the parameters for the adaptive BP algorithm are chosen as in Example 2.8.1).

3. Repeat step 2 for $\sigma^2 = 2, 3, 4$ and draw conclusions.

Note that this is a more complex problem compared with those considered before, and the required number of hidden layer nodes is higher than that in the examples discussed previously. Note also that for the FNN with 16 hidden-layer nodes for $s = 1$ and 4, no satisfactory solution is obtained, although the network is, in principle, capable of learning the classification task (the FNN with 14 hidden-layer nodes performs much better). This may be because the landscape of the cost function $J(w)$ is such that it prevents the algorithm from converging to a good solution. That is, the algorithm may be trapped in a local minimum of the cost function that does not correspond to a satisfactory solution for the classification problem at hand.

Data Transformation
Feature Generation and Dimensionality Reduction

3.1 INTRODUCTION

In this chapter, we deal with linear and nonlinear transformation techniques, which are used to generate a set of features from a set of measurements or from a set of originally generated features. The goal is to obtain new features that encode the classification information in a more compact way compared with the original features. This implies a reduction in the number of features needed for a given classification task, which is also known as *dimensionality reduction* because the dimension of the new feature space is now reduced. The goal, of course, is to achieve this dimensionality reduction in some optimal sense so that the loss of information, which in general is unavoidable after reducing the original number of features, is as small as possible.

3.2 PRINCIPAL COMPONENT ANALYSIS

Principal component analysis (PCA) is one of the most popular techniques for dimensionality reduction. Starting from an original set of l samples (features), which form the elements of a vector $x \in \mathcal{R}^l$, the goal is to apply a linear transformation to obtain a new set of samples:

$$y = A^T x$$

so that the components of y are uncorrelated. In a second stage, one chooses the most significant of these components. The steps are summarized here:

1. Estimate the covariance matrix S. Usually the mean value is assumed to be zero, $E[x] = 0$. In this case, the covariance and autocorrelation matrices coincide, $R \equiv E[xx^T] = S$. If this is not the case, we subtract the mean. Recall that, given N feature vectors, $x_i \in \mathcal{R}^l$, $i = 1, 2, \ldots, N$, the autocorrelation matrix estimate is given by

$$R \approx \frac{1}{N} \sum_{i=1}^{N} x_i x_i^T \tag{3.1}$$

2. Perform the eigendecomposition of S and compute the l eigenvalues/eigenvectors, λ_i, $a_i \in \mathcal{R}^l$, $i = 0, 2, \ldots, l-1$.

3. Arrange the eigenvalues in descending order, $\lambda_0 \geq \lambda_1 \geq \cdots \geq \lambda_{l-1}$.
4. Choose the m largest eigenvalues. Usually m is chosen so that the gap between λ_{m-1} and λ_m is large. Eigenvalues $\lambda_0, \lambda_1, \ldots, \lambda_{m-1}$ are known as the m *principal components*.
5. Use the respective (column) eigenvectors a_i, $i = 0, 1, 2, \ldots, m-1$ to form the transformation matrix

$$A = \begin{bmatrix} a_0 & a_1 & a_2 & \cdots & a_{m-1} \end{bmatrix}$$

6. Transform each l-dimensional vector x in the original space to an m-dimensional vector y via the transformation $y = A^T x$. In other words, the ith element $y(i)$ of y is the *projection* of x on a_i $\left(y(i) = a_i^T x \right)$.

As pointed out in [Theo 09, Section 6.3], the total variance of the elements of x, $\sum_{i=0}^{l-1} E[x^2(i)]$ (for zero mean), is equal to the sum of the eigenvalues $\sum_{i=0}^{l-1} \lambda_i$. After the transformation, the variance of the ith element, $E[y^2(i)]$, $i = 0, 2, \ldots, l-1$, is equal to λ_i. Thus, selection of the elements that correspond to the m largest eigenvalues retains the maximum variance.

To compute the principal components, type

$$[eigenval, eigenvec, explain, Y, mean\_vec] = pca\_fun(X, m)$$

where

> X is an $l \times N$ matrix with columns that are the data vectors,
>
> m is the number of the most significant principal components taken into account,
>
> *eigenval* is an m-dimensional column vector containing the m largest eigenvalues of the covariance matrix of X in descending order,
>
> *eigenvec* is an $l \times m$-dimensional matrix, containing in its columns the eigenvectors that correspond to the m largest eigenvalues of the covariance matrix of X,
>
> *explain* is an l-dimensional column vector whose ith element is the percentage of the total variance retained along (in the MATLAB terminology *explained* by) the ith principal component,
>
> Y is an $m \times N$ matrix containing the projections of the data points of X to the space spanned by the m vectors of *eigenvec*,
>
> *mean_vec* is the mean vector of the column vectors of X.

Example 3.2.1

1. Generate a set X_1 of $N = 500$ 2-dimensional vectors from a Gaussian distribution with zero mean and covariance matrix

$$S_1 = \begin{bmatrix} 0.3 & 0.2 \\ 0.2 & 1.0 \end{bmatrix}$$

Perform PCA on X_1; that is, compute the two eigenvalues/eigenvectors of the estimate $\hat{S}_1$ of S_1 obtained using the vectors of X_1. Taking into account that the ith eigenvalue "explains" the variance along the direction of the ith eigenvector of $\hat{S}_1$, compute the percentage of the total variance explained

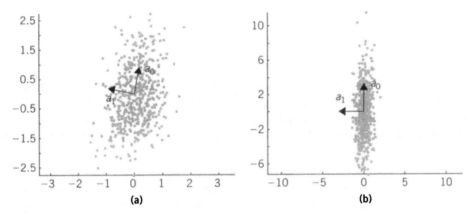

FIGURE 3.1

Data points of X_1(a) and X_2(b) considered in Example 3.2.1, together with the (normalized) eigenvectors of $\hat{S}_1$ and $\hat{S}_2$, respectively.

by each of the two components as the ratio $\frac{\lambda_i}{\lambda_0 + \lambda_1}$, $i = 0, 1$. Plot the data set X_1 as well as the eigenvectors of $\hat{S}_1$. Comment on the results.

2. Similarly generate a data set X_2, now with the covariance matrix $S_2 = \begin{bmatrix} 0.3 & 0.2 \\ 0.2 & 9.0 \end{bmatrix}$. Repeat the previous experiment.

Solution. Take the following steps:

Step 1. To generate the data set X_1, type

```
randn('seed',0)   %For reproducubility of the results
S1=[.3 .2; .2 1];
[l,l]=size(S1);
mv=zeros(1,l);
N=500;
m=2;
X1=mvnrnd(mv,S1,N)';
```

To apply PCA on X_1 and to compute the percentage of the total variance explained by each component, type

```
[eigenval,eigenvec,explained,Y,mean_vec]=pca_fun(X1,m);
```

To plot the points of the data set X_1 together with the (normalized) eigenvectors of $\hat{S}_1$, type (see Figure 3.1(a))

```
figure(1), hold on
figure(1), plot(X1(1,:),X1(2,:),'r.')
```

```
figure(1), axis equal
figure(1), line([0; eigenvec(1,1)],[0; eigenvec(2,1)])
figure(1), line([0; eigenvec(1,2)],[0; eigenvec(2,2)])
```

The percentages of the total variance explained by the first and second components are 78.98% and 21.02%, respectively. This means that if we project the points of X_1 along the direction of the principal eigenvector (that corresponds to the largest eigenvalue of $\hat{S}_1$), we retain 78.98% of the total variance of X_1; 21.02% of the total variance, associated with the second principal component, will be "lost."

Step 2. To generate the data set X_2, repeat the previous code, where now X_1 and S_1 are replaced by X_2 and S_2, respectively. In this case, the percentages of the total variance explained by the first and second components are 96.74% and 3.26%, respectively. This means that if we project the points of X_2 along the direction of the eigenvector that corresponds to the largest eigenvalue of $\hat{S}_1$, we retain almost all the variance of X_2 in the 2-dimensional space (see Figure 3.1(b)). Explain this using physical reasoning.   ■

The goal of the next example is to demonstrate that projecting in a lower-dimensional space, so as to retain most of the variance, does not necessarily guarantee that the classification-related information is preserved.

Example 3.2.2
1. **a.** Generate a data set X_1 consisting of 400 2-dimensional vectors that stem from two classes. The first 200 stem from the first class, which is modeled by the Gaussian distribution with mean $m_1 = [-8, 8]^T$; the rest stem from the second class, modeled by the Gaussian distribution with mean $m_2 = [8, 8]^T$. Both distributions share the covariance matrix

$$S = \begin{bmatrix} 0.3 & 1.5 \\ 1.5 & 9.0 \end{bmatrix}$$

   b. Perform PCA on X_1 and compute the percentage of the total amount of variance explained by each component.
   c. Project the vectors of X_1 along the direction of the first principal component and plot the data set X_1 and its projection to the first principal component. Comment on the results.
2. Repeat on data set X_2, which is generated as X_1 but with $m_1 = [-1, 0]^T$ and $m_2 = [1, 0]^T$.
3. Compare the results obtained and draw conclusions.

Solution. Take the following steps:

Step 1(a). To generate data set X_1 and the vector y_1, whose ith coordinate contains the class label of the ith vector of X_1, type

```
randn('seed',0)   %For reproducibility of the results
S=[.3 1.5; 1.5 9];
[l,l]=size(S);
mv=[-8 8; 8 8]';
N=200;
```

```
X1=[mvnrnd(mv(:,1),S,N); mvnrnd(mv(:,2),S,N)]';
y1=[ones(1,N), 2*ones(1,N)];
```

Step 1(b). To compute the eigenvalues/eigenvectors and variance percentages required in this step, type

```
m=2;
[eigenval,eigenvec,explained,Y,mean_vec]=pca_fun(X1,m);
```

Step 1(c). The projections of the data points of X_1 along the direction of the first principal component are contained in the first row of Y, returned by the function *pca_ fun*. To plot the data vectors of X_1 as well as their projections, type

```
%Plot of X1
figure(1), hold on
figure(1), plot(X(1,y==1),X(2,y==1),'r.',X(1,y==2),X(2,y==2),'bo')
%Computation of the projections of X1
w=eigenvec(:,1);
t1=w'*X(:,y==1);
t2=w'*X(:,y==2);
X_proj1=[t1;t1].*((w/(w'*w))*ones(1,length(t1)));
X_proj2=[t2;t2].*((w/(w'*w))*ones(1,length(t2)));
%Plot of the projections
figure(1), plot(X_proj1(1,:),X_proj1(2,:),'k.',...
X_proj2(1,:),X_proj2(2,:),'ko')
figure(1), axis equal
%Plot of the eigenvectors
figure(1), line([0; eigenvec(1,1)], [0; eigenvec(2,1)])
figure(1), line([0; eigenvec(1,2)], [0; eigenvec(2,2)])
```

The percentages of the total amount of variance explained by the first and second components are 87.34% and 12.66%, respectively. That is, the projection to the direction of the first component retains most of the total variance of X_1.

Step 2(a). To generate X_2, the code for X_1 is executed again, with $m_1 = [-1, 0]^T$ and $m_2 = [1, 0]^T$.

Step 2(b)–(c). The codes in the (b)–(c) branches of step 1 are executed for X_2. The percentages of the total amount of variance explained by the two principal components are 90.19% and 9.81%, respectively.

Step 3. In the two previous cases approximately 90% of the total variance of the data sets is retained after projecting along the first principal component. However, there is no guarantee that class discrimination is retained along this direction. Indeed, in the case of X_1 the data in the two classes, after projection along the first principal eigenvector, remain well separated. However, this is not the case for data set X_2 (see Figure 3.2). ■

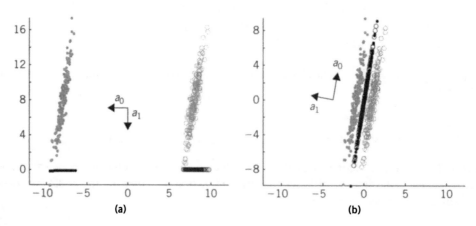

FIGURE 3.2

Data points (gray) of X_1 (a) and X_2 (b) considered in Example 3.2.2, along with the (normalized) eigenvectors of $\hat{S}_1$ and $\hat{S}_2$, respectively. The data points of the two classes of X_1, after projection along the first principal eigenvector (black), remain well separated. This is not the case for X_2.

Exercise 3.2.1

Take the following steps:

1. Generate a data set X_1 consisting of 400 3-dimensional vectors that stem from two classes. The first half of them stem from the first class, which is modeled by the Gaussian distribution with mean $m_1 = [-6,\ 6,\ 6]^T$; the rest stem from the second class, modeled by the Gaussian distribution with mean $m_2 = [6,\ 6,\ 6]^T$. Both distributions share the covariance matrix

$$S = \begin{bmatrix} 0.3 & 1.0 & 1.0 \\ 1.0 & 9.0 & 1.0 \\ 1.0 & 1.0 & 9.0 \end{bmatrix}$$

Perform PCA on X_1 and compute the percentage of the total amount of variance explained by each principal component. Project the vectors of X_1 on the space spanned by the first two principal components Y_1 and Y_2. Plot the data in the X_{11}-X_{12}, X_{11}-X_{13}, X_{12}-X_{13}, Y_1-Y_2, Y_1-Y_3, Y_2-Y_3 subspaces (six MATLAB figures in total).

2. Generate a data set X_2 as in step 1, now with $m_1 = [-2,\ 0,\ 0]^T$ and $m_2 = [2,\ 0,\ 0]^T$. Repeat the process as described in step 1.

3. Compare the results obtained from each data set and draw conclusions.

3.3 THE SINGULAR VALUE DECOMPOSITION METHOD

Given an $l \times N$ matrix, X, there exist square *unitary* matrices U and V of dimensions $l \times l$ and $N \times N$, respectively, so that

$$X = U \begin{bmatrix} \Lambda^{\frac{1}{2}} & O \\ O & 0 \end{bmatrix} V^T$$

where Λ is a square $r \times r$ matrix, with $r \le \min\{l, N\}$ (r is equal to the rank of X). Since matrices U and V are unitary, their column vectors are, by definition, orthonormal and $UU^T = I$ and $VV^T = I$. Matrix $\Lambda^{\frac{1}{2}}$ is given by

$$\Lambda^{\frac{1}{2}} = \begin{bmatrix} \sqrt{\lambda_0} & & & \\ & \sqrt{\lambda_1} & & \\ & & \ddots & \\ & & & \sqrt{\lambda_{r-1}} \end{bmatrix}$$

where λ_i, $i = 0, 2, \dots, r - 1$, are the r *nonzero* eigenvalues of XX^T, which are the same with the eigenvalues of $X^T X$ [Theo 09, Section 6.4], and known as the *singular values* of X. Equivalently, we can write

$$X = \sum_{i=0}^{r-1} \sqrt{\lambda_i} u_i v_i^T \tag{3.2}$$

where u_i, v_i, $i = 0, 1, \dots, r - 1$, are the corresponding eigenvectors of XX^T and $X^T X$, respectively. Moreover, u_i and v_i, $i = 0, \dots, r - 1$ are the first r column vectors of U and V, respectively. The rest of the column vectors of U and V correspond to zero eigenvalues.

If we retain $m \le r$ terms in the summation of Eq. (3.2), that is,

$$\hat{X} = \sum_{i=0}^{m-1} \sqrt{\lambda_i} u_i v_i^T \tag{3.3}$$

then $\hat{X}$ is the best approximation (in the Frobenius sense) of X of rank m [Theo 09, Section 6.4].

To compute the Singular Value Decomposition (SVD) of a matrix X, type

$$[U, s, V, Y] = svd\_fun(X, m)$$

where

   X is an $l \times N$ matrix whose columns contain the data vectors,

   m is the number of the largest singular values that will be taken into account,

   U is an $l \times l$ matrix containing the eigenvectors of XX^T in descending order,

   s is an r-dimensional vector containing the singular values in descending order,

   V is an $N \times N$ matrix containing the eigenvectors of $X^T X$ in descending order,

   Y is an $m \times N$ matrix containing the projections of the data points of X on the space spanned by the m leading eigenvectors contained in U.

More on SVD can be found in [Theo 09, Section 6.4].

Exercise 3.3.1

1. Consider the data set X_1 of Exercise 3.2.1. Perform singular value decomposition using *svd_fun*. Then project the vectors of X_1 on the space spanned by the m leading eigenvectors contained in U (that correspond to Y_1 and Y_2). Finally, plot the data in the X_{11}-X_{12}, X_{11}-X_{13}, X_{12}-X_{13}, Y_1-Y_2, Y_1-Y_3, Y_2-Y_3 spaces (six MATLAB figures in total).

2. Repeat for the data set X_2 of Exercise 3.2.1 and compare the results.
   Observe that the results obtained for the SVD case are similar to those obtained in Exercise 3.2.1 for the PCA case (why?).

Example 3.3.1. Generate a data set of $N = 100$ vectors of dimensionality $l = 2000$. The vectors stem from the Gaussian distribution with a mean equal to the l-dimensional zero vector and a diagonal covariance matrix, S, having all of its nonzero elements equal to 0.1 except $S(1,1)$ and $S(2,2)$, which are equal to 10,000. Apply PCA and SVD on the previous data set and draw your conclusions.

Solution. To generate matrix X, containing the vectors of the data set, type

```
N=100;
l=2000;
mv=zeros(1,l);
S=0.1*eye(l);
S(1,1)=10000;
S(2,2)=10000;
randn('seed',0)
X=mvnrnd(mv,S,N)';
```

Note that the data exhibit significant spread along the first two axes, that is, along the vectors $e_1 = [1, \overbrace{0,\ldots,0}^{l-1}]^T$ and $e_2 = [0, 1, \overbrace{0,\ldots,0}^{l-2}]^T$.

To run PCA and SVD on X and to measure the execution time of each method, type

```
%PCA
t0=clock;
m=5;
[eigenval,eigenvec,explain,Y]=pca_fun(X,m);
time1=etime(clock,t0)
'-----'
%SVD
t0=clock;
m=min(N,l);
[U,S,V,Y]=svd_fun(X,m);
time2=etime(clock,t0)
```

From the previously obtained results, two conclusions can be drawn.

First, both methods identify (approximately) e_1 and e_2 as the most significant directions. To verify this, compare the first two columns of *eigenvec* produced by PCA with the first two columns of U, that is, $U(:,1:2)$, produced by SVD, by typing

```
[eigenvec(:,1:2) U(:,1:2)]'
```

Second, provided that enough computer memory is available, PCA will take orders of magnitude more time than SVD (if not enough memory is available, PCA will not run at all). The difference in the performance of the two methods lies in the fact that in PCA we perform eigendecomposition on the $l \times l$ covariance matrix while in SVD we perform eigendecomposition on the $N \times N$ $X^T X$ and then, with a simple transformation, compute the eigenvectors of XX^T (which may be viewed as a scaled approximation of the autocorrelation matrix). Moreover, it has to be emphasized that, in general for such cases where $N < l$, the obtained estimate of the autocorrelation matrix is not a good one. Such cases, where $N < l$, arise in image-processing applications, in Web mining, in microarray analysis, and the like. ∎

3.4 FISHER'S LINEAR DISCRIMINANT ANALYSIS

In PCA, the dimensionality reduction is performed in an unsupervised mode. Feature vectors are projected on the subspace spanned by the dominant eigenvectors of the covariance (autocorrelation) matrix. In this section, computation of the subspace on which one projects, in order to reduce dimensionality, takes place in a supervised mode. This subspace is also determined via the solution of an eigendecomposition problem, but the corresponding matrix is different.

In the 2-class case, the goal is to search for a *single* direction, w, so that the respective projections y of the l-dimensional feature vectors $x \in \mathcal{R}^l$ maximize Fisher's discriminant ratio.

Fisher's discriminant ratio of a *scalar* feature y in a 2-class classification task is defined as

$$FDR = \frac{(\mu_1 - \mu_2)^2}{\sigma_1^2 + \sigma_2^2}$$

where μ_1, μ_2 are the mean values of y, and σ_1^2, σ_2^2 are the variances of y in the two classes, respectively. In other words, after the projection on w the goal is for the mean values of the data points in the two classes to be as far apart as possible and for the variances to be as small as possible. It turns out that w is given by the maximum eigenvector of the matrix product $S_w^{-1} S_b$ [Theo 09, Section 5.8], where for two equiprobable classes

$$S_w = \frac{1}{2}(S_1 + S_2)$$

is known as the *within-class scatter matrix*, with S_1, S_2 being the respective covariance matrices. S_b is known as the *between-class scatter matrix*, defined by

$$S_b = \frac{1}{2}(m_1 - m_0)(m_1 - m_0)^T + \frac{1}{2}(m_2 - m_0)(m_2 - m_0)^T$$

where m_0 is the overall mean of the data x in the original $\mathcal{R}^l$ space and m_1, m_2 are the mean values in the two classes, respectively [Theo 09, Section 5.6.3]. It can be shown, however, that in this special 2-class case the eigenanalysis step can be bypassed and the solution directly given by

$$w = S_w^{-1}(m_1 - m_2)$$

In the c-class case, the goal is to find the $m \leq c - 1$ directions (m-dimensional subspace) so that the so-called J_3 criterion, defined as

$$J_3 = \text{trace}\{S_w^{-1} S_b\}$$

is maximized. In the previous equation

$$S_w = \sum_{i=1}^{c} P_i S_i, \; S_b = \sum_{i=1}^{c} P_i (m_i - m_0)(m_i - m_0)^T$$

and the P_i's denote the respective class a priori probabilities. This is a generalization of the FDR criterion in the multiclass case with different a priori probabilities. The m directions are given by the m dominant eigenvectors of the matrix product $S_w^{-1} S_b$.

It must be pointed out that the rank of the S_b matrix is $c - 1$ at the most (although it is given as a sum of c matrices, only $c - 1$ of these terms are independent [Theo 09, Section 5.6.3]. This is the reason that m was upper-bounded by $c - 1$; only the $c - 1$ largest eigenvalues (at most) are nonzero. In some cases, this may be a drawback because the maximum number of features that this method can generate is bounded by the number of classes [Theo 09, Section 5.8].

Example 3.4.1

1. Apply linear discriminant analysis (LDA) on the data set X_2 generated in the second part of Example 3.2.2.
2. Compare the results obtained with those obtained from the PCA analysis.

Solution. Take the following steps:

Step 1. To estimate the mean vectors of each class using the available samples, type

```
mv_est(:,1)=mean(X2(:,y2==1)')';
mv_est(:,2)=mean(X2(:,y2==2)')';
```

To compute the within-scatter matrix S_w, use the *scatter_mat* function, which computes the within class (S_w), the between class (S_b), and the mixture class (S_m) [Theo 09, Section 5.6.3] for a c-class classification problem based on a set of data vectors. This function is called by

```
[Sw,Sb,Sm]=scatter_mat(X2,y2);
```

Since the two classes are equiprobable, the direction w along which Fisher's discriminant ratio is maximized is computed as $w = S_w^{-1}(m_1 - m_2)$. In MATLAB terms this is written as

```
w=inv(Sw)*(mv_est(:,1)-mv_est(:,2))
```

Finally, the projection of the data vectors of X_2 on the direction w as well as the plot of the results is carried out through the following statements (see Figure 3.3)

```
%Plot of the data set
figure(1), plot(X(1,y==1),X(2,y==1),'r.',...
X(1,y==2),X(2,y==2),'bo')
figure(1), axis equal
%Computation of the projections
t1=w'*X(:,y==1);
```

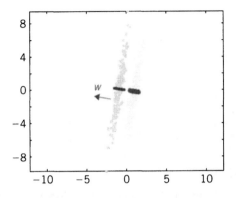

FIGURE 3.3

Points of the data set X_2 (gray) and their projections (black) along the direction of w, from Example 3.4.1.

```
t2=w'*X(:,y==2);
X_proj1=[t1;t1].*((w/(w'*w))*ones(1,length(t1)));
X_proj2=[t2;t2].*((w/(w'*w))*ones(1,length(t2)));
%Plot of the projections
figure(1), hold on
figure(1), plot(X_proj(1,y==1),X_proj(2,y==1),'y.',...
X_proj(1,y==2),X_proj(2,y==2),'co')
```

Step 2. Comparing the result depicted in MATLAB figure 1, which was produced by the execution of the previous code, to the corresponding result obtained by the PCA analysis, it is readily observed that the classes remain well separated when the vectors of X_2 are projected along the w direction that results from Fisher's discriminant analysis. In contrast, classes were heavily overlapped when they were projected along the principal direction provided by PCA. ■

Example 3.4.2

1a. Generate a data set of 900 3-dimensional data vectors, which stem from two classes—the first 100 vectors from a zero-mean Gaussian distribution with covariance matrix

$$S_1 = \begin{bmatrix} 0.5 & 0 & 0 \\ 0 & 0.5 & 0 \\ 0 & 0 & 0.01 \end{bmatrix}$$

The rest grouped in 8 groups of 100 vectors. Each group stems from a Gaussian distribution. All of these distributions share the covariance matrix

$$S_2 = \begin{bmatrix} 1 & 0 & 0 \\ 0 & 1 & 0 \\ 0 & 0 & 0.01 \end{bmatrix}$$

while their means are

- $m_1^2 = [a, 0, 0]^T$
- $m_2^2 = [a/2, a/2, 0]^T$
- $m_3^2 = [0, a, 0]^T$
- $m_4^2 = [-a/2, a/2, 0]^T$
- $m_5^2 = [-a, 0, 0]^T$
- $m_6^2 = [-a/2, -a/2, 0]^T$
- $m_7^2 = [0, -a, 0]^T$
- $m_8^2 = [a/2, -a/2, 0]^T$

where $a = 6$ (m_i^2 denotes the mean of the ith Gaussian distribution of the second class).

Take the following steps:

1b. Plot the 3-dimensional data set and view it from different angles to get a feeling of how the data are spread in the 3-dimensional space (use the Rotate-3D MATLAB utility).

1c. Perform Fisher's discriminant analysis on the previous data set. Project the data on the subspace spanned by the eigenvectors that correspond to the nonzero eigenvalues of the matrix product $S_w^{-1} S_b$. Comment on the results.

2. Repeat step 1 for a 3-class problem where the data are generated like those in step 1, with the exception that the last group of 100 vectors, which stem from the Gaussian distribution with mean m_8^2, is labeled class 3.

Solution. Take the following steps:

Step 1(a). To generate a 3×900-dimensional matrix whose columns are the data vectors, type

```
%Initialization of random number generator
randn('seed',10)
%Definition of the parameters
S1=[.5 0 0; 0 .5 0; 0 0 .01];
S2=[1 0 0; 0 1 0; 0 0 .01];
a=6;
mv=[0 0 0; a 0 0; a/2 a/2 0; 0 a 0; -a/2 a/2 0;...
 -a 0 0; -a/2 -a/2 0; 0 -a 0; a/2 -a/2 0]';
N=100;
% Generation of the data set
X=[mvnrnd(mv(:,1),S1,N)];
for i=2:9
    X=[X; mvnrnd(mv(:,i),S2,N)];
end
X=X';
c=2; %No of classes
y=[ones(1,N) 2*ones(1,8*N)]; %Class label vector
```

Step 1(b). To plot the data set X in the 3-dimensional space, type

```
figure(1), plot3(X(1,y==1),X(2,y==1),X(3,y==1),'r.',...
X(1,y==2),X(2,y==2),X(3,y==2),'b.')
figure(1), axis equal
```

With the Rotate-3D button of MATLAB figure 1, you can view the data set from different angles. It is easy to notice that the variation of data along the third direction is very small (because of the small values of $S_1(3,3)$ and $S_2(3,3)$). The data set in the 3-dimensional space may be considered as lying across the $x - y$ plane, with a very small variation along the z axis.

Clearly, the projection of the data set in the $x - y$ plane retains the separation of the classes, but this is not the case with the projections on the $x - z$ and $y - z$ planes. In addition, observe that there is no single direction (1-dimensional space) w that retains the separation of the classes after projecting X on it.

Step 1(c). To perform Fisher's discriminant analysis, first compute the scatter matrices S_w and S_b; then perform eigendecomposition on the matrix $S_w^{-1}S_b$; finally, project the data on the subspace spanned by the eigenvectors of $S_w^{-1}S_b$ that correspond to the nonzero eigenvalues. The following MATLAB code may be used:

```
% Scatter matrix computation
[Sw,Sb,Sm]=scatter_mat(X,y);
% Eigendecomposition of Sw^(-1)*Sb
[V,D]=eig(inv(Sw)*Sb);
% Sorting the eigenvalues in descending order
% and rearranging accordingly the eigenvectors
s=diag(D);
[s,ind]=sort(s,1,'descend');
V=V(:,ind);
% Selecting in A the eigenvectors corresponding
% to non-zero eigenvalues
A=V(:,1:c-1);
% Project the data set on the space spanned by
% the column vectors of A
Y=A'*X;
```

Here we used the code for the multiclass case with $c = 2$. Since the number of classes is equal to 2, only one eigenvalue of $S_w^{-1}S_b$ is nonzero (0.000234). Thus, Fisher's discriminant analysis gives a single direction (1-dimensional space) along which the data will be projected.

To plot the projections of X on the subspace spanned by the eigenvector of $S_w^{-1}S_b$, which corresponds to the nonzero eigenvalue, type

```
figure(2), plot(Y(y==1),0,'ro',Y(y==2),0,'b.')
figure(2), axis equal
```

Observe that the projections of the data of the two classes coincide. Thus, in this case Fisher's discriminant analysis cannot provide a smaller subspace where the class discrimination is retained. This happens because the number of classes is equal to 2 and so the dimensionality of the reduced subspace is at most 1, which is not sufficient for the current problem.

Step 2(a). To generate a 3×900-dimensional matrix whose columns are data vectors, repeat the code given in step 1(a), replacing the last two lines with

```
% Definition of the number of classes
c=3;
% Definition of the class label of each vector
y=[ones(1,N) 2*ones(1,7*N) 3*ones(1,N)];
```

Step 2(b). To plot the data set X in the 3-dimensional space, type

```
figure(1), plot3(X(1,y==1),X(2,y==1),X(3,y==1),'r.',X(1,y==2),...
X(2,y==2),X(3,y==2),'b.',X(1,y==3),X(2,y==3),X(3,y==3),'g.')
figure(1), axis equal
```

Step 2(c). Adopt the MATLAB code of step 1(c) for the current data set. In this case, since there are three classes, we may have at most two nonzero eigenvalues of $S_w^{-1}S_b$. Indeed, the nonzero eigenvalues now turn out to be 0.222145 and 0.000104.

To plot the projections of X on the space spanned by the eigenvectors of $S_w^{-1}S_b$ that correspond to the nonzero eigenvalues (2-dimensional space), type

```
figure(3), plot(Y(1,y==1),Y(2,y==1),'ro',...
Y(1,y==2),Y(2,y==2),'b.',Y(1,y==3),Y(2,y==3),'gx')
figure(3), axis equal
```

In this case, observe that the projection in the 2-dimensional subspace retains the separation among the classes at a satisfactory level.

Finally, keep in mind that there are data sets where the dimensionality reduction from projection in any subspace of the original space may cause substantial loss of class discrimination. In such cases, nonlinear techniques may be useful. ■

3.5 THE KERNEL PCA

The three methods considered so far for dimensionality reduction are *linear*. A subspace of low dimension is first constructed as, for example, the span of the m dominant directions in the original $\mathcal{R}^l$, $l > m$ space.

The choice of dominant directions depends on the method used. In a second stage, all vectors of interest in $\mathcal{R}^l$ are (linearly) projected in the low-dimensional subspace. Such techniques are appropriate whenever our data in $\mathcal{R}^l$ lie (approximately) on a linear manifold (e.g., hyperplane). However, in many

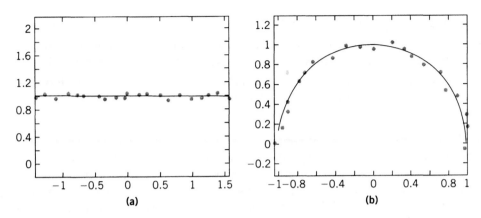

FIGURE 3.4

(a) The 2-dimensional data points lying (approximately) on a line (linear manifold). (b) The 2-dimensional data points lying (approximately) on a semicircle (nonlinear manifold).

cases the data are distributed around a lower-dimensional manifold, which is not linear (e.g., around a circle or a sphere in a 3-dimensional space).

Figures 3.4(a,b) show two cases where data in the 2-dimensional space lie (approximately) on a linear and a nonlinear manifold, respectively. Both manifolds are 1-dimensional since a straight line and the circumference of a circle can be parameterized in terms of a *single* parameter.

The kernel PCA is one technique for dimensionality reduction when the data lie (approximately) on a nonlinear manifold. According to the method, data are first mapped into a high-dimensional space via a *nonlinear* mapping:

$$x \in \mathcal{R}^l \mapsto \phi(x) \in H$$

PCA is then performed in the new space H, chosen to be an RKHS. The inner products can be expressed in terms of the kernel trick, as discussed in Section 2.5.

Although a (linear) PCA is performed in the RKHS space H, because of the nonlinearity of the mapping function $\phi(\cdot)$, the method is equivalent to a nonlinear function in the original space. Moreover, since every operation can be expressed in inner products, the explicit knowledge of $\phi(\cdot)$ is not required. All that is necessary is to adopt the kernel function that defines the inner products. More details are given in [Theo 09, Section 6.7.1].

To use the kernel PCA, type

$$[s, V, Y] = kernel\_PCA(X, m, choice, para)$$

where

X is an $l \times N$ matrix whose columns contain the data vectors,

m is the number of (significant) principal components that will be considered,

choice is the type of kernel function to be used ('*pol*' for polynomial, '*exp*' for exponential),

para is a 2-dimensional vector containing the parameters for the kernel function; for polynomials it is $(x^T y + para(1))^{para(2)}$ and for exponentials it is $exp(-(x-y)^T(x-y)/(2para(1)^2))$,

s is an N-dimensional vector that contains the computed eigenvalues after applying the kernel PCA,

V is an $N \times N$ matrix whose columns are the eigenvectors corresponding to the principal components of the Gram matrix, $\mathcal{K}$, which is involved in the kernel PCA [Theo 09, Section 6.7.1],

Y is an $m \times N$ dimensional matrix that contains the projections of the data vectors of X on the subspace spanned by the m principal components.

Example 3.5.1. This example illustrates the rationale behind the kernel PCA. However, since kernel PCA implies, first, a mapping to a higher-dimensional space, visualization of the results is generally not possible. Therefore, we will "cheat" a bit and use a mapping function $\phi(\cdot)$ that does not correspond to a kernel function $k(\cdot,\cdot)$. (After all, the mapping to an RKHS is required only for the computational tractability needed to compute inner products efficiently.) However, this function allows transformation of a 2-dimensional space, where our data points lie around a nonlinear manifold, into another 2-dimensional space, where the data points are mapped around a linear manifold.

Consider a data set X consisting of 21 2-dimensional points of the form $x_i = (x_i(1), x_i(2)) = (\cos \theta_i + s_i, \sin \theta_i + s_i')$, where $\theta_i = (i-1) * (\pi/20)$, $i = 1, \ldots, 21$ and s_i, s_i' are random numbers that stem from the uniform distribution in $[-0.1, 0.1]$ (see Figure 3.5(a)). These points lie around the semicircle modeled by $x^2(1) + x^2(2) = 1$, which is centered at the origin and is positive along the x_2 axis.

The mapping function $\phi(\cdot)$ is defined as

$$\phi\left(\begin{bmatrix} x(1) \\ x(2) \end{bmatrix}\right) = \begin{bmatrix} \tan^{-1}\left(\frac{x(2)}{x(1)}\right) \\ \sqrt{x^2(1) + x^2(2)} \end{bmatrix}$$

By applying $\phi(\cdot)$ on the data set X, we get the set $Y = \{y_i = \phi(x_i), i = 1, \ldots, 21\}$, which is illustrated in Figure 3.5(b). Note that the points of Y lie around a linear manifold (straight line) in the transformed domain. Then we apply linear PCA on Y and keep only the first principal component, since almost all of the total variance of the data set (99.87%) is retained along this direction.[1] Let $Z = \{z_i = [z_i(1), z_i(2)]^T, i = 1, \ldots, 21\}$ be the set containing the projections of y_i's on the first principal component in the transformed space (see Figure 3.5(c)). Mapping z_i's back to the original space via the inverse function of $\phi(\cdot)$, which is given by

$$\phi^{-1}\left(\begin{bmatrix} z(1) \\ z(2) \end{bmatrix}\right) = \begin{bmatrix} z(2)\cos z(1) \\ z(2)\sin z(1) \end{bmatrix} \equiv \begin{bmatrix} x'(1) \\ x'(2) \end{bmatrix}$$

the points $(x'(1), x'(2))$ are obtained that lie on the semicircle defined by $x^2(1) + x^2(2) = 1$, with $x(2) > 0$ (see Figure 3.5(d)).

---

[1] Linear PCA requires subtraction of the mean of the data vectors (which is performed in the *pca_fun* function). In our case, this vector equals $[0, 1]^T$. After PCA, this vector is added to each projection of the points along the direction of the first principal component.

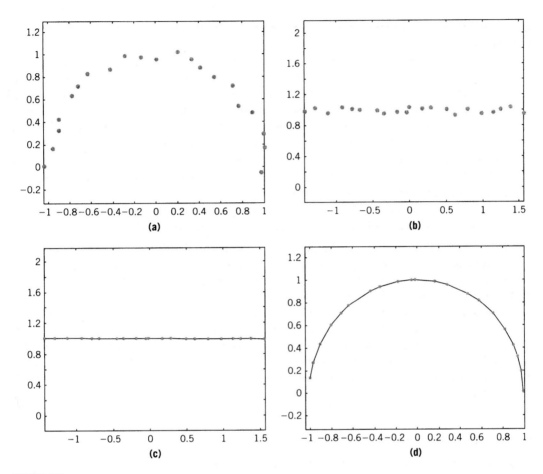

FIGURE 3.5

Example 3.5.1: (a) Data set in the original space (around a semicircle). (b) Data set in the transformed space (around a straight line). (c) Direction corresponding to the first principal component and the images (projections) of the points on it in the transformed space. (d) Images of the points in the original space.

Remark

- Observe that the nonlinear mapping transformed the original manifold to a linear one. Thus, the application of the (linear) PCA on the transformed domain is fully justified. Of course, in the general case one should not expect to be so "lucky"—that is, to have the transformed data lying across a linear manifold.

In the next example we consider kernel PCA in the context of a classification task. More specifically, the goal is to demonstrate the potential of the kernel PCA to transform a nonlinear classification problem, in the (original) l-dimensional space, into a linear one in an $m(< l)$ dimensional space. If this is achieved, the original classification problem can be solved in the transformed space by a linear classifier.

Example 3.5.2

1. Generate two data sets X and X_{test}, each one containing 200 3-dimensional vectors. In each, the first $N_1 = 100$ vectors stem from class 1, which is modeled by the uniform distribution in $[-0.5, 0.5]^3$, while the rest, $N_2 = 100$, stem from class -1 and lie around the sphere with radius $r = 2$ and centered at the origin. The N_2 points for each data set are generated as follows.

   Randomly select a pair of numbers, $x(1)$ and $x(2)$, that stem from the uniform distribution in the range $[-2, 2]$, and check if $x^2(1) + x^2(2)$ is less than r^2. If this is not the case, choose a different pair. Otherwise, generate two points of the sphere as $(x(1), x(2), \sqrt{r^2 - x^2(1) - x^2(2)} + \varepsilon_1)$ and $(x(1), x(2), -\sqrt{r^2 - x^2(1) - x^2(2)} + \varepsilon_2)$, where ε_1 and ε_2 are random numbers that stem from the uniform distribution in the interval $[-0.1, 0.1]$.

   Repeat this procedure $N_2/2$ times to generate N_2 points. Also generate the vectors y and y_{test} which contain the class labels of the points of X and X_{test}, respectively. Then plot the data sets.

2. Perform kernel PCA on X using the exponential kernel function with $\sigma = 1$ and keep only the first two most significant principal components. Project the data points of X onto the subspace spanned by the two principal components and let Y be the set of these projections (plot Y).

3. Design a least squares (LS) classifier based on Y.

4. Evaluate the performance of the previous classifier based on X_{test} as follows: For each vector in $x \in X_{test}$, determine its projection onto the space spanned by the two most significant principal components, computed earlier, and classify it using the LS classifier generated in step 3. Assign x to the class where its projection has been assigned. Plot the projections of the points of X_{test} onto the subspace spanned by the two principal components along with the straight line that realizes the classifier.

5. Repeat steps 2 through 4 with $\sigma = 0.6$.

Solution. Take the following steps:

Step 1. To generate the points of X that belong to class 1, type

```
rand('seed',0)
noise_level=0.1;
n_points=[100 100];  %Points per class
l=3;
X=rand(l,n_points(1))- (0.5*ones(l,1))*ones(1,n_points(1));
```

To generate the points of X that belong to class -1, type

```
r=2; %Radius of the sphere
for i=1:n_points(2)/2
    e=1;
    while(e==1)
        temp=(2*r)*rand(1,l-1)-r;
        if(r^2-sum(temp.^2)>0)
```

```
                    e=0;
              end
        end
        t=sqrt(r^2-sum(temp.^2))+noise_level*(rand-0.5);
        qw=[temp t; temp -t]';
        X=[X qw];
    end
```

The data set X_{test} is generated similarly (use the value 100 as the seed for the *rand* function). To define the class labels of the data vectors, type

```
[l,N]=size(X);
y=[ones(1,n_points(1)) -ones(1,n_points(2))];
y_test=[ones(1,n_points(1)) -ones(1,n_points(2))];
```

To plot the data set X, type[2]

```
figure(1), plot3(X(1,y==1),X(2,y==1),X(3,y==1),'r.',...
X(1,y==-1),X(2,y==-1),X(3,y==-1),'b+')
figure(1), axis equal
```

X_{test} is plotted similarly. Clearly, the two classes are nonlinearly separable.

Step 2. To perform kernel PCA with kernel exponential and $\sigma = 1$, type

```
[s,V,Y]=kernel_PCA(X,2,'exp',[1 0]);
```

Note that Y contains in its columns the images of the points of X on the space spanned by the first two principal components, while V contains the respective principal components.

To plot Y, type

```
figure(2), plot(Y(1,y==1),Y(2,y==1),'r.',Y(1,y==-1),Y(2,y==-1),'b+')
```

Step 3. To design the LS classifier based on Y, type

```
w=SSErr([Y; ones(1,sum(n_points))],y,0);
```

Note that each column vector of Y has been augmented by 1. The resulting w is [33.8001, 2.4356, −0.8935].

Step 4. Type the following to generate the Y_{test} set, containing in its columns the projections of the vectors of X_{test} to the space spanned by the principal components:

```
[l,N_test]=size(X_test);
```

---

[2]Use the Rotate 3D button to observe the data set from different angles.

```
Y_test=[];
for i=1:N_test
    [temp]=im_point(X_test(:,i),X,V,2,'exp',[1 0]);
    Y_test=[Y_test temp];
end
```

To classify the vectors of X_{test} (Y_{test}) and compute the classification error, type

```
y_out=2*(w'*[Y_test; ones(1,sum(n_points))]>0)-1;
class_err=sum(y_out.*y_test<0)/sum(n_points);
```

Figure 3.6(a) shows the Y_{test} set together with the line that corresponds to the linear classifier. This is produced by typing

```
figure(6), plot(Y_test(1,y==1),Y_test(2,y==1),'r.',...
Y_test(1,y==-1),Y_test(2,y==-1),'b+')
figure(6), axis equal
% Ploting the linear classifier (works only if w(1)~=0)
y_lin=[min(Y_test(2,:)') max(Y_test(2,:)')];
x_lin=[(-w(3)-w(2)*y_lin(1))/w(1) (-w(3)-w(2)*y_lin(2))/w(1)];
figure(6), hold on
figure(6), line(x_lin,y_lin)
```

Step 5. For this step, repeat the codes given in steps 2 through 4. Now in the call of the kernel PCA function (step 2), [1, 0] is replaced by [0.6, 0] (see also Figure 3.6(b)).

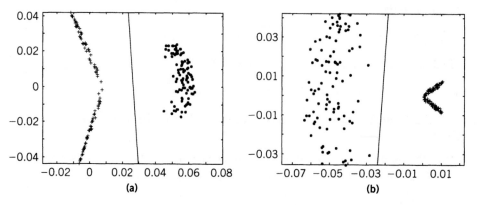

(a)   (b)

FIGURE 3.6

Y_{test} set produced in step 4 and linear classifier determined in step 3 of Example 3.5.2 for $\sigma = 1$ (a) and $\sigma = 0.6$ (b).

The previous steps having been performed, three conclusions can be drawn:

- First, kernel PCA *may* lead to mappings in lower-dimensional spaces, where the involved classes can be linearly separated, even though this is not the case in the original space. This cannot be achieved with linear PCA.
- Second, the choice of the kernel function parameters is critical. To verify this, try step 5 with $\sigma = 3$. In this case, the arrangement of the classes in the transformed space looks very similar to the arrangement in the original space.
- Third, for this problem the two classes remain linearly separable even in the 1-dimensional space as defined by the first principal component.

■

Example 3.5.3

1. Generate two data sets X_1 and X_2 as follows:
    - X_1 consists of 300 2-dimensional points. The first $N_1 = 100$ points stem from class 1, which is modeled by the uniform distribution in the region $[-2.5, -1.5] \times [-0.5, 0.5]$; the next $N_2 = 100$ points stem from class 2, which is modeled by the uniform distribution in the area $[0.5, 1.5] \times [-2.5, -1.5]$; and the final, $N_3 = 100$ points stem from class 3 and lie around the circle C with radius $r = 4$ and centered at the origin.

      More specifically, the last N_3 points are generated as follows: The points of the form $x_i = -r + \frac{2r}{N_2/2-1}i, i = 0,\ldots, N_2/2 - 1$ in the x axis are selected (they lie in the interval $[-2, 2]$). For each x_i the quantities $v_i^1 = \sqrt{r^2 - x_i^2} + \varepsilon_i^1$ and $v_i^2 = -\sqrt{r^2 - x_i^2} + \varepsilon_i^2$ are computed, where $\varepsilon_i^1, \varepsilon_i^2$ stem from the uniform distribution in the interval $[-0.1, 0.1]^T$. The points (x_i, v_i^1) and (x_i, v_i^2), $i = 0,\ldots, N_2 - 1$, lie around C.
    - X_2 consists of 300 2-dimensional points. Points $N_1 = 100$, $N_2 = 100$, and $N_3 = 100$ stem from classes 1, 2, and 3, respectively. They lie around the circles centered at the origin and having radii $r_1 = 2$, $r_2 = 4$, and $r_3 = 6$, respectively (the points of each class are generated by adopting the procedure used for generating the last N_3 points of the previous data set, X_1).

    Generate the vectors y_1 and y_2, which contain the class labels of the data points of the sets X_1 and X_2, respectively. Plot X_1 and X_2.
2. Perform kernel PCA on X_1, using the exponential kernel function with $\sigma = 1$ and keep only the first two principal components. Determine and plot the set Y_1, which contains the projections of the data points of X_1 onto the subspace spanned by the two principal components. Repeat the steps for X_2 and draw conclusions.

Solution. Take the following steps:

Step 1. To generate the data set X_1, type

```
rand('seed',0)
noise_level=0.1;
%%%
n_points=[100 100 100];
```

```
l=2;
% Production of the 1st class
X1=rand(l,n_points(1))- [2.5 0.5]'*ones(1,n_points(1));
% Production of the 2nd class X1=[X1
rand(l,n_points(2))- [-0.5 2.5]'*ones(1,n_points(2))];
% Production of the 3rd class
c1=[0 0];
r1=4;
b1=c1(1)-r1;
b2=c1(1)+r1;
step=(b2-b1)/(n_points(2)/2-1);
for t=b1:step:b2
    temp=[t c1(2)+sqrt(r1^2-(t-c1(1))^2)+noise_level*(rand-0.5);...
    t c1(2)-sqrt(r1^2-(t-c1(1))^2)+noise_level*(rand-0.5)]';
    X1=[X1 temp];
end
```

To generate the vector of the labels y_1, type

```
y1=[ones(1,n_points(1)) 2*ones(1,n_points(2)) 3*ones(1,n_points(3))];
```

To plot the data set X_1, type

```
figure(1), plot(X1(1,y1==1),X1(2,y1==1),'r.',...
X1(1,y1==2),X1(2,y1==2),'bx',...
X1(1,y1==3),X1(2,y1==3),'go')
```

Step 2. To perform kernel PCA on X_1 with the exponential kernel function ($\sigma = 1$), type

```
m=2;
[s,V,Y1]=kernel_PCA(X1,m,'exp',[1 0]);
```

To plot Y_1, type

```
figure(2), plot(Y1(1,y1==1),Y1(2,y1==1),'r.',...
Y1(1,y1==2),Y1(2,y1==2),'bx',...
Y1(1,y1==3),Y1(2,y1==3),'go')
```

Work similarly for X_2.

In Y_1 the classes are linearly separable, but this is not the case in Y_2. That is, kernel PCA does not necessarily transform nonlinear classification problems into linear ones.

Exercise 3.5.1

In this exercise, we see how the original space is transformed using kernel PCA. To ensure visualization of the results, we consider a 2-dimensional problem, which will be mapped to the 2-dimensional space spanned by the first two principal components that result from the kernel PCA. More specifically, go through the following steps:

Step 1. Generate a data set X, which contains 200 2-dimensional vectors. $N_1 = 100$ vectors stem from class 1, which is modeled by the uniform distribution in $[-0.5, 0.5]^2$; $N_2 = 100$ vectors stem from class -1 and lie around the circle with radius 1 and centered at the origin. The N_2 points are produced as the last N_3 points of the X_1 data set in Example 3.5.3.

Step 2. Repeat step 1 from Example 3.5.2, with $\sigma = 0.4$.

Step 3. Repeat step 2 from Example 3.5.2.

Step 4. Consider the points x of the form $(-2 + i * 0.1, -2 + j * 0.1)$, $i, j = 0, \ldots, 40$ (these form a rectangular grid in the region $[-2, 2]^2$) and their images in the space spanned by the two principal components, determined in step 2. Classify the image of each point x using the LS classifier designed in step 3 and produce two figures. The first corresponds to the transformed space and an image point is plotted with a green o if it is classified to the first class (+1) and with a cyan x if it is classified to the second class (−1). The second figure corresponds to the original space and the corresponding points x are drawn similarly. Observe how the implied nonlinear transformation deforms the space.

Step 5. Repeat steps 2 through 4, with $\sigma = 1$.

Hint

To generate X, work as in Example 3.5.3. To define the class labels of the data vectors and to plot X, work as in Example 3.5.2. To perform kernel PCA and define the linear classifier, also work as in Example 3.5.2. To carry out step 4, use the MATLAB function *plot_orig_trans_kPCA* by typing

```
m=2;
choice='exp';
para=[0.4 0];
reg_spec=[-2 0.1 2; -2 0.1 2];
fig_or=5;
fig_tr=6;
plot_orig_trans_kPCA(X,V,m,choice,para,w,reg_spec,fig_or,fig_tr)
```

The results are shown in Figure 3.7. Observe how the points inside the circle (denoted by o) in the original space are expanded in the transformed space. Also notice the difference between the transformed spaces for $\sigma = 0.4$ and $\sigma = 1$, respectively (Figure 3.7(a, c)).

3.6 LAPLACIAN EIGENMAP

The Laplacian eigenmap method belongs to the family of so-called graph-based methods for dimensionality reduction. The idea is to construct a graph, $G(V, E)$, where nodes correspond to the data points x_i, $i = 1, 2, \ldots, N$. If two points are close, the corresponding nodes are connected via an edge, which is weighted accordingly. The closer two points are the higher the value of the weight of the respective edge.

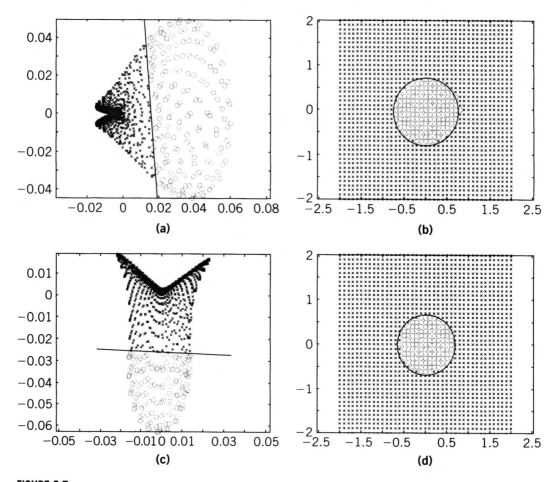

FIGURE 3.7

(a) Linear classifier in the space spanned by the first two principal components resulting from the kernel PCA, using exponential kernel function with $\sigma = 0.4$, from Exercise 3.5.1. (b) Equivalent of the linear classifier in the original space. (c) Linear classifier in the space spanned by the first two principal components using the exponential kernel function with $\sigma = 1$, from Exercise 3.5.1. (d) Equivalent of the linear classifier in the original space. Observe the influence of the value of σ.

Closeness is determined via a threshold value. For example, if the squared Euclidean distance between two points, $||x_i - x_j||^2$, is less than a user-defined threshold, say e, the respective nodes are connected and are said to be *neighbors*. The corresponding weight can be defined in different ways. A common choice for the weights $W(i, j)$ between the nodes i and j is, for some user-defined variable σ^2,

$$W(i,j) = \begin{cases} \exp\left(-\frac{||x_i - x_j||^2}{\sigma^2}\right), & \text{if } ||x_i - x_j||^2 < e \\ 0 & \text{otherwise} \end{cases}$$

Thus, the graph encodes the *local information* in the original, high-dimensional, space $\mathcal{R}^l$.

It is further assumed that the data $x_i \in \mathcal{R}^l$ lie on a *smooth* manifold of dimension m. The value of m is assumed to be known. For example, the original data may live in the 3-dimensional space $\mathcal{R}^3$, but lie around a sphere. The latter is a 2-dimensional smooth manifold since two parameters suffice to describe the surface of a sphere.

The goal of the method is to obtain an m-dimensional representation of the data so that the *local neighborhood information* in the manifold is *optimally* retained. In this way, the local geometric structure of the manifold is reflected in the obtained solution.

The Laplacian eigenmap turns out to be equivalent to an eigenvalue/eigenvector problem of the so-called *Laplacian matrix*. This matrix encodes the local information as described by the weights of the edges in the graph [Theo 09, Section 6.7.2].

To use the Laplacian eigenmap, type

$$y = lapl\_eig(X, e, sigma2, m)$$

where

e is the value of the threshold,

$sigma2$ is the σ^2 parameter,

y is an $m \times N$ matrix whose ith column defines the projection of the ith data vector to the m-dimensional subspace.

Example 3.6.1. Generate a 3-dimensional Archimedes spiral as a pack of 11 identical 2-dimensional Archimedes spirals, one above the other. A 2-dimensional spiral is described in polar coordinates by the equation $r = a\theta$, where a is a user-defined parameter. In our case, the points of a 3-dimensional spiral are generated as follows: For θ, take the values from θ_{init} to θ_{fin} with step θ_{step} and compute

$r = a\theta$
$x = r\cos\theta$
$y = r\sin\theta$

The 11 points of the form (x, y, z), where $z = -1, -0.8, -0.6, \ldots, 0.8, 1$, are points of the spiral. Use $a = 0.1$, $\theta_{init} = 0.5$, $\theta_{fin} = 2.05 * \pi$, $\theta_{step} = 0.2$.

Plot the 3-dimensional spiral so that all points of the same 2-dimensional spiral are plotted using the same symbol and all groups of 11 points of the form (x, y, z), where x and y are fixed and z takes the values $-1, -0.8, -0.6, \ldots, 0.8, 1$, are plotted using the same color.

1. Perform the Laplacian eigenmap on the points of the previous data set for manifold dimension $m = 2$. Plot the results.
2. Perform linear PCA on the same data set, using the first two principal components. Plot the results.
3. Compare the results obtained in steps 1 and 2.

Solution. To generate and plot the 3-dimensional spiral, call the function *spiral_3D* by typing

```
a=0.1;
init_theta=0.5;
```

```
fin_theta=2.05*pi;
step_theta=0.2;
plot_req=1; % Request for plot the spiral
fig_id=1;   % Number id of the figure
% Producing the 3D spiral
[X,color_tot,patt_id]=spiral_3D(a,init_theta,...
fin_theta,step_theta,plot_req,fig_id);
[l,N]=size(X);
```

Use Rotate 3D to see the spiral from different viewpoints.
Do the following:

Step 1. To perform the Laplacian eigenmap, call the function *lapl_eig* by typing

```
e=0.35;
sigma2=sqrt(0.5);
m=2;
y=lapl_eig(X,e,sigma2,m);
```

To plot the results, type

```
figure(2), hold on
for i=1:N
      figure(2), plot(y(1,i),y(2,i),patt_id(i),'Color',color_tot(:,i)')
end
```

Step 2. To perform linear PCA, call the function *pca_fun* by typing:

```
[eigenval,eigenvec,explain,Y]=pca_fun(X,m);
```

To plot the results, type

```
figure(3), hold on
for i=1:N
      figure(3), plot(Y(1,i),Y(2,i),patt_id(i),'Color',color_tot(:,i)')
end
```

Step 3. Observing MATLAB figure 1 on the computer screen, notice how the color of each 2-dimensional spiral varies from red to yellow to green to cyan to blue. On the mapping produced by the Laplacian eigenmap method (MATLAB figure 2), the following two comments are in order: Each 2-dimensional spiral is "stretched" so that the points are placed on a line segment (horizontal direction); in each vertical direction the succession of the colors observed in MATLAB figure 1 is the same as that observed in MATLAB figure 2. Thus, for the given choice of parameters for the Laplacian eigenmap, the method successfully "unfolds" the 3-dimensional spiral.

The linear PCA (MATLAB figure 3) also succeeds in "stretching" each 2-dimensional spiral so that the points are placed on a line segment (horizontal direction). However, the succession of colors in the vertical direction is not the same as that observed in MATLAB figure 1 (green, yellow, red, cyan, blue). This indicates that after the projection produced by PCA, points that are distant from each other in the 3-dimensional space lie close in the 2-dimensional representation (see, for example, the red and cyan points in the original 3-dimensional space and in the reduced 2-dimensional space).

Finally, the results obtained by the Laplacian eigenmap are sensitive to the choice of parameters. If, for example, the previous experiment is performed for $e = 0.5$ and $sigma2 = 1$, the Laplacian eigenmap fails to completely "unfold" the spiral (in this case, red is close to green). However, this unfolding, although not perfect, is still better than the one produced by linear PCA. In general, extensive experimentation is required before choosing the right values for the parameters involved in the Laplacian eigenmap method. ■

Exercise 3.6.1

1. Generate a "cut cylinder" of radius $r = 0.5$ in the 3-dimensional space as a pack of 11 identical "cut circles," one above the other, as in Example 3.6.1. For the jth circle, with center $c_j = [c_{j1}, c_{j2}]^T$, the following points are selected:

   - $(x_i, c_{j2} + \sqrt{r^2 - (x_i - c_{j1})^2})$ for x_i ranging from $c_{j1} - r$ to $c_{j1} + r$, with step $(2r)/(N-1)$.
   - $(x_i, c_{j2} - \sqrt{r^2 - (x_i - c_{j1})^2})$ for x_i ranging from $c_{j1} + r$ down to $(c_{j1} - r)/4$, with the previously chosen step, where N is the number of points on which x_i is sampled in the range $[c_{j1} - r, c_{j1} + r]$.

   Plot the cut cylinder so that all points of the same 2-dimensional cut circle are plotted using the same symbol, and all groups of 11 points of the form (x, y, z), where x and y are fixed and z takes the values $-1, -0.8, -0.6, \ldots, 0.8, 1$ are plotted using the same color.

2. Perform the Laplacian eigenmap on the points of the previous data set for manifold dimension $m = 2$. Plot the results.

3. Perform linear PCA on the same data set using the first two principal components and plot the results.

4. Compare the results obtained in steps 2 and 3.

Hints

1. To generate and plot the 3-dimensional cut cylinder, call the function *cut_cylinder_3D* by typing

   ```
   r=0.5;
   center=[0 0];
   N=25;
   plot_req=1; %Request for plot the cylinder
   fig_id=1;   %Number id of the figure
   % Producing the 3D cut cylinder
   [X,color_tot,patt_id]=cut_cylinder_3D(r,center,N,plot_req,...
   fig_id);
   [l,N]=size(X);
   ```

   Use Rotate 3D to observe the cut cylinder from different viewpoints.

2. Apply step 1 of Example 3.6.1, using the same parameters for the Laplacian eigenmap method.

3. Apply step 2 of Example 3.6.1.
4. Observe that, once again, the Laplacian eigenmap gives better results compared with those of the linear PCA. However, this is not the case when the cut cylinder has a radius equal to 5. (Why? Compare the height of the cylinder with its radius.)

Feature Selection

4.1 INTRODUCTION

In this chapter we present techniques for the selection of a subset of features from a larger pool of available features. The goal is to select those that are rich in discriminatory information with respect to the classification problem at hand. This is a crucial step in the design of any classification system, as a poor choice of features drives the classifier to perform badly. Selecting highly informative features is an attempt (a) to place classes in the feature space far apart from each other (large between-class distance) and (b) to position the data points within each class close to each other (small within-class variance).

Another major issue in feature selection is choosing the number of features l to be used out of an original $m > l$. Reducing this number is in line with our goal of avoiding overfitting to the specific training data set and of designing classifiers that result in good generalization performance—that is, classifiers that perform well when faced with data outside the training set. The choice of l depends heavily on the number of available training patterns, N. For more details see [Theo 09, Chapter 5].

Before feature selection techniques can be used, a preprocessing stage is necessary for "housekeeping" purposes, such as removal of outlier points and data normalization.

4.2 OUTLIER REMOVAL

An outlier is a point that lies far away from the mean value of the corresponding random variable; points with values far from the rest of the data may cause large errors during the classifier training phase. This is not desirable, especially when the outliers are the result of noisy measurements. For normally distributed data, a threshold of 1, 2, or 3 times the standard deviation is used to define outliers. Points that lie away from the mean by a value larger than this threshold are removed. However, for non-normal distributions, more rigorous measures should be considered (e.g., cost functions).

Example 4.2.1. Generate $N = 100$ points using a 1-dimensional Gaussian distribution of mean value $m = 1$ and variance $\sigma^2 = 0.16$. Then add six outlier points, namely, $6.2, -6.4, 6.8, 4.2, 15$. Note that all of them are away from the mean value by more than 3σ. These numbers are inserted in random positions among the rest of the points. Use the m-file *simpleOutlierRemoval.m* to identify and print the outliers as well as the corresponding indices in the array.

Solution. Generate the data set.

```
randn('seed',0);
m=1; var=0.16;
stdevi=sqrt(var);
norm_dat=m+stdevi*randn(1,100);
```

Generate the outliers.

```
outl=[6.2 -6.4 4.2 15.0 6.8];
```

Add outliers at the end of the data.

```
dat=[norm_dat';outl'];
```

Scramble the data.

```
rand('seed',0); % randperm() below calls rand()
y=randperm(length(dat));x=dat(y);
```

Identify outliers and their corresponding indices.

```
times=1; % controls the tolerance threshold
[outliers,Index,new_dat]=simpleOutlierRemoval(x,times);
[outliers Index]
```

The *new_dat* file contains the data after the outliers have been rejected. The program output should look like this:

```
outliers          index
   4.2              3
   6.8             49
   15              58
   6.2             60
  -6.4             84
```

where *index* indicates the position of each outlier in *x*. By changing the variable *times* (i.e., the tolerated threshold) a different number of outliers may be detected. Try running the program with different values for the *times* variable.   ■

4.3 DATA NORMALIZATION

Data normalization is a useful step often adopted, prior to designing a classifier, as a precaution when the feature values vary in different dynamic ranges. In the absence of normalization, features with large values have a stronger influence on the cost function in designing the classifier. Data normalization restricts the values of all features within predetermined ranges.

A common technique is to normalize the features to zero mean and unit variance via linear methods. Assume that our training data contain N values of a specific feature, x. Let $\bar{x}$ and σ be the respective mean value and standard deviation, computed using the values of the specific feature, x, from all classes. The values of the feature, after normalization, become

$$\widehat{x}_i = \frac{x_i - \bar{x}}{\sigma}, \quad i = 1, 2, \ldots, N \tag{4.1}$$

where $\widehat{x}_i$ is the normalized value.

Alternatively, values may be normalized by restricting the range of the allowed values to lie between a minimum and a maximum as, for example, in the interval [0,1] or [−1,1]. A third technique is employed in cases where the data are not evenly distributed around the mean; one may adopt nonlinear methods—*softmax* scaling, for example, squashes data values nonlinearly in the interval [0,1]. That is,

$$\widehat{x}_i = \frac{1}{1 + \exp(-y)} \tag{4.2}$$

where $y = \frac{x_i - \bar{x}}{r\sigma}$ and r is a user-defined parameter.

Example 4.3.1. To demonstrate the data normalization procedure using the three techniques just mentioned, we will use realistic data coming from medical images in the area of histopathology. Two images are shown in Figure 4.1. For both, the mean value and the skewness of the gray levels of the pixels within the five regions defined by the squares will be used as features. These regions are known as *regions of interest* (ROI). Each image consists of a number of nuclei. The nuclei in Figure 4.1(a) correspond to

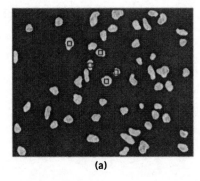
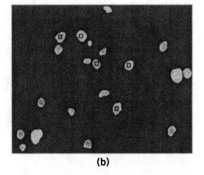

(a)   (b)

FIGURE 4.1

Histopathology images of (a) high-grade and (b) low-grade astrocytomas. The differences between the two grades are not visually evident. Squares denote the ROIs.

Table 4.1 Mean Value and Skewness from Five Extracted ROIs in Images of High-Grade and Low-Grade Astrocytomas

High-Grade Astrocytomas		Low-Grade Astrocytomas	
Mean Value	**Skewness**	**Mean Value**	**Skewness**
114.36	0.11	150.07	0.35
100.44	0.27	153.09	−0.28
109.42	−3.69	113.58	0.55
109.75	−0.07	130.84	0.47
104.41	−3.79	158.74	−0.30

a so-called high-grade astrocytoma and are different from those in Figure 4.1(b), which correspond to low-grade astrocytoma.

Obviously, the goal of a pattern recognition (PR) system would be to distinguish between the two grades of astrocytoma. Table 4.1 shows the derived values for the two features for each one of the five ROIs and for each one of the two pathological cases. It is readily observed that the values of the two features differ significantly in dynamic range. The goal is to normalize the values for both classes.

Solution. By making use of the provided m-files *normalizeStd.m*, *normalizeMnmx.m*, and *normalizeSoftmax.m*, the values can be normalized by the following steps:

Step 1. Insert the values from Table 4.1 into two files, *class1.dat* and *class2.dat*; store the files in the hard drive; and load the respective features into two arrays, *class1* and *class2*:

```
class1=load('class1.dat')';
class2=load('class2.dat')';
```

Step 2. Normalize the data in both classes to zero mean and standard deviation equal to 1, using *normalizeStd*:

```
[c1,c2]=normalizeStd(class1,class2);
```

Step 3. Normalize the data so that they lie in $[-1,1]$:

```
[c1,c2]=normalizeMnmx(class1,class2,-1,1);
```

Step 4. Normalize the data in $[0,1]$ using *softmax*:

```
[c1,c2]=normalizeSoftmax(class1,class2,0.5);
```

Print matrices c_1 and c_2 after each normalization procedure; the results should look like those in Table 4.2. Observe that the values of both features now vary in the same dynamic range.

Table 4.2 Results of Normalization

Normalized to zero mean and unit variance			
High-Grade Astrocytomas		Low-Grade Astrocytomas	
Mean Value	Skewness	Mean Value	Skewness
−0.46	0.45	1.17	0.60
−1.10	0.55	1.30	0.22
−0.69	−1.84	−0.50	0.72
−0.67	0.34	0.29	0.67
−0.91	−1.90	1.56	0.20
Normalized in [−1 1] using minmax			
−0.52	0.80	0.70	0.91
−1.00	0.87	0.81	0.62
−0.69	−0.95	−0.55	1.00
−0.68	0.71	0.04	0.96
−0.86	−1.00	1.00	0.61
Normalized in [0 1] using softmax			
0.28	0.71	0.91	0.77
0.10	0.75	0.93	0.61
0.20	0.02	0.27	0.81
0.21	0.66	0.64	0.79
0.14	0.02	0.96	0.60

4.4 HYPOTHESIS TESTING: THE *t*-TEST

The first step in feature selection is to look at each feature *individually* and check whether or not it is an informative one. If not, the feature is discarded. To this end, statistical tests are commonly used. The idea is to test whether the mean values that a feature has in two classes differ *significantly*. In the case of more than two classes, the test may be applied for each class pair. Assuming that the data in the classes are *normally distributed*, the so-called *t*-test is a popular choice.

The goal of the statistical *t*-test is to determine which of the following two hypotheses is true:

H_1: The mean values of the feature in the two classes are different.

H_0: The mean values of the feature in the two classes are equal.

The first is known as the *alternative hypothesis* (the values in the two classes differ significantly); the second, as the *null hypothesis* (the values do not differ significantly). If the null hypothesis holds true, the feature is discarded. If the alternative hypothesis holds true, the feature is selected. The hypothesis test is carried out against the so-called *significance level*, ρ, which corresponds to the probability of committing an error in our decision. Typical values used in practice are $\rho = 0.05$ and $\rho = 0.001$. (More on this statistical test can be found in [Theo 09, Section 5.4].

Example 4.4.1. Assume that a feature follows Gaussian distributions in both classes of a 2-class classification problem. The respective mean values are $m_1 = 8.75$ and $m_2 = 9$; their common variance is $\sigma^2 = 4$.

1. Generate the vectors x_1 and x_2, each containing $N = 1000$ samples from the first and the second distribution, respectively.
2. Pretend that the means m_1 and m_2, as well as the variance σ^2, are unknown. Assumed to be known are the vectors x_1 and x_2 and the fact that they come from distributions with equal (yet unknown) variance. Use the t-test to check whether the mean values of the two distributions differ significantly, using as significance level the value $\rho = 0.05$.
   Repeat this procedure for $\rho = 0.001$ and draw conclusions.

Solution. Do the following:

Step 1. To generate the vectors x_1 and x_2, type

```
randn('seed',0)
m1=8.75;
m2=9;
stdevi=sqrt(4);
N=1000;
x1=m1+stdevi*randn(1,N);
x2=m2+stdevi*randn(1,N);
```

Step 2. Apply the t-test using the MATLAB *ttest2* function, typing

```
rho=0.05;
[h] = ttest2(x1,x2,rho)
```

where

   $h = 0$ (corresponding to the null hypothesis H_0) indicates that there is no evidence, at the ρ significance level, that the mean values are not equal

   $h = 1$ (corresponding to the alternative hypothesis H_1) indicates that the hypothesis that the means are equal can be rejected, at the ρ significance level.

If the latter case is the outcome, the feature is selected; otherwise, it is rejected. In our case, the result is $h = 1$, which implies that the hypothesis of the equality of the means can be rejected at the 5% significance level. The feature is thus selected.

Step 3. Repeating for $\rho = 0.001$, obtain $h = 0$, which implies that there is no evidence to reject the hypothesis of the equality of the means, at significance level of 0.1%. Thus, the feature is discarded. Comparing this result with that of step 2, we can conclude that the smaller the ρ (i.e., the more confident we want to be in our decision), the harder to reject the equality hypothesis. ■

Exercise 4.4.1

Repeat the *t*-test using for the variance the values 1 and 16. Compare and explain the obtained results.

Remark

• The *t*-test assumes that the values of the features are drawn from normal distributions. However, in real applications this is not always the case. Thus, each feature distribution should be tested for *normality* prior to applying the *t*-test. Normality tests may be of the *Lilliefors* or the *Kolmogorov-Smirnov* type, for which MATLAB functions are provided (*lillietest* and *kstest*, respectively).

   If the feature distributions turn out not to be normal, one should choose a nonparametric statistical significance test, such as the *Wilcoxon* rank sum test, using the *ranksum* MATLAB function, or the *Fisher* ratio, provided in the current library and described in Section 4.6.

4.5 THE RECEIVER OPERATING CHARACTERISTIC CURVE

The receiver operating characteristic (ROC) curve is a measure of the class-discrimination capability of a specific feature. It measures the overlap between the pdfs describing the data distribution of the feature in two classes [Theo 09, Section 5.5]. This overlap is quantified in terms of an area between two curves, also known as AUC (*area under the receiver operating curve*). For complete overlap, the AUC value is 0, and for complete separation it is equal to 0.5 [Theo 09, Section 5.5].

Example 4.5.1. Consider two 1-dimensional Gaussian distributions with mean values $m_1 = 2$ and $m_2 = 0$ and variances $\sigma_1^2 = \sigma_2^2 = 1$, respectively.

1. Generate 200 points from each distribution.
2. Plot the respective histograms, using the function *plotHist*.
3. Compute and plot the corresponding AUC values using the function ROC.

Solution. Do the following:

Step 1. Generate the two classes, typing

```
randn('seed',0);
N=200;
m1=2;m2=0;var1=1;var2=1;
class1=m1+var1*randn(1,N);
class2=m2+var2*randn(1,N);
```

Step 2. Plot the histogram of the resulting values, typing

```
plotHist(class1,class2);
```

The following *classlabels* array contains the class labels of the respective points generated from the Gaussian distributions and it is a prerequisite of the ROC function.

```
classlabels = [1*ones(N,1); -1*ones(N,1)];
```

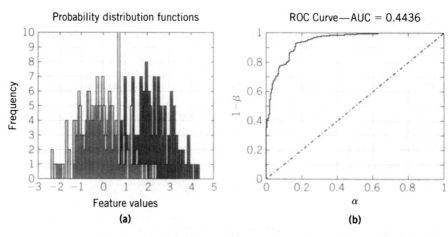

FIGURE 4.2

(a) Distributions with partial overlap between pdfs of the two classes. (b) Corresponding ROC curve.

Step 3. Calculate and plot the results (Figure 4.2) utilizing the ROC function. Type

```
[AUC_Value] = ROC([class1 class2]',classlabels,1);
% The last argument has been set to 1, because a plot
% will be generated.
```

Exercise 4.5.1

Repeat the previous experiment with (a) $m_1 = 0$ and $m_2 = 0$, and (b) $m_1 = 5$ and $m_2 = 0$. Comment on the results.

4.6 FISHER'S DISCRIMINANT RATIO

Fisher's discriminant ratio (FDR) is commonly employed to quantify the discriminatory power of individual features between two equiprobable classes. In other words, it is independent of the type of class distribution. Let m_1 and m_2 be the respective mean values and σ_1^2 and σ_2^2 the respective variances associated with the values of a feature in two classes. The FDR is defined as

$$\text{FDR} = \frac{(m_1 - m_2)^2}{(\sigma_1^2 + \sigma_2^2)} \tag{4.3}$$

Example 4.6.1. Generate $N = 200$ 5-dimensional data vectors that stem from two equiprobable classes, ω_1 and ω_2. The classes are modeled by Gaussian distributions with, respectively, means

$m_1 = [1, 1, 0, 6, 3]^T$ and $m_2 = [11.5, 11, 10, 6.5, 4]^T$ and covariance matrices

$$S_1 = \begin{bmatrix} 0.06 & 0 & 0 & 0 & 0 \\ 0 & 0.5 & 0 & 0 & 0 \\ 0 & 0 & 3 & 0 & 0 \\ 0 & 0 & 0 & 0.001 & 0 \\ 0 & 0 & 0 & 0 & 3 \end{bmatrix} S_2 = \begin{bmatrix} 0.06 & 0 & 0 & 0 & 0 \\ 0 & 0.6 & 0 & 0 & 0 \\ 0 & 0 & 4 & 0 & 0 \\ 0 & 0 & 0 & 0.001 & 0 \\ 0 & 0 & 0 & 0 & 4 \end{bmatrix}$$

Compute the FDR values for the five features and draw conclusions.

Solution. Do the following:

Step 1. To generate the data vectors from the first class, type

```
randn('seed',0)
N=200;
m1=[1 1 0 6 3];
S1=diag([.06 .5 3 .001 3]);
class1=mvnrnd(m1,S1,fix(N/2))';
```

The data vectors of the second class are generated similarly.

Step 2. Compute the FDR for each feature, typing

```
l=length(m1);
for i=1:l
    FDR(i)= Fisher(class1(i,:)',class2(i,:)');
end
FDR
```

The FDR values for the five features are 930.521, 79.058, 13.771, 107.284, and 0.057, respectively.

Step 3. The results indicate that for features having large differences between the means of the classes and small variances in each class, a high value of FDR will be obtained. In addition, if two features have the same absolute mean difference and a different sum of variances ($\sigma_1^2 + \sigma_2^2$), the one with the smallest sum of variances will get a higher FDR value (e.g., features 2 and 3). On the other hand, if two features have the same sum of variances and different absolute mean differences, the feature with the larger absolute mean difference will get a higher FDR value (e.g., features 3 and 5). ■

Example 4.6.2. The goal of this example is to demonstrate the use of the FDR criterion in ranking a number of features with respect to their class-discriminatory power. We turn our attention once more to a realistic example coming from ultrasound imaging.

Figure 4.3(a) is an ultrasound image of a human liver diagnosed with *liver cirrhosis*. Figure 4.3(b) is an image corresponding to *fatty liver infiltration*. Obviously, the ultimate goal of a related PR system

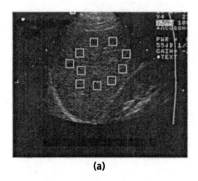 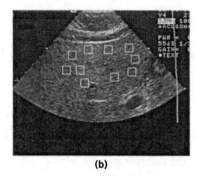

(a)   (b)

FIGURE 4.3

Selected ROIs from (a) cirrhotic liver and (b) liver with fatty infiltration.

is this: Given an unknown ultrasound image, "diagnose" whether it belongs to the first or to the second type of disease. To this end, given an image, an ROI (indicated by a square in the figure) is marked and features are computed from this region.

In this example, the features used are

- The mean value of the gray levels of pixels in each ROI
- The corresponding standard deviation
- The skewness
- The kurtosis

The mathematical definition of these quantities is provided in [Theo 09, Section 7.2.1].

To test the discriminatory power of each of the listed features, we select ten ROIs from the individual images (as indicated in Figure 4.3) available for training. The resulting values are shown in Table 4.3. To derive the respective features from each ROI, the MATLAB m-files *mean2.m, std2.m, skewness.m,*

Table 4.3 Features Calculated from 10 ROIs in Images of Cirrhotic and Fatty Liver Types

Cirrhotic Liver				Fatty Liver			
Mean	**Std**	**Skew**	**Kurtosis**	**Mean**	**Std**	**Skew**	**Kurtosis**
73.73	20.72	0.19	2.38	100.85	24.83	1.11	6.27
77.84	22.07	0.32	3.10	111.77	26.31	0.19	2.29
78.43	19.47	0.53	3.37	114.13	25.89	0.06	2.45
70.56	19.65	0.41	2.91	98.67	20.61	0.24	2.71
70.27	20.81	0.78	3.95	96.96	20.78	0.32	2.46
71.91	16.79	0.44	2.80	111.33	20.38	0.28	2.76
71.35	18.40	0.84	4.61	114.76	23.04	0.22	2.54
59.02	17.84	0.47	2.51	122.71	28.27	0.90	4.73
67.36	16.48	0.25	2.72	106.44	22.00	0.27	2.43
72.42	21.33	0.92	5.32	103.36	22.31	0.18	2.67

and *kurtosis.m,* have been used. The goal is to use the values of Table 4.3 and compute the FDR for each feature and rank it accordingly.

Solution. The values of the features given in Table 4.3 are stored in two files, *cirrhoticLiver.dat* and *fattyLiver.dat*, corresponding to the *Cirrhotic* and *Fatty Infiltration* classes, respectively. In the following steps, we compute the FDR value and rank features in FDR-descending order.

Step 1. Load the values of Table 4.3 into two files, *cirrhoticLiver.dat* and *fattyLiver.dat*; store the files in the hard drive; and load the respective features in two arrays, *class1* and *class2*:

```
class1=load('cirrhoticLiver.dat')';
class2=load('fattyLiver.dat')';
feature_names={'Mean','Std','Skewness','Kurtosis'};
```

Step 2. Calculate each feature's FDR, typing

```
[NumOfFeatures,N]=size(class1);
for i=1:NumOfFeatures
    FDR_value(i)=Fisher(class1(i,:),class2(i,:));
end
```

Step 3. Sort features in descending FDR value, typing

```
[FDR_value,feature_rank]=sort(FDR_value,'descend');
FDR_value', feature_names(feature_rank)'
```

The printout of these commands is the following:

```
FDR_value          feature_names
  13.888              'Mean'
   1.492              'Std'
   0.105              'Skewness'
   0.021              'Kurtosis'
```

If one has to choose the most informative feature, according to the FDR criterion, this is the *mean*. The next most informative is the *standard deviation*, and so on. Note that for this example images were taken under the same scanning conditions, which justifies the use of the mean value as a feature. ∎

4.7 CLASS SEPARABILITY MEASURES

In the previous sections, measures that quantify the class-discriminatory power of individual features were discussed. In this section, we turn our attention from individual features to combinations of features (i.e., feature vectors) and describe measures that quantify class separability in the respective feature space.

Three class-separability measures are considered: divergence (implemented by the MATLAB function *divergence*), Bhattacharyya distance (*divergenceBhata*), and scatter matrices (*ScatterMatrices*).

4.7.1 Divergence

The definition of the divergence measure, for the general case, can be found in [Theo 09, Section 5.6]. Assume that we are given two normally distributed classes in the *l*-dimensional space. The divergence between them is defined as

$$d_{1,2} = \frac{1}{2}\text{trace}\left\{S_1^{-1}S_2 + S_2^{-1}S_1 - 2I\right\} + \frac{1}{2}(m_1 - m_2)^T\left(S_1^{-1} + S_2^{-1}\right)(m_1 - m_2) \tag{4.4}$$

where S_i is the covariance matrix; m_i, $i = 1, 2$ is the respective mean vector of the *i*th class; and I is the $l \times l$ identity matrix.

The divergence measure exhibits a strong dependence on the variances. It turns out that, even for equal mean values, $d_{1,2}$ can take large values provided that the variances in the two classes are significantly different. This becomes evident from the following example.

Example 4.7.1. We consider two classes and assume the features to be independent and normally distributed in each one. Specifically, the first (second) class is modeled by the Gaussian distribution with mean $m_1 = [3,3]^T$ $(m_2 = [2.3, 2.3]^T)$ and covariance matrix $S_1 = 0.2I$ $(S_2 = 1.9I)$.

Generate 100 data points from each class. Then compute the divergence between the two classes and plot the data.

Solution. Do the following:

Step 1. To generate data for the two classes, type

```
m1=[3 3]';S1=0.2*eye(2);
m2=[2.3 2.3]';S2=1.9*eye(2);
randn('seed',0);
class1=mvnrnd(m1,S1,100)';
randn('seed',100);
class2=mvnrnd(m2,S2,100)';
```

Step 2. Compute the divergence, employing the *divergence* function by typing

```
Distance=divergence(class1,class2);
```

The value of the divergence between the two classes is 5.7233. Plot the data, using the *plotData.m* function as follows:

```
featureNames={'1','2'};
plotData(class1,class2,1:2,featureNames);
```

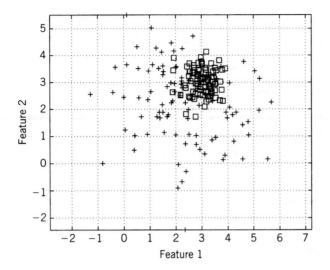

FIGURE 4.4

Plot of the data in Example 4.7.1. Observe the small difference in mean values and the large difference in variances. The points in the two classes are denoted by "pluses" and "squares," respectively.

The program output is shown in Figure 4.4. Observe that, in spite of the fact that the mean values of the two classes are very close, the variances of the features differ significantly, so the divergence measure results in a large value.

Exercise 4.7.1

Repeat the previous experiment considering the following cases:

Case 1. $m_1 = [3,3]^T$ and $S_1 = 0.2I$; $m_2 = [2.3, 2.3^T]$ and $S_2 = 0.2I$. That is, this corresponds to small differences between mean values and equal variances.

Case 2. $m_1 = [1,1]^T$ and $S_1 = 0.2I$; $m_2 = [4,4]^T$ and $S_2 = 0.2I$. That is, this corresponds to large differences between mean values and equal variances.

Case 3. $m_1 = [1,1]^T$ and $S_1 = 0.2I$; $m_2 = [4,4]^T$ and $S_2 = 1.9I$. That is, this corresponds to large differences between mean values and large differences between variances.

Comment on the results.

4.7.2 Bhattacharyya Distance and Chernoff Bound

Considering Gaussian distributions in both classes, the Bhattacharyya distance bears a close relationship to the error of the Bayesian classifier [Theo 09, Section 5.6.2]. The Bhattacharyya distance $B_{1,2}$ between two classes is defined as

$$B_{1,2} = \frac{1}{8}(m_1 - m_2)^T \left(\frac{S_1 + S_2}{2} \right)^{-1} (m_1 - m_2) + A \tag{4.5}$$

where $A = 0.5 \ln \frac{0.5(|S_1+S_2|)}{\sqrt{|S_1||S_2|}}$ and $|\cdot|$ denotes the determinant of the respective matrix. The Chernoff bound is an upper bound of the optimal Bayesian error and is given by

$$e_{CB} = \exp(-B_{1,2})\sqrt{P(\omega_1)P(\omega_2)} \tag{4.6}$$

where $P(\omega_1), P(\omega_2)$ are the a priori class probabilities.

Example 4.7.2. Consider a 2-class 2-dimensional classification problem with two equiprobable classes ω_1 and ω_2 modeled by the Gaussian distributions $\mathcal{N}(m_1, S_1)$ and $\mathcal{N}(m_2, S_2)$, respectively, where $m_1 = [3,3]^T$ and $S_1 = 0.2I$, and $m_2 = [2.3, 2.3]^T$ and $S_2 = 1.9I$. This is the case of small differences between mean values and large differences between variances.

Compute the Bhattacharyya distance and the Chernoff bound between the two classes.

Solution. Do the following:

Step 1. To generate data for the two classes, type

```
m1=[3 3]';S1=0.2*eye(2);
m2=[2.2 2.2]';S2=1.9*eye(2);
randn('seed',0);
class1=mvnrnd(m1,S1,100)';
randn('seed',100);
class2=mvnrnd(m2,S2,100)';
```

Step 2. To compute the Bhattacharyya distance and the Chernoff bound, type

```
BhattaDistance=divergenceBhata (class1,class2);
ChernoffBound=0.5*exp(-BhattaDistance);
```

The resulting values are 0.3730 and 0.3443, respectively.

Exercise 4.7.2
Consider the three cases in Exercise 4.7.1 and compute the Bhattacharyya distance and the Chernoff bound. Comment on the results.

4.7.3 Measures Based on Scatter Matrices

Scatter matrices are among the most popular measures for quantifying the way feature vectors "scatter" in the feature space. Because of their rich physical meaning, a number of class-separability measures are built around them. Three such measures are the following [Theo 09, Section 5.6.3]:

$$J_1 = \frac{trace\{S_m\}}{trace\{S_w\}} \tag{4.7}$$

$$J_2 = \frac{|S_m|}{|S_w|} \tag{4.8}$$

$$J_3 = trace\{S_w^{-1}S_b\} \tag{4.9}$$

where S_m is the *mixture* scatter matrix, S_w is the *within-class* scatter matrix, and S_b is the *between-class* scatter matrix.

The respective definitions are

$$S_w = \sum_{i=1}^{c} P_i S_i \tag{4.10}$$

where P_i denotes the a priori probability of class $i = 1, 2, \ldots, c$ and S_i is the respective covariance matrix of class i.

$$S_b = \sum_{i=1}^{c} P_i (m_i - m_0)(m_i - m_0)^T \tag{4.11}$$

where $m_0 = \sum_{i=1}^{c} P_i m_i$ is the global mean vector (considering the data from all classes). It can be shown that

$$S_m = S_w + S_b \tag{4.12}$$

Large values of J_1, J_2, and J_3 indicate that data points in the respective feature space have small within-class variance and large between-class distance.

━━━

Example 4.7.3. In this example, the previously defined J_3 measure will be used to choose the best l features out of $m > l$ originally generated features. To be more realistic, we will consider Example 4.6.2, where four features (mean, standard deviation, skewness, and kurtosis) were used. From Table 4.3 we have ten values for each feature and for each class. The goal is to select three out of the four features that will result in the best J_3 value.

1. Normalize the values of each feature to have zero mean and unit variance.
2. Select three out of the four features that result in the best J_3 value.
3. Plot the data points in the 3-dimensional space for the best feature combination.

Solution. Do the following:

Step 1. Load files *cirrhoticLiver.dat* and *fattyLiver.dat* containing the feature values from the ROIs in Example 4.6.2:

```
class1=load('cirrhoticLiver.dat')';
class2=load('fattyLiver.dat')';
```

To normalize features using the provided *normalizeStd* function, type

```
[class1,class2]=normalizeStd(class1,class2);
```

Step 2. Evaluate J_3 for the 3-feature combination [1,2,3], where 1 stands for mean, 2 for standard deviation, and so on, by typing

```
[J]=ScatterMatrices(class1([1 2 3],:),class2([1 2 3],:));
```

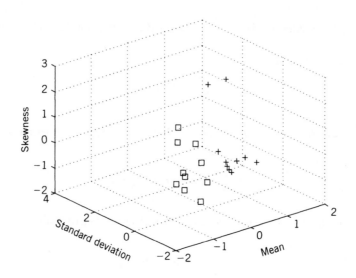

FIGURE 4.5

Plot of the (normalized) 3-feature combination (mean value, standard deviation, and skewness). This combination leads to good class separation.

Work similarly to evaluate the J_3 for the remaining 3-feature combinations: $[1,2,4], [1,3,4], [2,3,4]$. The results are 3.9742, 3.9741, 3.6195, and 1.3972 for the combinations $[1,2,3], [1,2,4], [1,3,4]$, and $[2,3,4]$, respectively.

Step 3. To plot the results of the feature combination $[1,2,3]$, utilize the provided *plotData* function:

```
featureNames = {'mean','standart dev','skewness','kurtosis'};
plotData(class1,class2,[1 2 3],featureNames);
```

The program output is shown in Figure 4.5.   ■

Exercise 4.7.3

Repeat the experiment for all of the 3-feature combinations. Compare the results with those obtained in Example 4.7.3 and comment.

4.8 FEATURE SUBSET SELECTION

We now build on experience gained from the previous sections to address the feature selection stage. There are two major steps involved:

- Reduce the number of features by discarding the less informative ones, using scalar feature selection.
- Consider the features that survive from the previous step in different combinations in order to keep the "best" combination.

The first step is required to reduce the overall number of computations required in searching for the "best" combination.

4.8.1 Scalar Feature Selection

One way of reducing the available features is to consider them individually and use one of the related criteria, such as the t-test, ROC, or FDR, to discard and/or rank them in descending order; then choose the top, say, l features. Such an approach does not take into account existing correlations among the features, so here the cross-correlation coefficient between them is considered and the following procedure may be followed [Theo 09, Section 5.7.1].

First, features are ranked in descending order according to some criterion C. Let i_1 be the index of the best one. Next, the cross-correlations among the first (top-ranked) feature with each of the remaining features are computed. The index, i_2, of the second most important feature, x_{i_2}, is computed as

$$i_2 = \max_j \{a_1 C_j - a_2 |\rho_{i_1,j}|\}, \quad j \neq i_1 \qquad (4.13)$$

which incorporates the value of the criterion C for the jth feature, as well as the cross-correlations ($\rho_{i_1,j}$) between the best feature (i_1) and feature $j \neq i_1$. The parameters a_1 and a_2 are user defined.

The rest of the features are ranked according to

$$i_k = \max_j \left\{ a_1 C_j - \frac{a_2}{k-1} \sum_{r=1}^{k-1} |\rho_{i_r,j}| \right\}, \quad j \neq i_r, \quad r = 1,2,\ldots,k-1 \qquad (4.14)$$

for $k = 3,4,\ldots,m$. Observe that the *average correlation* with all the previously considered features is taken into account.

▬▬▬

Example 4.8.1. This example demonstrates the ranking of a given number of features according to their class-discriminatory power. We will use the same data as in Example 4.6.2. Recall that there are two classes and four features (*mean, standard deviation, skewness, and kurtosis*); their respective values for the two classes are summarized in Table 4.3.

1. Normalize the features so as to have zero mean and unit variance. Then use the FDR criterion to rank the features by considering each one independently (see Example 4.6.2).
2. Use the scalar feature selection technique described before to rank the features. Use the FDR in place of the criterion C. Set $a_1 = 0.2$ and $a_2 = 0.8$.
3. Comment on the results.

Solution. Do the following:

Step 1. Load files *cirrhoticLiver.dat* and *fattyLiver.dat* containing the features from the ROIs in Example 4.6.2:

```
class1=load('cirrhoticLiver.dat')';
class2=load('fattyLiver.dat')';
```

To normalize and rank the features using the FDR criterion with the *ScalarFeature-SelectionRanking* function, type

```
[class1,class2]=normalizeStd(class1,class2);
[T]=ScalarFeatureSelectionRanking(class1,class2,'Fisher');
```

Step 2. To rank the features use their cross-correlation with the *compositeFeaturesRanking* function:

```
featureNames = {'mean ','st. dev.','skewness','kurtosis'};
a1=0.2;a2=0.8;
[p]= compositeFeaturesRanking (class1,class2,a1,a2,T);
```

Print out the results, typing

```
fprintf('\n Scalar Feature Ranking  \n');
for i=1:size(T,1)
   fprintf('(%10s) \n',featureNames{T(i,2)});
end
fprintf('\n Scalar Feature Ranking with correlation \n');
for i=1:size(p,1)
   fprintf('(%10s) \n',featureNames{p(i)});
end
```

The program output is

```
Scalar Feature Ranking
(      mean )
(   st. dev.)
(   skewness)
(   kurtosis)

Scalar Feature Ranking with correlation
(      mean)
(   kurtosis)
(   st. dev.)
(   skewness)
```

Step 3. As can be seen, the rank order provided by the FDR class-separability criterion differs from the ranking that results when both the FDR and the cross-correlations are considered. It must be emphasized that different values for coefficients a_1 and a_2 (see Eq. (4.14)) may change the ranking. ■

4.8.2 Feature Vector Selection

We assume that m features have survived from the scalar feature selection. The goal now is to find the "best" combination of features. Usually, either the number l of the feature space or an upper limit of it is chosen a priori. Such a choice heavily depends on the number of available training data, as already stated. One idea is to examine all possible combinations of the m features (i.e., combinations of $2, 3, \ldots, m$), use each combination to design the classifier, evaluate the classifier's performance by one of the available methods (e.g., leave-one-out), and end up with the best combination. The computational burden of such an approach can be prohibitive in real problems. Thus, other, less computationally expensive methods may be employed. To assess the computational effort involved, we will examine three techniques:

- *Exhaustive search*
- *Sequential forward* and *backward selection*
- *Forward floating search selection*

Exhaustive Search

According to this technique, all possible combinations will be "exhaustively" formed and for each combination its class separability will be computed. Different class separability measures will be used.

Example 4.8.2. We will demonstrate the procedure for selecting the "best" feature combination in the context of computer-aided diagnosis in mammography. In digital X-ray breast imaging, *microcalcifications* are concentrations of small white spots representing calcium deposits in breast tissue (see Figure 4.6). Often they are assessed as a noncancerous sign, but depending on their shape and concentration patterns, they may indicate cancer. Their significance in breast cancer diagnosis tasks makes it important to have a pattern recognition system that detects the presence of microcalcifications in a mammogram. To this end, a procedure similar to the one used in Example 4.6.2 will be adopted here.

Four features are derived for each ROI: *mean, standard deviation, skewness*, and *kurtosis*. Figure 4.6 shows the selected ROIs for the two classes (10 for normal tissue; 11 for abnormal tissue with microcalcifications).

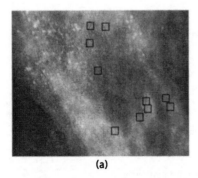 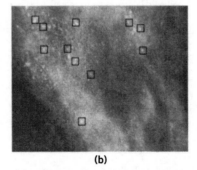

(a) (b)

FIGURE 4.6

Mammogram showing (a) ten ROIs selected from regions of normal tissue and (b) eleven ROIs from regions with abnormal tissue containing microcalcifications.

Table 4.4 Feature Values Calculated from ROIs of Abnormal and Normal Mammogram Regions

Ten ROIs from normal regions				Eleven ROIs with microcalcification			
Mean	Std	Skew	Kurt	Mean	Std	Skew	Kurt
129.53	20.21	0.37	2.72	127.88	19.20	1.14	4.59
107.07	20.47	0.68	3.96	120.42	22.27	1.11	3.61
94.97	14.66	0.35	3.89	109.86	17.71	0.89	3.72
109.50	17.83	0.31	2.36	118.30	14.32	0.71	4.40
102.47	21.14	0.26	2.45	123.44	19.11	0.68	4.31
142.68	28.17	0.30	2.63	103.10	12.65	0.55	3.95
74.16	12.05	0.30	2.17	106.85	12.44	0.38	3.23
118.49	32.67	0.51	2.89	145.46	16.74	0.65	4.53
104.65	17.72	0.23	2.69	96.95	15.14	0.79	5.90
91.09	20.00	0.82	3.73	118.29	13.12	0.69	4.65
--	--	--	--	116.56	13.87	0.48	3.76

Table 4.4 lists the values of the respective features for each class.

1. Employ the exhaustive search method to select the best combination of three features out of the four previously mentioned, according to the divergence, the Bhattacharyya distance, and the J_3 measure associated with the scatter matrices.
2. Plot the data in the subspace spanned by the features selected in step 1.

Solution. Do the following:

Step 1. Load the values from the preceding table into the following two files: *breastMicrocalcifications .dat* and *breastNormalTissue.dat*. Store the files on the hard drive. To load the respective features in two arrays, *class1* and *class2*, type

```
class1=load('breastMicrocalcifications.dat')';
class2=load('breastNormalTissue.dat')';
```

To normalize the features so that all of them have zero mean and unit variance, type

```
[class1,class2]=normalizeStd(class1,class2);
```

Select the best combination of features using the J_3 criterion:

```
costFunction='ScatterMatrices';
[cLbest,Jmax]=exhaustiveSearch(class1,class2, costFunction,[3]);
```

where

   costFunction is a string identifying the employed criterion,

   cLbest is an array containing the best combination of features,

   Jmax is the criterion value for the feature combination *cLbest*.

The value 3 in the bracket indicates our interest in the best 3-feature combination

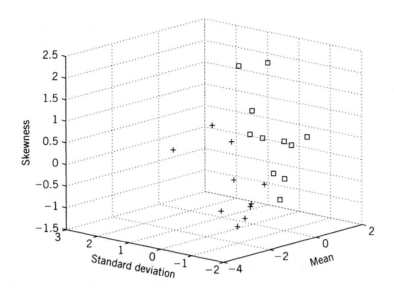

FIGURE 4.7

Output of the J_3 class-separability measure showing the best feature combination—mean, standard deviation, and skewness—using exhaustive search. Pluses and squares indicate points into the two classes, respectively.

Work similarly for the divergence and the Bhattacharyya distance, where now *costFunction* is set equal to *'divergence'* and *'divergenceBhata'*, respectively.

Step 2. To form the classes c_1 and c_2 using the best feature combination, type

```
c1 = class1(cLbest,:);c2 = class2(cLbest,:);
```

Plot the data using the provided *plotData* function:

```
featureNames = {'mean ','st. dev.','skewness','kurtosis'};
plotData(c1,c2,cLbest,featureNames);
```

The program output is shown in Figure 4.7.   ■

Exercise 4.8.2

Compute the J_3 measure for the feature combination *mean, skewness, kurtosis* in Example 4.8.2 and compare the results with those obtained there.

Suboptimal Searching Techniques

Although exhaustive search is an optimal scheme, it is computationally expensive and often may not be feasible, especially in cases where the number of available features is large. In such cases, there are computationally efficient suboptimal searching techniques, such as *sequential forward selection* (SFS), *sequential backward selection* (SBS), *sequential forward floating selection* (SFFS), and *sequential backward floating selection* (SBFS) [Theo 09, Section 5.7.2].

Example 4.8.3. The goal of this example is to demonstrate the (possible) differences in accuracy between the suboptimal feature selection techniques SFS, SBS, and SFFS and the optimal *exhaustive search* technique, which will be considered as the "gold standard." This time, we will work with an example inspired by the field of texture classification in images. Texture classification is an important application of pattern recognition [Petr 06].

We assume that we are given two images of different textures. We associate each texture with a different class. In each of the two images, we form 25 ROIs (see Figure 4.8). These 50 total patterns form the training set, which will be used for selecting the "best" combination of features. Thus, for each pattern (ROI) 20 features are generated:

- Four first-order statistics: the *mean, standard deviation, skewness,* and *kurtosis* of each ROI
- Sixteen second-order (textural) features, derived from the four co-occurrence matrices of each ROI, for the directions $0°$, $90°$, $45°$, $135°$ [Theo 09, Section 7.2]. From each matrix, the extracted (four) features are *contrast, correlation, energy,* and *homogeneity.*

The features are ordered so that the first four are the first-order statistics, the next four are the contrasts of the four co-occurrence matrices, the next four are the correlations of the four co-occurrence matrices, and so on.

Once the feature generation phase is completed, two 25×20 arrays are formed: *dataClass1.dat* and *dataClass2.dat.*

We assume that we are working in a 2-dimensional feature space, and we evaluate the performance of the four feature selection methods in determining the best 2-feature combination, employing the functions *exhaustiveSearch, SequentialForwardSelection, SequentialBackwardSelection,* and *SequentialForwardFloatingSelection.* Work as follows:

1. Normalize the features to have zero mean and unit variance. Then rank them utilizing scalar feature selection, which employs the FDR criterion and a cross-correlation measure between pairs of features (see Section 4.8.1). Set $a_1 = 0.2$ and $a_2 = 0.8$.

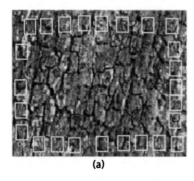 

(a)   (b)

FIGURE 4.8

Terrain images and superimposed image ROIs used to form the training data set for Examples 4.8.3 and 4.8.4.

2. Select the 14 highest-ranked features and employ the exhaustive search method with the J_3 criterion to select the best combination of two features.

3. Repeat step 2 for SFS, SBS, and SFFS and comment on the results obtained.

Solution. To load the data sets of the two classes, type

```
class_1=load('testClass1.dat')';
class_2=load('testClass2.dat')';
```

and then do the following:

Step 1. Normalize and rank features in FDR descending order, typing

```
[class_1,class_2]=normalizeStd(class_1,class_2);
[TFisher]=ScalarFeatureSelectionRanking(...
    class_1,class_2,'Fisher');
[pFisher]= compositeFeaturesRanking (...
    class_1,class_2,0.2,0.8,TFisher);
```

Step 2. Select the 14 highest-ranked features, typing

```
NumOfFeats=14;
inds=sort(pFisher,'ascend');
```

Use function *exhaustiveSearch* and the J_3 criterion to determine the best combination of two features, typing

```
[cLbest,Jmax]=exhaustiveSearch(...
class_1(inds,:),class_2(inds,:),'ScatterMatrices',2);
```

Print out the results, typing

```
fprintf('\n Exhaustive Search -> Best of two:');
fprintf('(%d)',inds(cLbest));
```

Step 3. Working similarly for the suboptimal searching techniques (sequential forward selection, sequential backward selection, and floating search), type

```
[cLbestSFS,JSFS]=SequentialForwardSelection(...
class_1(inds,:),class_2(inds,:),'ScatterMatrices',2);
fprintf('\n Sequential Forward Selection -> Best of two:');
fprintf('(%d)',inds(cLbestSFS));

[cLbestSBS,JSBS]=SequentialBackwardSelection(...
    class_1(inds,:),class_2(inds,:),'ScatterMatrices',2);
```

```
fprintf('\n Sequential Backward Selection -> Best of two:');
fprintf('(%d)',inds(cLbestSBS));

[cLbestSFFS,JSFFS]=sequentialForwardFloatingSelection(...
    class_1(inds,:),class_2(inds,:),'ScatterMatrices',2);
fprintf('\n Floating Search Method -> Best of two:');
fprintf('(%d)',inds(cLbestSFFS));
fprintf('\n');
```

The program outputs are

```
Exhaustive Search -> Best of two: (1) (6)

Sequential Forward Selection -> Best of two: (1) (5)

Sequential Backward Selection -> Best of two: (2) (9)

Floating Search Method -> Best of two: (1) (6)
```

It can be seen that the results of exhaustive search and floating search coincide, whereas the sequential forward selection and sequential backward selection result in different feature combinations. In practice, floating search has become very popular. Although it is suboptimal and is inspired by a rationale similar to that behind the sequential techniques, it has a unique advantage; the potential to correct some wrong decisions made in previous iterations. Of course, this is gained at the expense of some extra computation. ■

Exercise 4.8.3
Experiment with different numbers of the highest-ranked features, such as four, eight, ten, twenty. Comment on the results.

Example 4.8.4. Designing a Classification System
The goal of this example is to demonstrate the various stages involved in the design of a classification system. We will adhere to the 2-class texture classification task of Figure 4.8.

The following five stages will be explicitly considered:

- Data collection for training and testing
- Feature generation
- Feature selection
- Classifier design
- Performance evaluation

Data collection. A number of different images must be chosen for both the training and the test set. However, for this specific case study, one can select the data by selecting different ROIs from two images (one for each class). To form the training data set, 25 ROIs are selected from each image representing the two classes (see Figure 4.8). The same procedure is followed for the test set. However, this time different ROIs must be selected. The ROIs are collected via the provided program *RoisGen.m.*

Many times it is not possible to have different sets for training and testing, since the number of the available data is usually small. In such cases, the same data have to be utilized for training as well as testing. Of course, this has to be "cleverly" done to make sure that the error estimation is based on patterns that have not been considered in the training. (We will come to this point later; see also [Theo 09, Section 10.3].)

Feature generation. From each of the selected ROIs, a number of features is generated. We have decided on 20 different texture-related features. In practice, the number depends on the application as well as on the expert's experience in the field of application. One can employ already known and previously used features, but new features often may have to be generated in order to capture more (classification-related) information for the specific problem. The expert's knowledge and imagination are critical at this stage.

For our example, the following features are generated from each ROI:

- Four first-order statistics textural features (*mean, standard deviation, skewness*, and *kurtosis*) derived from the respective histogram.
- Sixteen second-order textural features—four (*contrast, correlation, energy*, and *homogeneity*) from each of the four co-occurrence matrices [Theo 09, Section 7.2.1] associated with each ROI. Function *FeatGen* is employed to generate the features.

Feature selection. Of the 20 generated features, some may turn out not to be very informative or some may exhibit high mutual correlation. In the latter case, there is no point in using all of them because they do not carry complementary information. Moreover, one has to keep in mind that the number of features, l (i.e., the dimension of the feature space in which the design of the classifier will take place), must be relatively small with respect to the number of training/test points to ensure good generalization performance of the designed classifier.

A rule of thumb is to keep l less than one-third of the training points. In our case, we chose $l = 3$ because that turns out to result in good performance and also gives us the possibility of visualization of the data for pedagogic purposes. In practice, one has to experiment with different values of l and choose the one that results in the best performance as measured by an appropriate criterion.

In this example, feature selection is achieved as follows. First, we use scalar feature selection (function *compositeFeaturesRanking*), discussed in Section 4.8.1, which employs the FDR criterion as well as a cross-correlation measure between pairs of features in order to rank them. The highest-ranked are identified and exhaustive search is employed to select the combination that maximizes the J_3 criterion (function *exhaustiveSearch*). The reader may experiment with other techniques that have been discussed. During this stage, feature preprocessing (e.g., feature normalization) also takes place.

Classifier design. During this stage, different classifiers are employed in the the selected feature space; the one that results in the best performance is chosen. In this example we use the k-nearest neighbor (k-NN) classifier. Note that this is a special classifier that needs no training; it suffices to have access to the training data set. (The reader is encouraged to experiment with the different classifiers discussed in this book.)

Performance evaluation. The performance of the classifier, in terms of its error rate, is measured against the test data set. However, in order to cover the case where the same data must be used for both training and testing, the leave-one-out (LOO) method will be employed. LOO is particularly useful in cases where only a limited data set is available.

The idea behind LOO is the following. Given N training points, use $N - 1$ for training the classifier and the remaining point for testing. Repeat the procedure N times, each time leaving out a different sample. Finally, average out the number of errors committed by the N different test points. Although the method is computationally expensive, since the classifier has to be trained N times, the same data set is utilized for training and testing and, at the same time, the testing is carried out on points that have not been used in the training.

For more details on LOO and other related techniques, see [Theo 09, Section 10.3].

Solution. As a first option, you may create your own data sets by typing

```
RoisGen;
FeatGen;
```

Four data sets will result: *trainingClass1.dat*, *trainingClass2.dat*, *testClass1.dat*, and *testClass2.dat*. If you follow this option, skip the first two lines of the code that follows. Alternatively, you may use the data sets that are provided on the website associated with this book. If this is the case, follow all the lines of code given.

Step 1. Read the training data and normalize the feature values:

```
c1_train=load('trainingClass1.dat')';
c2_train=load('trainingClass2.dat')';

% Normalize dataset
superClass=[c1_train c2_train];
for i=1:size(superClass,1)
    m(i)=mean(superClass(i,:)); % mean value of i-th feature
    s(i)=std (superClass(i,:)); % std of i-th feature
    superClass(i,:)=(superClass(i,:)-m(i))/s(i);
end
c1_train=superClass(:,1:size(c1_train,2));
c2_train=superClass(:,size(c1_train,2)+1:size(superClass,2));
```

Step 2. Rank the features using the normalized training data set. We have adopted the scalar feature-ranking technique, which employs FDR in conjunction with feature correlation. The ranking results are returned in variable p.

```
[T]=ScalarFeatureSelectionRanking(c1_train,c2_train,'Fisher');
[p]= compositeFeaturesRanking (c1_train,c2_train,0.2,0.8,T);
```

Step 3. To reduce the dimensionality of the feature space, work with the seven highest-ranked features:

```
inds=sort(p(1:7),'ascend');
c1_train=c1_train(inds,:);
c2_train=c2_train(inds,:);
```

Step 4. Choose the best feature combination consisting of three features (out of the previously selected seven) using the exhaustive search method.

```
[cLbest,Jmax] = exhaustiveSearch(c1_train,c2_train,'ScatterMatrices',[3]);
```

Step 5. Form the resulting training data set (using the best feature combination) along with the corresponding class labels.

```
trainSet=[c1_train c2_train];
trainSet=trainSet(cLbest,:);
trainLabels=[ones(1,size(c1_train,2)) 2*ones(1,size(c2_train,2))];
```

Step 6. Load the test data set and normalize it using the mean and standard deviation (computed over the training data set Why?). Form the vector of the corresponding test labels.

```
c1_test=load('testClass1.dat')';
c2_test=load('testClass2.dat')';
for i=1:size(c1_test,1)
    c1_test(i,:)=(c1_test(i,:)-m(i))/s(i);
    c2_test(i,:)=(c2_test(i,:)-m(i))/s(i);
end
c1_test=c1_test(inds,:);
c2_test=c2_test(inds,:);
testSet=[c1_test c2_test];
testSet=testSet(cLbest,:);
testLabels=[ones(1,size(c1_test,2)) 2*ones(1,size(c2_test,2))];
```

Step 7. Plot the test data set by means of function *plotData* (Figure 4.9). Observe the good separation of the classes. This is a consequence of the fact that the two selected types of textures are quite different, leading to an "easy" problem, if the right combination of features is selected. Obviously, in practice, such "easy" problems are the exception rather than the rule.

```
%Provide names for the features
featureNames={'mean','stand dev','skewness','kurtosis',...
    'Contrast 0','Contrast 90','Contrast 45','Contrast 135',...
    'Correlation 0','Correlation 90','Correlation 45','Correlation 135',...
    'Energy 0','Energy 90','Energy 45','Energy 135',...
```

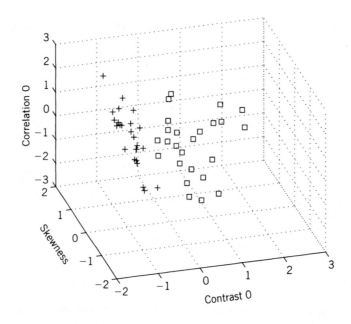

FIGURE 4.9

Plot of the patterns of the two classes, employing a 3-feature combination. Observe that this combination results in well-separated classes in the 3-dimensional feature space.

```
    'Homogeneity 0','Homogeneity 90','Homogeneity 45','Homogeneity 135'};
fNames=featureNames(inds);
fNames=fNames(cLbest);
plotData(c1_test(cLbest,:),c2_test(cLbest,:),1:3,fNames);
```

Step 8. Classify the feature vectors of the test data using the *k*-NN classifier (*k* = 3) and compute the classification error. For this, use functions *k_nn_classifier* and *compute_error*, which were introduced in Chapter 1.

```
[classified]=k_NN_classifier(trainSet,trainLabels,3,testSet);
[classif_error]=compute_error(testLabels,classified);
```

We now employ the LOO method to evaluate the performance of the classifier, so this time we do not make use of the testing data sets.

Step 9. Load all data, normalize them, and create class labels.

```
c1_train=load('trainingClass1.dat')';
c1=c1_train;
Labels1=ones(1,size(c1,2));
```

```
c2_train=load('trainingClass2.dat')';
c2=c2_train;
Labels2=2*ones(1,size(c2,2));

[c1,c2]=normalizeStd(c1,c2);
AllDataset=[c1 c2];
Labels=[Labels1 Labels2];
```

Step 10. Keep features of the best feature combination (determined previously) and discard the rest.

```
AllDataset=AllDataset(inds,:);
AllDataset=AllDataset(cLbest,:);
```

Step 11. Apply LOO on the *k*-NN classifier ($k = 3$) and compute the error.

```
[M,N]=size(AllDataset);
for i=1:N
    dec(i)=k_nn_classifier([AllDataset(:,1:i-1) AllDataset(:,i+1:N)],...
        [Labels(1,1:i-1) Labels(1,i+1:N)],3,AllDataset(:,i));
end
LOO_error=sum((dec~=Labels))/N;
```

The LOO error is 1%.   ∎

Template Matching

5

5.1 INTRODUCTION

In this chapter, we assume that each class is represented by a single pattern. A set of such *reference* patterns (or *prototypes*) is available and stored in a database. Given an unknown *test* pattern, template matching consists of searching the database for the reference pattern most "similar" to the given test pattern. This is equivalent to defining a matching cost that quantifies similarity between the test pattern and the reference patterns.

Template-matching techniques are very common in string matching, speech recognition, alignment of molecular sequences, image retrieval, and so forth. They often come with different names depending on the application. For example, in speech recognition the term *dynamic time warping* is used, whereas in string matching *Edit* (or *Levenstein*) *distance* is quite common.

This chapter is devoted to a series of examples of increasing complexity, culminating in an example from speech recognition.

5.2 THE EDIT DISTANCE

A *string* pattern is defined as an *ordered sequence of symbols* taken from a discrete and finite set. For example, if the finite set consists of the letters of the alphabet, the strings are words. The *Edit distance* between two string patterns A and B, denoted $D(A,B)$, is defined as the minimum total number of changes (C), insertions (I), and deletions (R) required to change pattern A into pattern B,

$$D(A,B) = \underbrace{\min}_{j}[C(j) + I(j) + R(j)] \tag{5.1}$$

where j runs over all possible combinations of symbol variations in order to obtain B from A. If the two strings are exactly the same, then $D(A,B) = 0$. For every symbol "change," "insertion," or "deletion," the cost increases by one.

The required minimum is computed by means of the dynamic programming methodology [Theo 09, Section 8.2.1]. That is, an optimal path is constructed in the 2-dimensional grid formed by the two sequences in the 2-dimensional space, by locating one sequence across the horizontal axis and the other across the vertical axis. The Edit distance is commonly used in spell-checking systems where the prototypes stem from the vocabulary of words.

Example 5.2.1. Compute the Edit distance between the words "book" and "bokks," taking the former as the reference string. Plot the optimal matching path and comment on the sequence of operations needed to change "bokks" to "book." Repeat for the words "template" (reference) and "teplatte."

Solution. Use function *editDistance* by typing

```
[editCost,Pred]=editDistance('book','bokks');
```

The Edit distance equals 2 and is stored in the variable *editCost*. The value of 2 is the result of a symbol change (*k* to *o*) and a deletion (*s* at the end of the word). To extract the matching path, give matrix *Pred* as input to function *BackTracking* as follows:

```
L_test=length('bokks'); % number of rows of the grid
L_ref=length('book'); % number of columns of the grid
[BestPath]=BackTracking(Pred,L_test,L_ref,1,'book','bokks');
% The fourth input argument indicates that a plot of the best
% path will be generated. The last two arguments serve as labels for the
resulting axes.
```

The resulting best path is stored in the vector variable *BestPath* and is presented in Figure 5.1(a), where the reference pattern has been placed on the horizontal axis. Each element of vector *BestPath* is a complex number and stands for a node in the path. The real part of the element is the node's row index and the imaginary part is its column index. Inspection of the path in Figure 5.1(a) reveals that the first

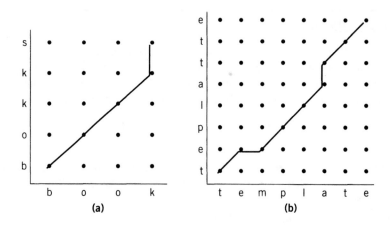

(a)   (b)

FIGURE 5.1

(a) Optimal matching path between "book" and "bokks." (b) Optimal matching path between "template" and "teplatte." A diagonal transition between two successive nodes amounts either to zero cost (if the corresponding symbols are the same) or to one (if the corresponding symbols are different). Horizontal transitions (symbol insertions) and vertical transitions (deletions) contribute one to the total cost.

occurrence of k in "bokks" has been changed to o. In addition, the vertical segment of the best path is interpreted as the deletion of s in "bokks." A total of one symbol change and one symbol deletion is needed to convert "bokks" to "book" in an optimal way.

Similarly, the Edit cost for matching "teplatte" against "template" equals 2, and the resulting best path can be seen in Figure 5.1(b). In this case, an insertion (horizontal segment) and a deletion (vertical segment) are required to convert "teplatte" to the reference pattern in an optimal way. ∎

Exercise 5.2.1
Given the words "impose," "ignore," and "restore" as prototypes, determine which one stands for the most likely correction of the mistyped word "igposre" in terms of the edit distance. Note that, as is the case with most spell checkers, ties result in multiple correction possibilities.

5.3 MATCHING SEQUENCES OF REAL NUMBERS

In this section, we focus on a slightly different task, that of matching sequences of real numbers. In contrast to Section 5.2, where the goal was to change one string pattern to another, the aim here is to measure how similar/dissimilar are two given *ordered* sequences of numbers. For example, if we are given two real numbers, x, y, their similarity can be quantified by the absolute value of their difference. If we are given two vectors (i.e., two strings of real numbers of *equal* length), we can use the respective Euclidean distance. A more interesting case is when two sequences of numbers are of different length. One approach to this problem is to allow local "stretching"/"compressing," known as *warping*, achieved by constructing the optimal (low-cost) path through nodes of the respective grid. The grid is formed by the two sequences in the 2-dimensional space by locating one sequence along the horizontal axis and the other along the vertical axis.

Assuming that the reference sequence is placed on the horizontal axis, the dimensions of the grid are $J \times I$, where I and J are the lengths of the reference and test sequences, respectively. In the simplest case, the cost assigned to each node of the grid is equal to the absolute value of the difference between the respective numbers associated with a specific node. The type and the allowable degree of expansion/compression are determined by the so-called local constraints. Popular choices include the Sakoe-Chiba and Itakura constraints [Theo 09, Section 8.2]. Basically, these are constraints imposed on the allowable jumps among nodes in the grid.

The purpose of matching sequences of numbers is pedagogical and is used as an intermediate step to help the reader acquire a better understanding of the concepts underlying dynamic time warping for speech recognition, which is treated in the next section (see [Theo 09, Section 8.2.3]).

Example 5.3.1. Let $P = \{-1, -2, 0, 2\}$ be the prototype and $T = \{-1, -2, -2, 0, 2\}$ be the unknown pattern.

1. Compute the matching cost and the resulting best path by adopting the Sakoe-Chiba local constraints. Comment on the shape of the resulting best path.
2. Repeat with $T = \{-1, -2, -2, -2, -2, 0, 2\}$.

Solution

Step 1. For $T = \{-1, -2, -2, -2, -2, 0, 2\}$, use function *DTW Sakoe* and type

```
P=[-1,-2,0,2];
T=[-1,-2,-2,0,2];
[MatchingCost,BestPath,D,Pred]=DTWSakoe(P,T,1);
```

where D is the array having as elements the costs associated with optimally reaching each node of the grid. The value 1 is used if a plot is required; if not, 0 is used. Although the two sequences differ by one symbol, the matching cost equals 0. This is due to the fact that a) the absolute difference was employed as the (node) cost and b) the only difference between the two sequences is symbol repetition.

To further interpret the result, observe the respective best path in Figure 5.2(a). It can be seen that the vertical segment of the path corresponds to a local stretching operation; that is, the symbol -2 of the prototype (horizontal axis) is matched against two consecutive occurrences of -2 in sequence T.

Step 2. To repeat the experiment with $T = \{-1, -2, -2, -2, -2, 0, 2\}$ type

```
P=[-1,-2,0,2];
T=[-1,-2,-2,-2,-2,0,2];
[MatchingCost,BestPath,D,Pred]=DTWSakoe(P,T,1);
```

The matching cost remains 0 and the resulting best path is presented in Figure 5.2(b). It can be seen that the vertical segment of the path is now four nodes long. This should not come as a surprise

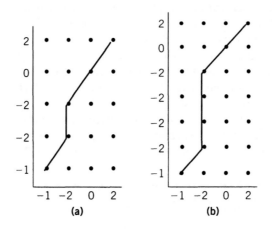

(a)   (b)

FIGURE 5.2

(a) Best path for $P = \{-1, -2, 0, 2\}$ and $T = \{-1, -2, -2, 0, 2\}$. (b) Best path for $P = \{-1, -2, 0, 2\}$ and $T = \{-1, -2, -2, -2, -2, 0, 2\}$.

because, as before, T differs from P in terms of *symbol repetition. The length of repetition does not affect the cost*; it only causes a more intense time-warping effect. To draw an analogy with speech, we may have the same phoneme but one time it is said fast and another time slowly. Long horizontal or vertical segments are very common when the Sakoe-Chiba local constraints are employed. If no global constraints are specified, the horizontal (vertical) segments can become arbitrarily long. This behavior is often undesirable with real-world signals, such as in speech. ■

Example 5.3.2. Let $P = \{1, 0, 1\}$ be the prototype, and let $T_1 = \{1, 1, 0, 0, 0, 1, 1, 1\}$, $T_2 = \{1, 1, 0, 0, 1\}$ be two unknown patterns. Compute the matching cost for the standard Itakura local constraints between P and T_1 and between P and T_2.

Solution. To compute the matching cost for the two unknown patterns using the standard Itakura local constraints, use function *DTWItakura* and type

```
P=[1,0,1];
T1=[1,1,0,0,0,1,1,1];
T2=[1,1,0,0,1];
[MatchCost1,BestPath1,D1,Pred1]=DTWItakura(P,T1,1);
[MatchCost2,BestPath2,D2,Pred2]=DTWItakura(P,T2,1);
```

The returned value of *MatchCost*1 is ∞, whereas the value of *MatchCost*2 is 0. This is because one property of the standard Itakura constraints is that the maximum allowed stretching factor for the prototype is 2. In other words, the length of the unknown pattern has to be, in the worst case, twice the length of the prototype. If this rule is violated, the *DTWItakura* function returns ∞. In the case of P and T_2, this rule is not violated and the best path can be seen in Figure 5.3.

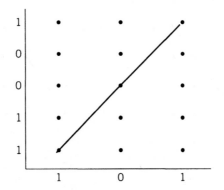

FIGURE 5.3

Best path for $P = \{1, 0, 1\}$ and $T = \{1, 1, 0, 0, 1\}$ using the standard Itakura local constraints. ■

Example 5.3.3. This example demonstrates the importance of the endpoint constraints [Theo 09, Section 8.2.3]. Let the sequence $P = \{-8, -4, 0, 4, 0, -4\}$ be a prototype. Also let the sequence $T = \{0, -8, -4, 0, 4, 0, -4, 0, 0\}$ be the unknown pattern.

1. Compute the matching cost by adopting the Sakoe-Chiba local constraints and comment on the result.
2. Repeat, allowing for endpoint constraints. Specifically, omit at most two symbols from each endpoint of T.

Solution

Step 1. For the first case, type

```
P=[-8,-4,0,4,0,-4];
T=[0,-8,-4,0,4,0,-4,0,0];
[MatchingCost,BestPath,D,Pred]=DTWSakoe(P,T,1);
```

The matching cost turns out to be 16. In practice, the cost is normalized by dividing it by the length of the best path. In this example, the best path is 9 nodes long, as can be seen in Figure 5.4(a), and so the normalized cost is 1.778. Hence, although P and T can be considered practically the same (they only differ in the trailing zeros), the matching cost is nonzero.

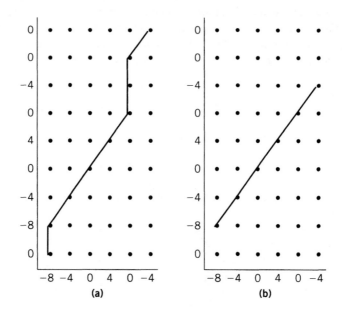

(a)   (b)

FIGURE 5.4

(a) Best path for $P = \{-8, -4, 0, 4, 0, -4\}$ and $T = \{0, -8, -4, 0, 4, 0, -4, 0, 0\}$, no endpoint constraints.
(b) Previous sequences matched while allowing endpoint constraints.

Inspection of Figure 5.4(a) reveals that time stretching occurs at the beginning and end of the path and is due to the existence of zeros at the endpoints. This is a common situation; that is, the unknown pattern contains "garbage" near the endpoints. As a remedy, we can resort to a variation of the standard matching scheme, where it is possible to omit a number of symbols at the endpoints of the unknown pattern; it suffices to specify the maximum number of symbols to omit. This type of enhancement to the standard matching mechanism can be easily embedded in the dynamic programming methodology.

Step 2. To employ the endpoint constraints in the current example, use function *DTWSakoeEndp* and type

```
P=[-8,-4,0,4,0,-4];
T=[0,-8,-4,0,4,0,-4,0,0];
[MatchingCost,BestPath,D,Pred]=DTWSakoeEndp(P,T,2,2,1);
```

In this function call, the third and fourth arguments stand for the number of symbols that can be omitted at each endpoint (2 in this example). The fifthindicates that a plot of the best path will be generated. The resulting matching cost is zero, as can be verified from Figure 5.4(b), where the first row and the last two rows of the grid have been skipped by the algorithm.

Endpoint constraints are very useful in speech recognition because the unknown pattern usually has silence periods around the endpoints, whereas the prototypes are free of such phenomena. ■

5.4 DYNAMIC TIME WARPING IN SPEECH RECOGNITION

Here we focus on a simple task in speech recognition known as *isolated word recognition (IWR)*. We assume that the spoken utterance consists of discrete words; that is, there exist sufficient periods of silence between successive words (hence the term "isolated"). This is a convenient assumption, since it allows for employing segmentation algorithms capable of locating the boundaries (endpoints) of the spoken words with satisfactory precision. Note that in practice a certain amount of silence/noise is likely to exist close to the endpoints of the detected word after the segmentation stage.

At the heart of any IWR system is an architecture consisting of a set of reference patterns (prototypes) and a distance measure. Recognition of a test (unknown) pattern is achieved by searching for the best match between the test and each one of the reference patterns, on the basis of the adopted measure.

As a first stage, a feature extraction algorithm converts each signal into a sequence of feature vectors—instead of matching sequences of real numbers, the task is computing the matching cost between two sequences of vectors. However, the rationale is the same, and the only difference lies in replacing the absolute value with the Euclidean distance between vectors. In speech recognition, this type of matching is known as *dynamic time warping* (DTW).

We now develop a simple, speaker-dependent IWR system for a 10-word vocabulary consisting of "zero," "one," ..., "nine" and uttered by a single male speaker. We are actually building an "isolated digit recognition" system. We need a total of 10 utterances to use as prototypes and a number of utterances for testing.

At this point, you may record your own audio files or you may use the files available via this book's website. If you record your own files, name the prototypes as follows: *zero.wav*, *one.wav*, and so on, for the sake of compatibility, and place all 10 in a single folder (this is the naming convention we have adopted for the audio samples on the website). Note that "clean" prototypes are desirable. That is, make sure silence/noise has been removed, at least to the extent possible, from the endpoints of the prototypes before storing. Such care need not be taken with the samples that will be used for testing. In addition, the file names for the test patterns need not follow any naming convention and it suffices to store the unknown patterns in the folder where the prototypes are held.

To build the system, we use short-term energy and short-term zero-crossing rate as features [Theo 09, Section 7.5.4], so that each signal is represented by a sequence of 2-dimensional feature vectors. Note that this is not an optimal feature set in any sense and has only been adopted for simplicity.

The feature extraction stage is accomplished by typing the following code:

```
protoNames={'zero','one','two','three','four','five',...
    'six','seven','eight','nine'};
for i=1:length(protoNames)
    [x,Fs,bits]=wavread(protoNames{i});
    winlength = round(0.02*Fs); % 20 ms moving window length
    winstep = winlength; % moving window step. No overlap
    [E,T]=stEnergy(x,Fs,winlength,winstep);
    [Zcr,T]=stZeroCrossingRate(x,Fs,winlength,winstep);
    protoFSeq{i}=[E;Zcr];
end
```

which performs feature extraction per prototype and uses a single cell array (*protoFSeq*) to hold the feature sequences from all prototypes. To extract the features, a moving windows technique is employed [Theo 09, Section 7.5.1]. The length of the moving windows is equal to 20 milliseconds and there is no overlap between successive windows.

To find the best match for an unknown pattern—for example, a pattern stored in file *upattern1.wav*—type the following code:

```
[test,Fs,bits]=wavread('upattern1');
winlength = round(0.02*Fs); % use the same values as before
winstep = winlength;
[E,T]=stEnergy(test,Fs,winlength,winstep);
[Zcr,T]=stZeroCrossingRate(test,Fs,winlength,winstep);
Ftest=[E;Zcr];

tolerance=0.1;
LeftEndConstr=round(tolerance/winstep); % left endpoint constraint
RightEndConstr = LeftEndConstr;
for i=1:length(protoNames)
    [MatchingCost(i),BestPath{i},D{i},Pred{i}]=DTWSakoeEndp(...
        protoFSeq{i},Ftest,LeftEndConstr,RightEndConstr,0);
end
```

```
[minCost,indexofBest]=min(MatchingCost);
fprintf('The unknown pattern has been identified as %s \n',...
        protoNames{indexofBest});
```

This code uses the standard Sakoe local constraints and allows for endpoint constraints. Specifically, it is assumed that the length of silence/noise at each endpoint may not exceed 0.1 seconds (i.e., at most 5 frames can be skipped from each endpoint of the test utterance). Note that, instead of using the function *DTWSakoeEndp* to compute the matching cost, we could have used *DTWItakuraEndp*. To avoid repeating the code for each unknown pattern, the whole system is available on the website as a single m-file under the name *IsoDigitRec.m*.

Remarks

- Errors may occur in the experiments. This is also expected in practice, and is even more true here since only two features have been used for pedagogic simplicity.
- Moreover, this a speaker-dependent speech recognition example. Hence, if you record your own voice and test the system using the provided prototypes, the performance may not to be a good one, especially if the accent of the speaker is very different from the accent we used to record the prototypes. You can reconstruct the whole example by using your own voice for both the test data and the prototypes.

Hidden Markov Models

6

6.1 INTRODUCTION

In general, a hidden Markov model (HMM) is a type of stochastic modeling appropriate for nonstationary stochastic sequences whose statistical properties undergo *distinct* random transitions among a set of, say, k different stationary processes. In other words, HMMs are used to model piecewise stationary processes. A stationary process is one whose statistical properties do not change with time.

We assume that we are given a set of observations (feature vectors), $x_1, x_2, \ldots, x_N \in \mathcal{R}^l$. In contrast to what has been assumed in previous chapters, here we allow each observation to be generated (emitted) by a different source. Each source is described by different statistical properties. For example, assuming two sources (stationary processes), $k = 2$, one may generate data points sequentially, according to either a Gaussian or a Chi-square distribution. Hence, each observation may have been emitted by either of the two sources, but we do not have access to this information. A hidden Markov model is a way to model such a nonstationary process.

6.2 MODELING

An important issue concerning any HMM is its modeling. We first assume that the number of sources, k, that emit the observations is known. In practice, this has to be inferred by exploiting any available knowledge about the problem at hand following some physical reasoning. Each emitting source is associated with a *state*, and k is known as the number of states.

The next set of parameters that need to be specified are the probability densities describing each state, that is, $p(x|j)$, $j = 1, \ldots, k$. This is natural, since each state is an emitting source statistically described by the respective pdf.

Since the process undergoes random jumps from one state to another, the model should also have access to the set of *state transition* probabilities, $P(i|j)$, $i, j = 1, \ldots, k$, where $P(i|j)$ is the probability of the system jumping from state j to state i.

Finally, since any observation sequence must have an origin, x_1, one needs to know the a priori probability $P(i), i = 1, \ldots, k$—that is, the probability of the first observation being emitted by state i.

If the observation sequence is discrete, taken from a finite alphabet set, the pdfs $p(x|j)$ become probabilities.

In summary, an HMM is described by the following set of parameters:

- The number of states, k.
- The probability densities, $p(x|j)$, $j = 1,\ldots,k$. For discrete variables, where $x = r$, $r = 1,\ldots,L$, the *observation probability matrix* that is defined as

$$B = \begin{bmatrix} P(x=1|1) & P(x=1|2) & \cdots & P(x=1|k) \\ \vdots & \vdots & \vdots & \vdots \\ P(x=L|1) & p(x=L|2) & \cdots & P(x=L|k) \end{bmatrix}$$

- The state transition matrix, A,

$$A = \begin{bmatrix} P(1|1) & p(2|1) & \cdots & p(k|1) \\ \vdots & \vdots & \vdots & \vdots \\ P(1|k) & P(2|k) & \cdots & P(k|k) \end{bmatrix}$$

- The vector π of the initial probabilities,

$$\pi = \begin{bmatrix} P(1) \\ P(2) \\ \vdots \\ P(k) \end{bmatrix}$$

6.3 RECOGNITION AND TRAINING

During recognition, we assume that we have more than one HMM, each one described by a different set of parameters. Obviously, each HMM models a different piecewise stationary process. For example, one may model a process consisting of two emitting sources (e.g., one Gaussian and one Chi-square, two states); another may correspond to a process consisting of three sources (e.g., three Gaussians with different mean values and covariance matrices).

Given an observation sequence and a number, M, of HMMs (each one modeling a different process), the goal of the recognition phase is to decide which one of the HMMs is more likely to have emitted the received sequence. The so-called *any path* or *Baum-Welch* and *best path* or *Viterbi* are two approaches used for recognition [Theo 09, Section 9.6]. Both provide a probability-related score for each involved HMM; the HMM scoring the maximum is considered as the most probable to have emitted the specific observation sequence. The recognition stage assumes that all parameters that define the involved HMMs have been estimated and are known.

In the training phase the parameters describing an HMM are estimated. To this end, one (or more) long enough observation sequence that has been generated by the corresponding stochastic process is used to estimate the unknown parameters (e.g., using Maximum Likelihood parameter estimation arguments). The *Baum-Welch* and *Viterbi* techniques are commonly used for training [Theo 09, Section 9.6].

Example 6.3.1. In this example, two coins (C_1, C_2) are used to generate a sequence of observations consisting of heads (H) or tails (T). Both coins are not fair toward the heads or tails outcome. We have chosen $P(H|C_1) = 0.8$ ($P(T|C_1) = 0.2$) and $P(H|C_2) = 0.3$ ($P(T|C_2) = 0.7$). Somebody is behind a curtain and tosses the coins provided to us, *sequentially*, the resulting outcomes, without, however, disclosing which one of the two coins was tossed. Moreover, there is an added difficulty. The person who performs the experiment behind the curtain does not toss the two coins in a "fair" way; instead he or she gives preference to one of them. To this end, the person uses a third coin, C_3, with $P(H|C_3) = 0.7$. Each time the outcome of C_3 is heads, coin C_1 generates the next observation; otherwise, coin C_2 does.

A little thought reveals that such an experiment corresponds to a state transition matrix equal to

$$A = \begin{bmatrix} 0.7 & 0.3 \\ 0.7 & 0.3 \end{bmatrix}$$

where two states have been considered, each one associated with one of the coins, C_1 or C_2, that generate the observation sequence. Let us assume that coin C_1 has just been used. Then the probability of tossing the *same* coin, C_1, is equal to 0.7—that is, $P(1|1) = 0.7$. Obviously, the probability of tossing C_2 is equal to the probability $P(T|C_3)$ (i.e., $P(2|1) = 0,3$). On the other hand, if C_2 was the last used, the probability of tossing the *same* coin, C_2, would be 0.3 and the probability of tossing C_1 would be 0.7—that is, $P(2|2) = 0.3$ and $P(1|2) = 0.7$.

Let *HHHTHHHHHTHHHHHTTHH* be the observation sequence of heads and tails that have resulted from the above experiment. We are also given two HMMs:

- $A_1 = \begin{bmatrix} 0.7 & 0.3 \\ 0.7 & 0.3 \end{bmatrix}$, $B_1 = \begin{bmatrix} 0.8 & 0.3 \\ 0.2 & 0.7 \end{bmatrix}$, $\pi_1 = [0.7, 0.3]^T$

- $A_2 = \begin{bmatrix} 0.6 & 0.4 \\ 0 & 1 \end{bmatrix}$, $B_2 = B_1, \pi_2 = \pi_1$

Compute the recognition probability of this sequence for each HMM and comment on the results.

Solution. First create the two HMMs. Type

```
% First HMM
A1  = [0.7 0.3;0.7 0.3];
B1  = [0.8 0.3;0.2 0.7];
pi1 = [0.7 0.3]';
% Second HMM
A2  = [0.6 0.4;0 1];
B2  = B1;
pi2 = pi1;
```

Then rewrite the sequence of heads and tails as a sequence of 1s and 2s, where 1 stands for heads and 2 for tails. To compute the recognition probabilities, say *Pr*1 and *Pr*2, use function *BWDoHMMst*, which implements the standard Baum-Welch (any-path) algorithm for discrete-observation HMMs. Type

```
O = [1 1 1 2 1 1 1 1 2 1 1 1 1 2 2 1 1];
[Pr1]=BWDoHMMst(pi1,A1,B1,O);
[Pr2]=BWDoHMMst(pi2,A2,B2,O);
Pr1, Pr2
```

The screen output is

```
Pr1 = 5.5481e-005
Pr2 = 6.2033e-007
```

It can be seen that the first model results in higher recognition probability. This is natural, since in this HMM the correct parameters associated with the experiment have been used. In real life, of course, access to the true values of the parameters is hardly the case. What one expects is that the training of the HMM is sufficient and that the estimated parameters have values close to the correct ones. The second model has a state transition matrix that corresponds to a completely different process. Indeed, A_2 is a so-called *left-to-right* HMM, meaning that its state transition matrix is upper triangular: Once the model reaches the second state, it will stay there until the whole observation sequence has been emitted. Naturally, this has nothing to do with the given observation sequence, where heads and tails interchange (with a bias toward heads Why?).

The goal of this example was to demonstrate the essence of the recognition phase; it attempts to "match" an observation sequence with the data emission "mechanism," which is implied by the respective HMM.

Concerning the matrices common in both HMMs (i.e., $B_1 = B_2$ and $\pi_1 = \pi_2$), observe that each column of B_1 (B_2) reflects the bias of the respective coin. Remember that C_1 is biased toward heads ($P(H|C_1) = 0.8$), and this is why $B_1(1,1) = 0.8$ and $B_1(2,1) = 0.2$. Following a similar reasoning, we assign the values $B_1(1,2) = 0.3$ and $B_1(2,2) = 0.7$. In addition, $\pi_1 = [0.7, 0.3]^T$ because it is C_3 that decides which coin is the first to be tossed. Once more, it has to be emphasized that in practice the values of B and π are estimated during training, using an appropriate observation sequence, for each model.

Hint

Function *BWDoHMMst* is a *nonscaled* version of the any-path (Baum-Welch) method. Because of the lack of scaling, if the observation sequence is too long, numerical problems (underflow) may occur, since the standard algorithm employs multiplications of probabilities. Fortunately, it is possible to avoid numerical instabilities by using a proper scaling technique in the method's implementation. The resulting function is *BWDoHMMsc*. If you replace *BWDoHMMst* with *BWDoHMMsc* in the last lines of the previous code, variables *Pr*1 and *Pr*2 become −4.25 and −6.27, respectively. The minus sign is the effect of the presence of a logarithm in the scaling process, which replaces multiplications with additions. Scaling is very useful in real-world applications, where symbol sequences can be very long [Theo 09, Section 9.6]. ∎

Example 6.3.2. For the setting of the previous example, compute the Viterbi score and the respective best-state sequence for each of the two HMMs. Comment on the results. By best-state, we mean associating each observation with a specific state. Identification of the best-state sequence is also known as *back-tracking*. This is an important part of the recognition stage. Once the winning HMM has been decided, one has to identify the state (source) from which individual points in the observation sequence have been emitted. In other words, it classifies observations to states.

Solution. To compute the Viterbi score, we use function *ViterbiDoHMMst*, which implements the standard Viterbi algorithm. This function returns both the score and the best-state sequence, the latter as a vector of complex numbers. The higher the score, the better the matching. Each element of the vector encodes a node of the best path. For implementation, we have made the assumption that the real part of each complex number stands for the y-coordinate of the node (state number); the imaginary part stands for the x-coordinate (observation (time) index). Therefore, we are only interested in the real part of variable *BestPath*.

Type

```
% First HMM
pi1 = [0.7 0.3]';
A1  = [0.7 0.3;0.7 0.3];
B1  = [0.8 0.3;0.2 0.7];
% Second HMM
pi2 = pi1;
A2  = [0.6 0.4;0 1];
B2  = B1;
O = [1 1 1 2 1 1 1 1 2 1 1 1 1 2 2 1 1];
[Score1, BestPath1] = VitDoHMMst(pi1,A1,B1,O);
[Score2, BestPath2] = VitDoHMMst(pi2,A2,B2,O);
BestStateSeq1 = real(BestPath1);
BestStateSeq2 = real(BestPath2);
Score1, Score2, BestStateSeq1, BestStateSeq2
```

The screen output is

```
Score1 = 1.0359e-006
Score2 = 9.2355e-008
BestStateSeq1 = 1 1 1 2 1 1 1 1 2 1 1 1 1 2 2 1 1
BestStateSeq2 = 1 1 1 1 1 1 1 1 1 1 1 1 1 2 2 2 2
```

As expected, the first HMM (A_1) has resulted in a significantly higher Viterbi score. Moreover, unveiling the best-state sequences justifies the outcome of the recognition stage; that is, the first of the two models is better matched to the observation sequence. Specifically, if *BestStateSeq1* is examined jointly with the sequence of observations, it can be seen that a 1 in the best-state sequence, indicating the first state, occurs whenever heads appears in the observation sequence. A similar observation holds for the second state, which occurs when tails appear. This ties in well with the statistical properties of the emitting process. State 1, associated with coin C_1, has higher probability of emitting heads. The opposite is true for state 2, associated with coin C_2.

On the other hand, the second HMM (A_2) spends 13 time instances in its first state, switches to the second state, and remains there until the end, because of the lack of backward transitions (i.e., from state 2 back to state 1). In other words, the best-state sequence, according to the second HMM, is not representative of the underlying coin-tossing statistical mechanism.

Hint (1)

The scaled version of function *ViterbiDoHMMst* is *ViterbiDoHMMsc*. We have employed the base-10 logarithm, and the respective scores are -5.9847 and -7.0345. Note that most often in practice Viterbi scoring gives results that compare with those of the Baum-Welch (any-path) method.

Hint (2)

In general, it is good to avoid zero entries in the HMM matrices. In such cases, it is common to replace zeros with small probabilities, say a value of 0.001 or even less. This is particularly true for the initialization of the respective HMM parameters in the training phase (an issue discussed in the next example). ∎

Example 6.3.3. So far, we have assumed the HMM parameters to be known, which is not realistic for the majority of real-word applications. In this example, we will focus on the training phase. We will estimate the HMM parameters given a set of training sequences. Specifically, we will use the first 70 out of 100 observation sequences, which are available in the *DOHMMTrainingData.mat* file located in the "Data" folder in the software that accompanies this book. Each sequence in the file was generated by the coin-tossing experiment of Example 6.3.1. Using multiple sequences for training is common in practice, where different realizations (observation instances) of the stochastic HMM process are available and are exploited in an averaging rationale.

Assume that we have decided to train a 2-state HMM and consider the following two initialization options:

$$A = \begin{bmatrix} 0.6 & 0.4 \\ 0.6 & 0.4 \end{bmatrix}, B = \begin{bmatrix} 0.6 & 0.2 \\ 0.4 & 0.8 \end{bmatrix}, \pi = [0.6, 0.4]^T$$

$$A = \begin{bmatrix} 0.6 & 0.4 \\ 0 & 1 \end{bmatrix}, B = \begin{bmatrix} 0.6 & 0 \\ 0.4 & 1 \end{bmatrix}, \pi = [0.5, 0.5]^T$$

For each initialization scheme, train the HMM with the Baum-Welch training method and comment on the results.

Solution. Load the training data stored in *DOHMMTrainingData.mat*. You will first need to switch to the respective folder and then type

```
load DOHMMTrainingData;
```

Variable *TrainingData* now resides in MATLAB's workspace. It is a cell array, with each cell containing a string of *H*s and *T*s, and is interpreted as a symbol sequence of the training set. For example, if you type

```
TrainingData{1}
```

the screen output is

```
HHHHTTHHTTTHTTHHHHTTHTHHHTHHHHTHHTTHTHTHHH
```
∎

Before we proceed, each string will be converted to a sequence of symbol IDs and stored in a new cell array, *NumericData*. This is convenient because, from an implementation point of view, it is easier to work with numbers. Assuming that *1* stands for heads and *2* for tails, type

```
L=length(TrainingData);
for i=1:L
    for j=1:length(TrainingData{i})
        if TrainingData{i}(j)=='H'
            NumericData{i}(j)=1;
        else
            NumericData{i}(j)=2;
        end
    end
end
```

Next, initialize the HMM with the first set of values. Type

```
pi_init_1 = [0.6 0.4]';
A_init_1  = [0.6 0.4; 0.6 0.4];
B_init_1  = [0.6 0.2; 0.4 0.8];
```

Then use function *MultSeqTrainDoHMMBWsc* to train the HMM with the Baum-Welch training algorithm. Type

```
maxEpoch=1000;
[piTrained_1, ATrained_1, BTrained_1, SumRecProbs_1]=...
    MultSeqTrainDoHMMBWsc(pi_init_1, A_init_1, B_init_1, ...
    NumericData(1:70), maxEpoch);
```

where

Input variable *maxEpoch* defines the maximum number of iterations during the training stage. Although we have set it to a large value, the training algorithm is expected to converge in a few iterations (less than 20) mainly because of the simplicity of the problem.

Function *MultSeqTrainDoHMMBWsc* implements the scaled version of the Baum-Welch training algorithm, which stops iterating when the sum of recognition probabilities of the training sequences ceases to increase.

Variable *SumRecProbs_1* is a vector whose *i*th element is the sum of recognition probabilities at the *i*th iteration of the training algorithm (obviously, the length of this vector is the number of iterations that took place).

If you now type

```
piTrained_1, ATrained_1, BTrained_1
```

the screen output is

```
piTrained_1 =    ATrained_1 =           BTrained_1 =
0.7141           0.6743    0.3257       0.7672    0.3544
0.2859           0.6746    0.3254       0.2328    0.6456
```

The training stage has terminated after only two iterations (the length of variable *SumRecProbs*_1), and the resulting HMM matrices are very close to the true ones, describing the generation mechanism of the observation sequences. This is also a consequence of the fact that the values used to initialize the HMM were already close to the true values.

We now repeat the training phase and initialize the HMM with the second set of parameter values. Type

```
pi_init_2 = [0.5 0.5]';
A_init_2  = [0.6 0.4; 0 1];
B_init_2  = [0.6 0; 0.4 1];
maxEpoch=1000;
[piTrained_2, ATrained_2, BTrained_2, SumRecProbs_2]=...
    MultSeqTrainDoHMMBWsc(pi_init_2, A_init_2, B_init_2, ...
    NumericData(1:70), maxEpoch);
piTrained_2, ATrained_2, BTrained_2
```

The screen output is

```
piTrained_2 =    ATrained_2 =        BTrained_2 =
1                1.0000  0.0000      0.6333          0
0                0       1.0000      0.3667    1.0000
```

This time, the training phase has terminated after 13 iterations (the length of variable *SumRecProbs*_2). For the second initialization scheme, the resulting estimates of the HMM matrices are quite different from the true ones. Interestingly, this second HMM can be interpreted as a single-coin model biased toward heads because, in the resulting state-transition matrix, $ATrained\_2(2,2) = 1$; that is, the HMM will never leave the first state. Furthermore, since $piTrained\_2(1) = 1$, the first state will always be the starting one.

Overall, the HMM will always start at the first state and stay there until the end. This is mainly due to the fact that zeros at initialization remain zeros at the end of the training stage, which is why, for example, $ATrained\_2(2,1)$ equals zero. In general, zeros at the initialization stage imply that we are certain that the respective events are not encountered in the training sequences. This is a very strict assumption, which must be fully justified by physical reasoning. In general, it is best to assign small values instead of zeros to the respective elements, if we expect that these elements must have small values. As a matter of fact, even if at the end of the training stage some elements end up with zero values (although initialized with nonzero values), it is advisable to set them manually to a small (enough) value because the resulting parameter estimates from the training phase can hardly be "exact" representations of the problem under study (and a zero does not allow for deviations).

Exercise 6.3.1
Repeat the training procedure for the second initialization scenario by replacing each zero with 0.01. Comment on the results.

Example 6.3.4. Repeat the experiment in Example 6.3.3 for the first initialization scenario. This time use Viterbi training. Comment on the results.

Solution. For training with the Viterbi algorithm, only change the training function. Type

```
[piTrained_1, ATrained_1, BTrained_1, SumRecProbs_1]=...
    MultSecTrainDoHMMVITsc(pi_init_1, A_init_1, B_init_1, ...
    NumericData(1:70), maxEpoch);
piTrained_1, ATrained_1, BTrained_1
```

The screen output is

```
piTrained_1 =     ATrained_1 =          BTrained_1 =
  0.6857            0.6278    0.3722     1    0
  0.3143            0.6288    0.3712     0    1
```

The training algorithm converged after three iterations. The main difference, with respect to the values obtained using the Baum-Welch method in Example 6.3.3, lies in the resulting estimate of the observation probability matrix. The obtained matrix indicates that the first state can only emit heads and, similarly, the second state can only emit tails. This is because of the simplicity of the Viterbi training method, which is based on computing frequencies of events [Theo 09, Section 9.6]. ∎

Example 6.3.5. Compute the Viterbi score for each of the remaining 30 symbol sequences in file *DOHMMTrainingData.mat*. Use both of the HMMs that resulted from the training stage of Example 6.3.3.

Solution. Assuming that the following variables still reside in MATLAB's workspace—*piTrained_*1, *ATrained_*1, *BTrained_*1, *piTrained_*2, *ATrained_*2, *BTrained_*2, and *NumericData*; so type

```
for i=71:100
    [ViterbiScoreScaled1(i),BestPath1{i}] = VitDoHMMsc(...
        piTrained_1,ATrained_1,BTrained_1,NumericData{i});
    [ViterbiScoreScaled2(i),BestPath2{i}] = VitDoHMMsc(...
        piTrained_2,ATrained_2,BTrained_2,NumericData{i});
end
```

After the termination of the *for* loop, the *i*th element of *ViterbiScoreScaled*1 (*ViterbiScoreScaled*2) is the Viterbi score of the *i*th symbol sequence for the first (second) HMM and, similarly, the *i*th cell of the variable *BestPath*1 (*BestPath*2) is the respective best path. ∎

Exercise 6.3.2
Compare the Viterbi scores of the two HMMs on the basis of each observation sequence used for testing. Comment on the results.

Example 6.3.6. In this example, we will work with observation sequences that consist of real numbers, thus departing from the assumption that the emissions are drawn from a finite and discrete alphabet. For this, we adopt an experimental setup in which two generators of real numbers are available. The first one, G_1, follows a Gaussian distribution with mean value and standard deviation both equal to 1.

The second generator, G_2, is also Gaussian with mean value and standard deviation equal to 3 and 1, respectively. At each time instance, one of the two generators is chosen to emit an observation (real number) based on the outcome of a coin toss; if the outcome is heads, G_1 is used to generate (emit) the real number; if the outcome is tails, G_2 is used to generate the observation. The coin is slightly biased toward heads ($P(H) = 0.55$).

Because we are now dealing with real numbers, the use of an observation probability matrix no longer makes sense. However, for the sake of uniformity in implementation, we will retain the notation of the B matrix but assign a different meaning to it. Specifically, if k is the number of states, the size of B is $2 \times k$, and each column contains the mean value and the standard deviation of the Gaussian that describes the pdf of the respective state observations. In other words, assuming that we know the functional form of the underlying pdfs, we use the corresponding parameters that define them. This will also be the case if non-Gaussian pdfs are chosen. Often in practice, mixture models are employed that are more representative of a number of real-life problems [Theo 09, Section 9.6], so more complicated modeling of more parameters (than the mean and standard deviation) is needed.

Let the following observation sequence be a realization of the previously stated experimental setup:

$$1.1 \quad 1.0 \quad 1.15 \quad 0.97 \quad 0.98 \quad 1.2 \quad 1.11 \quad 3.01 \quad 2.99 \quad 2.97 \quad 3.1 \quad 3.12 \quad 2.96$$

Compute the Viterbi score and the respective best-state path of this observation sequence for each of the following HMMs:

$$A_1 = \begin{bmatrix} 0.55 & 0.45 \\ 0.55 & 0.45 \end{bmatrix}, B_1 = \begin{bmatrix} 1 & 3 \\ 1 & 1 \end{bmatrix}, \pi_1 = [1, 0]^T$$

$$A_2 = A_1, B_2 = \begin{bmatrix} -1 & 1 \\ 3 & 2 \end{bmatrix}, \pi_2 = \pi_1$$

Solution. It can be observed that the difference between the two HMMs lies in the mean values and standard deviations associated with the probability densities per state. To proceed, we first create the two HMMs typing

```
pi1=[1 0]'; pi2=pi1;
A1=[0.55 0.45; 0.55 0.45]; A2=A1;
B1=[1 1; 3 1]';
B2=[-1 1; 3 2]';
O = [1.1 1.0 1.15 0.97 0.98 1.2 1.11 3.01 2.99 2.97 ...
       3.1 3.12 2.96];
```

We then compute the recognition scores, say $Pr1$ and $Pr2$, by typing

```
[Pr1,bp1] = VitCoHMMsc(pi1,A1,B1,O);
[Pr2,bp2] = VitCoHMMsc(pi2,A2,B2,O);
bs1=real(bp1);
bs2=real(bp2);
Pr1, Pr2
bs1, bs2
```

The screen output is

```
Pr1 = -8.8513
Pr2 = -15.1390

bs1 = 1  1  1  1  1  1  1  2  2  2  2  2  2
bs2 = 1  2  2  2  2  2  2  2  2  2  2  2  2
```

Note that we have used the scaled version of the Viterbi algorithm. The value of $Pr1$ is significantly higher because the observation pdfs of the first HMM more accurately model the experiment under study. This also becomes evident from the respective best-state sequences (variables $bs1$ and $bs2$). Justify the resulting sequence of states by comparing it with the observation sequence and using physical reasoning.   ▪

Exercise 6.3.3
Determine whether it is possible to treat the problem in the previous example in the discrete observation domain?

Hint
The answer is positive if we quantize the real numbers to the symbols of a finite discrete alphabet. There are many ways to accomplish this, including clustering algorithms. For simplicity, here we suggest using a simple thresholding technique. Any value less than $T_h = 2$ will be converted to 1 and, similarly, values greater that T_h will be quantized to 2. Type

```
Th=2;
for i=1:length(O)
    if O(i)<Th
        Oq(i)=1;
    else
        Oq(i)=2;
    end
end
```

Proceed as in Example 6.3.2.

Exercise 6.3.4
Load the contents of file *CoTrainData.mat* to create a cell array with 1100 cells in MATLAB's workspace. Each cell encapsulates a sequence of real numbers, which were recorded at the output of the experiment described in Example 6.3.6. Use the first 800 cells to train an HMM with the Baum-Welch method. Experiment with the initial conditions and the number of states. Finally, choose an HMM and compute the recognition probability for the remaining 300 sequences.

Clustering

7.1 INTRODUCTION

In previous chapters we dealt with supervised pattern recognition—that is, with problems where the class label for each training pattern was known. In this chapter we consider the unsupervised case, where this information is not available. The aim now is to determine "sensible" groups (clusters) formed by the available patterns in order to extract useful information concerning similarity or dissimilarity among them.

7.2 BASIC CONCEPTS AND DEFINITIONS

As has been the case so far, we assume that each training pattern is represented by a set of l features that form an l-dimensional vector $x = [x(1),\ldots,x(l)]^T$. Thus, *each training pattern corresponds to a point (vector) in an l-dimensional space.*

Definition of Clustering: Given a set of data vectors $X = \{x_1,\ldots,x_N\}$, group them such that "more similar" vectors are in the same cluster and "less similar" vectors are in different clusters. The set, $\Re$, containing these clusters is called a *clustering* of X. (A more rigorous definition of clustering can be found in [Theo 09, Section 11.1.3].)

Example 7.2.1. Consider the data vectors shown in Figure 7.1. Two clusterings that are in line with the definition just given are $\Re_1 = \{\{x_1, x_2\}, \{x_3, x_4\}, \{x_5, x_6, x_7\}\}$ and $\Re_2 = \{\{x_1, x_2, x_3, x_4\}, \{x_5, x_6, x_7\}\}$.

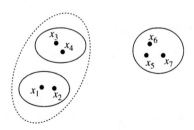

FIGURE 7.1

Clustering examples for Example 7.2.1.

DOI: 10.1016/B978-0-12-374486-9.00007-5

Both are "sensible," in the sense that the vectors close to each other are included in the same cluster. However, there is no extra data information to indicate which should be finally selected. In general, the best approach when dealing with clustering problems is to *consult an expert in the field of application.*

Another possibility would be the clustering $\Re_3 = \{\{x_1, x_7\}, \{x_3, x_4\}, \{x_5, x_6, x_2\}\}$, but this is not sensible since grouping x_1 and x_7, which are far from each other, seems to contradict physical reasoning. The same holds true for clustering x_2 together with x_5, x_6. ■

Remarks

- The previous definition of clustering is a loose one. Note, however, that *clustering has no rigorous definition.*[1] The inability to give a rigorous definition for the clustering problem stems from the fact that no external information (class labels) is available, and the term "similarity" is itself loose. As a consequence, *subjectivity is an inescapable feature of clustering we have to live with.*
- Any pattern may belong *exclusively* to a single cluster (*hard clustering*) or it may belong *simultaneously* to more than one cluster up to a certain degree (*fuzzy clustering*).
- The "amount of proximity" is quantified via a *proximity measure.* This can be a *similarity* (usually denoted s) or a *dissimilarity* (usually denoted d) measure. In addition, depending on the clustering method used, proximity may be defined (a) between vectors, (b) between a vector and a set of vectors (cluster), and (c) between sets of vectors (clusters) [Theo 09, Section 11.2].

7.3 CLUSTERING ALGORITHMS

The naive approach to determining the clustering that best fits a data set, X, is to consider all possible clusterings and select the one that is most sensible according to a criterion or rationale. For example, one may choose the clustering that optimizes a preselected criterion, which quantifies the requirement for more "similar" vectors to be in the same cluster and less "similar" vectors to be in different clusters. However, the number of all possible clusterings is huge, even for a moderate number of patterns, N. A way out of this situation is the development of *clustering algorithms*, which consider only a small fraction of the possible clusterings. The clusterings to be considered depend on the specific algorithmic procedure.

Several clustering algorithms have been developed. Some of them return a *single clustering*; others return a *hierarchy of clusterings*. The following rough classification contains most of the well-known clustering algorithms.

Algorithms that return a single clustering include

- *Sequential algorithms*, which are conceptually simple, performing a single pass or very few passes on the data set [Theo 09, Chapter 12].
- *Cost function optimization algorithms*, which adopt a cost function J that quantifies the term "sensible," and return a clustering that optimizes J. This category contains *hard clustering algorithms*, such as the celebrated k-means, *fuzzy clustering algorithms*, such as the fuzzy c-means (FCM), *probabilistic clustering algorithms*, such as the EM, and *possibilistic algorithms* [Theo 09, Chapter 14].

---

[1]Other definitions can be found in [Theo 09, Section 11.2].

- *Miscellaneous algorithms*, which do not fit the previous categories, for example, *competitive learning algorithms, valley-seeking algorithms, density-based algorithms,* and *subspace-clustering algorithms* [Theo 09, Chapter 15].

Algorithms that return a hierarchy of clusterings include

- *Agglomerative algorithms*, which generate a sequence of clusterings of a decreasing number of clusters, *m*. At each step, the pair of "closest" clusters in the current clustering is identified and merged into one (while the remaining clusters are unaltered) in order to give rise to the next clustering.
- *Divisive algorithms*, which, in contrast to the agglomerative algorithms, generate a sequence of clusterings of an increasing number of clusters, *m*. At each step, an appropriately chosen cluster is split into two smaller clusters [Theo 09, Chapter 13].

7.4 SEQUENTIAL ALGORITHMS

In this section, we consider the Basic Sequential Algorithmic Scheme (BSAS) as well as some of its refinements.

7.4.1 BSAS Algorithm

The BSAS algorithm performs a single pass on a given data set. In addition, each cluster is represented by the mean of the vectors that have been assigned to it.[2] BSAS works as follows. For each new vector x, presented to the algorithm, its distance from the already formed clusters is computed. If these distances are larger than a (user-defined) threshold of dissimilarity, Θ, and if the maximum allowable number of clusters, q, have not been reached, a new cluster containing x is created. Otherwise, x is assigned to its closest cluster and the corresponding representative is updated. The algorithm terminates when all data vectors have been considered once.

To apply BSAS on a data set X, type

$$[bel, repre] = BSAS(X, theta, q, order)$$

where

X is an $l \times N$ matrix containing the data vectors in its columns,

theta is the dissimilarity threshold,

q is the maximum allowable number of clusters,

order is an N-dimensional vector containing a permutation of the integers $1, 2, \ldots, N$, where its *i*th element specifies the order of presentation of the *i*th vector to the algorithm,

bel is an N-dimensional vector whose *i*th element indicates the cluster where the *i*th data vector is assigned,

repre is a matrix that contains the *l*-dimensional (mean) representative of the clusters in its columns.

---

[2]Other choices are possible. For example, each cluster might be represented by the first vector that has been assigned to it. Such a solution is less computationally demanding, but often leads to low-quality results because a randomly chosen vector of a cluster is not likely to be a good representative of it.

Remarks
- In its original form, BSAS is suitable for unraveling compact clusters (i.e., clusters whose points are aggregated around a specific point in the data space).
- The algorithm is sensitive to the order of data presentation and the choice of the parameter Θ. If the data are presented in a different order and/or the parameter Θ is given a different value, a different clustering may result.
- BSAS is *fast*, because it requires a single pass on the data set, X; thus, it is a good candidate for processing large data sets. However, in several cases the resulting clustering may be of low quality. Improvements can be achieved in a refinement step, as discussed in the following subsection.
- Sometimes, the clustering returned by BSAS is used as a starting point for other more sophisticated clustering algorithms, to generate clusterings of improved quality.
- BSAS results in a rough estimate of the number of clusters underlying the data set at hand.

To more accurately estimate the number of clusters in X, BSAS may be run for different values of Θ in a range $[\Theta_{min}, \Theta_{max}]$. For each value, r runs are performed using different orders of data presentation; then the number of clusters m_Θ most frequently met is identified and a plot of m_Θ versus Θ is performed. "Flat" areas in the plot is an indication of the existence of clusters; the flattest area is likely to correspond to the number of clusters underlying X (sometimes it is useful to also consider the second flattest area, provided that it is "significantly" large).

7.4.2 Clustering Refinement

Reassignment Procedure

This procedure is applied on a clustering that has already been obtained. It performs a single pass over the data set. The closest cluster for each vector, x, is determined. After all vectors have been considered, each cluster is redefined using the vectors identified as closest to it. If cluster representatives are used, they are re-estimated accordingly (a usual representative is the mean of all the vectors in a cluster).

To apply the reassignment procedure, type

$$[bel, new\_repre] = reassign(X, repre, order)$$

where *new_repre* contains in its columns the re-estimated values of the mean vectors of the clusters; all other parameters are defined as for function *BSAS*.

Merging Procedure

This procedure is also applied on a clustering $\mathfrak{R}$ of a given data set. Its aim is to merge clusters in $\mathfrak{R}$ that exhibit high "similarity" (low "dissimilarity"). Specifically, the cluster pair that, according to a pre-elected dissimilarity measure between sets (clusters), exhibits the lowest dissimilarity is determined. If this is greater than a (user-defined) cluster-dissimilarity threshold, M_1, the procedure is terminated. Otherwise, the two clusters are merged and the procedure is repeated on the resulting clustering.

Merging is sensitive to the value of parameter M_1, the choice of which mostly depends on the problem at hand. Loosely speaking, M_1 is chosen so that clusters lying "close" to each other and "away" from most of the rest are merged. This procedure should be used only in cases where the number of clusters is "large". In all cases, it is desirable to have the merging of clusters approved by an expert in the field of application.

The previously described procedures may be used to "refine" a "primitive" clustering obtained, for example, by a sequential algorithm (BSAS).

Example 7.4.1. Consider the 2-dimensional data set X consisting of the following vectors: $x_1 = [2, 5]^T, x_2 = [6, 4]^T, x_3 = [5, 3]^T, x_4 = [2, 2]^T, x_5 = [1, 4]^T, x_6 = [5, 4]^T, x_7 = [3, 3]^T, x_8 = [2, 3]^T, x_9 = [2, 4]^T, x_{10} = [8, 2]^T, x_{11} = [9, 2]^T, x_{12} = [10, 2]^T, x_{13} = [11, 2]^T, x_{14} = [10, 3]^T, x_{15} = [9, 1]^T$ (Figure 7.2). Plot the data set and perform a "visual" clustering on it.

1. Apply the BSAS algorithm on X, presenting its elements in the order $x_8, x_6, x_{11}, x_1, x_5, x_2, x_3, x_4, x_7, x_{10}, x_9, x_{12}, x_{13}, x_{14}, x_{15}$ for $\Theta = 2.5$ and $q = 15$.
2. Repeat step 1, now with the order of presentation of the data vectors to the algorithm as $x_7, x_3, x_1, x_5, x_9, x_6, x_8, x_4, x_2, x_{10}, x_{15}, x_{13}, x_{14}, x_{11}, x_{12}$.
3. Repeat step 1, now with $\Theta = 1.4$.
4. Repeat step 1, now with the maximum allowable number of clusters, q, equaling 2.

Solution. To generate the data set X (Figure 7.2), type

```
% Data set generation
X=[2 5; 6 4; 5 3; 2 2; 1 4; 5 4; 3 3; 2 3;...
2 4; 8 2; 9 2; 10 2; 11 2; 10 3; 9 1]';
[l,N]=size(X);
% Plot of the data set
figure (1), plot(X(1,:),X(2,:),'.')
figure(1), axis equal
```

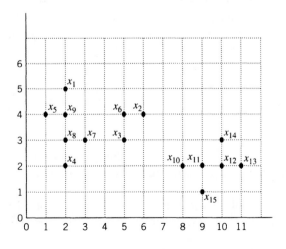

FIGURE 7.2

Setup of the data set from Example 7.4.1.

A "visual" inspection reveals three clusters: $C_1 = \{x_8, x_1, x_5, x_4, x_7, x_9\}$, $C_2 = \{x_6, x_2, x_3\}$, and $C_3 = \{x_{11}, x_{10}, x_{12}, x_{13}, x_{14}, x_{15}\}$.

Continue with the following steps.

Step 1. To apply the BSAS algorithm on X, type

```
q=15; % maximum number of clusters
theta=2.5; % dissimilarity threshold
order=[8 6 11 1 5 2 3 4 7 10 9 12 13 14 15];
[bel, repre]=BSAS(X,theta,q,order);
```

The resulting clustering is the same as that derived by the visual inspection in the previous step.

Step 2. Repeat the code given in step 1 for the new order of data presentation, ending with the following four clusters: $C_1 = \{x_7, x_3, x_6, x_2\}$, $C_2 = \{x_1, x_5, x_9, x_8, x_4\}$, $C_3 = \{x_{10}, x_{15}, x_{11}\}$, and $C_4 = \{x_{13}, x_{14}, x_{12}\}$. This shows the dependence of BSAS on the order of presentation of data vectors.

Step 3. Repeat the code given in step 1 for $\Theta = 1.4$ to obtain the following six clusters: $C_1 = \{x_4, x_7, x_8\}$, $C_2 = \{x_2, x_3, x_6\}$, $C_3 = \{x_{10}, x_{11}, x_{15}\}$, $C_4 = \{x_1, x_9\}$, $C_5 = \{x_5\}$, and $C_6 = \{x_{12}, x_{13}, x_{14}\}$. Compare with the results of step 2 to see the influence of Θ on the clustering results.

Step 4. Repeat step 1 for $q = 2$ to obtain the following clusters: $C_1 = \{x_1, x_4, x_5, x_7, x_8, x_9\}$, $C_2 = \{x_2, x_3, x_6, x_{10}, x_{11}, x_{12}, x_{13}, x_{14}, x_{15}\}$. The results show the influence of q on the formation of the clusters. Note that one should be very careful in imposing restrictions on the maximum number of allowable clusters, since an underestimation may prevent the algorithm from finding the clustering that best fits the data. ■

In the next example, we show how the BSAS algorithm may be utilized to estimate the number of (compact) clusters underlying a data set X.

Example 7.4.2. Generate and plot a data set X_1, that consists of $N = 400$ 2-dimensional data vectors. These vectors form four equally sized groups, each one of which contains vectors that stem from Gaussian distributions with means $m_1 = [0, 0]^T$, $m_2 = [4, 0]$, $m_3 = [0, 4]$, $m_4 = [5, 4]^T$, respectively, and respective covariance matrices

$$S_1 = I, \quad S_2 = \begin{bmatrix} 1 & 0.2 \\ 0.2 & 1.5 \end{bmatrix}, \quad S_3 = \begin{bmatrix} 1 & 0.4 \\ 0.4 & 1.1 \end{bmatrix}, \quad S_4 = \begin{bmatrix} 0.3 & 0.2 \\ 0.2 & 0.5 \end{bmatrix}$$

Then do the following:

1. Determine the number of clusters formed in X_1 by doing the following:
   a. Determine the maximum, d_{max}, and the minimum, d_{min}, (Euclidean) distances between any two points in the data set.[3]
   b. Determine the values of Θ for which the BSAS will run. These may be defined as $\Theta_{min}, \Theta_{min} + s, \Theta_{min} + 2s, \ldots, \Theta_{max}$, where $\Theta_{min} = 0.25\frac{d_{min}+d_{max}}{2}$ and $\Theta_{min} = 1.75\frac{d_{min}+d_{max}}{2}$ and

---

[3] Where N is large, approximations of these distances may be used.

$s = \frac{\Theta_{min}+\Theta_{max}}{n_\Theta -1}$, where n_Θ is the number of different (successive) values of Θ that will be considered. Use $n_\Theta = 50$.

c. For each of the previously defined values of Θ, run the BSAS algorithm $n_{times} = 10$, so that the data vectors are presented with different ordering to BSAS in each run. From the n_{times} estimates of the number of clusters, select the most frequently met value, m_Θ, as the most accurate. Let m_{tot} be the n_Θ-dimensional vector, which contains the m_Θ values.

d. Plot m_Θ versus Θ. Determine the widest flat region, r, of Θ's (excluding the one that corresponds to the single-cluster case) and let n_r be the number of Θ's in $\{\Theta_{min}, \Theta_{min} + s, \ldots, \Theta_{max}\}$ that also lie in r. If n_r is "significant" (e.g., greater than 10% of n_Θ), the corresponding number of clusters is selected as the best estimate, m_{best}, and the mean of the values of Θ in r is chosen as the corresponding best value for Θ (Θ_{best}). Otherwise, single-cluster clustering is adopted.

2. Run the BSAS algorithm for $\Theta = \Theta_{best}$ and plot the data set using different colors and symbols for points from different clusters.

3. Apply the reassignment procedure on the clustering results obtained in the previous step and plot the new clustering.

Solution. To generate the required data set, type

```
randn('seed',0)
m=[0 0; 4 0; 0 4; 5 4];
S(:,:,1)=eye(2);
S(:,:,2)=[1.0 .2; .2 1.5];
S(:,:,3)=[1.0 .4; .4 1.1];
S(:,:,4)=[.3 .2; .2 .5];

n_points=100*ones(1,4); %Number of points per group

X1=[];
for i=1:4
    X1=[X1; mvnrnd(m(i,:),S(:,:,i),n_points(i))];
end
X1=X1';
```

Plot the data set by typing

```
figure(1), plot(X1(1,:),X1(2,:),'.b')
figure(1), axis equal
```

As can be observed, X_1 consists of four (not very clearly separated) clusters.

Step 1. To estimate the number of clusters, proceed as follows:

a. Determine the minimum and the maximum distances between points of X_1 by typing

```
[l,N]=size(X1);
% Determination of the distance matrix
```

```
dista=zeros(N,N);
for i=1:N
    for j=i+1:N
        dista(i,j)=sqrt(sum((X1(:,i)-X1(:,j)).^2));
        dista(j,i)=dista(i,j);
    end
end

true_maxi=max(max(dista));
true_mini=min(dista(~logical(eye(N))));
```

b. Determine Θ_{min}, Θ_{max}, and s by typing

```
meani=(true_mini+true_maxi)/2;
theta_min=.25*meani;
theta_max=1.75*meani;
n_theta=50;
s=(theta_max-theta_min)/(n_theta-1);
```

c. Run BSAS n_{times} for all values of Θ, each time with a different ordering of the data, by typing

```
q=N;
n_times=10;
m_tot=[];
for theta=theta_min:s:theta_max
    list_m=zeros(1,q);
    for stat=1:n_times %for each value of Theta BSAS runs n_times times
        order=randperm(N);
        [bel, m]=BSAS(X1,theta,q,order);
        list_m(size(m,2))=list_m(size(m,2))+1;
    end
    [q1,m_size]=max(list_m);
    m_tot=[m_tot m_size];
end
```

d. Plot m_Θ versus Θ (see Figure 7.3(a)) by typing

```
theta_tot=theta_min:s:theta_max;
figure(2), plot(theta_tot,m_tot)
```

Determine the final estimate of the number of clusters and the corresponding Θ, as previously described, by typing:

```
% Determining the number of clusters
m_best=0;
theta_best=0;
siz=0;
```

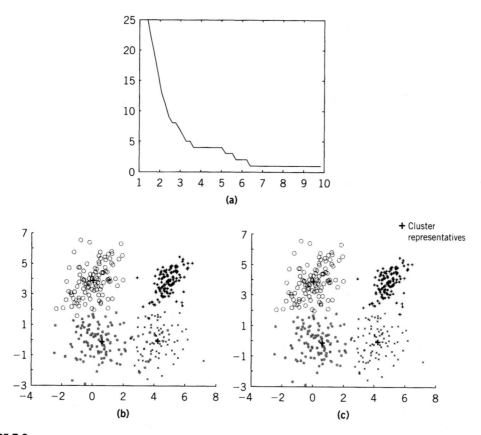

FIGURE 7.3

(a) Plot of m_Θ versus Θ for Example 7.4.2. (b) Clustering output of BSAS, using the value of Θ determined in step 2(d) of Example 7.4.2. (c) Result obtained after reassignment. Different clusters are indicated by different symbols.

```
for i=1:length(m_tot)
    if(m_tot(i)~=1) %Excluding the single-cluster clustering
        t=m_tot-m_tot(i);
        siz_temp=sum(t==0);
        if(siz<siz_temp)
            siz=siz_temp;
            theta_best=sum(theta_tot.*(t==0))/sum(t==0);
            m_best=m_tot(i);
        end
    end
end
%Check for the single-cluster clustering
```

```
if(sum(m_tot==m_best)<.1*n_theta)
    m_best=1;
    theta_best=sum(theta_tot.*(m_tot==1))/sum(m_tot==1);
end
```

Step 2. Run the BSAS algorithm for $\Theta = \Theta_{best}$:

```
order=randperm(N);
[bel, repre]=BSAS(X1,theta_best,q,order);
```

Plot the results (see Figure 7.3(b)), typing

```
figure(11), hold on
figure(11), plot(X1(1,bel==1),X1(2,bel==1),'r.',...
    X1(1,bel==2),X1(2,bel==2),'g*',X1(1,bel==3),X1(2,bel==3),'bo',...
    X1(1,bel==4),X1(2,bel==4),'cx',X1(1,bel==5),X1(2,bel==5),'md',...
    X1(1,bel==6),X1(2,bel==6),'yp',X1(1,bel==7),X1(2,bel==7),'ks')
figure(11), plot(repre(1,:),repre(2,:),'k+')
```

Step 3. To run the reassignment procedure, type

```
[bel,new_repre]=reassign(X1,repre,order);
```

Plot the results working as in the previous step (see Figure 7.3(c)). Compare the results obtained by the current and previous steps, observing the influence of reassignment on the results. ■

Exercise 7.4.1

Generate and plot a data set, X_2, that consists of 300 2-dimensional points stemming from the normal distribution with mean $m_1 = [0, \ 0]^T$ and covariance matrix equal to the 2×2 identity matrix. Repeat step 1 of Example 7.4.2 and draw conclusions.

Observe that X_2 contains no clusters.

7.5 COST FUNCTION OPTIMIZATION CLUSTERING ALGORITHMS

In this section, each cluster, C_j, in a clustering is parameterized by a vector of parameters θ_j. The aim is to identify the values of these parameter vectors, which characterize the clustering structure of X in an optimal sense. This is carried out via the optimization of appropriately defined functions.

7.5.1 Hard Clustering Algorithms

In the algorithms of this category, it is assumed that each data vector belongs *exclusively* to a single cluster.

k-Means, or Isodata, Algorithm

This is the most widely known clustering algorithm, and its rationale is very simple. In this case, the parameter vectors θ_j (also called *cluster representatives* or simply *representatives*) correspond to points in the l-dimensional space, where the vectors of data set X live. k-means assumes that the number of clusters underlying X, m, is known. Its aim is to move the points $\theta_j, j = 1,\dots,m$, into regions that are dense in points of X (clusters).

The k-means algorithm is of iterative nature. It starts with some initial estimates $\theta_1(0),\dots,\theta_m(0)$, for the parameter vectors $\theta_1,\dots,\theta_m$. At each iteration t,

- the vectors x_i that lie close to each $\theta_j(t-1)$ are identified and then
- the new (updated) value of θ_j, $\theta_j(t)$, is computed as the mean of the data vectors that lie closer to $\theta_j(t-1)$.

The algorithm terminates when no changes occur in θ_j's between two successive iterations. To run the k-means algorithm, type

$$[theta, bel, J] = k\_means(X, theta\_ini)$$

where

X is an $l \times N$ matrix whose columns contain the data vectors,

theta_ini is an $l \times m$ matrix whose columns are the initial estimates of θ_j (the number of clusters, m, is implicitly defined by the size of *theta_ini*),

theta is a matrix of the same size as *theta_ini*, containing the final estimates for the θ_j's,

bel is an N-dimensional vector whose ith element contains the cluster label for the ith data vector,

J is the value of the cost function given in Eq. (7.1) (see below) for the resulting clustering.

Remarks
- k-means is suitable for unraveling compact clusters.
- The k-means algorithm is a fast iterative algorithm because (a) in practice it requires only a few iterations to converge and (b) the computations required at each iteration are not complicated. Thus, it poses as a candidate for processing large data sets.
- It can be shown that the k-means algorithm minimizes the cost function

$$J(\theta, U) = \sum_{i=1}^{N} \sum_{j=1}^{m} u_{ij} \|x_i - \theta_j\|^2 \tag{7.1}$$

where $\theta = [\theta_1^T, \dots, \theta_m^T]^T$, $\|.\|$ stands for the Euclidean distance, and $u_{ij} = 1$ if x_i lies closest to θ_j; 0 otherwise. In words, *k-means minimizes the sum of the squared Euclidean distances of each data vector from its closest parameter vector.* When the data vectors of X form m compact clusters (with no significant difference in size), it is expected that J is minimized when each θ_j is placed (approximately) in the center of each cluster, provided that m is known. This is not necessarily the case when (a) the data vectors do not form compact clusters, or (b) their sizes differ significantly, or (c) the number of clusters, m, has not been estimated correctly.

- k-means cannot guarantee convergence to the global minimum of $J(\theta, U)$ (which, hopefully, corresponds to the best possible clustering). In other words, it returns clusterings corresponding to local minima of $J(\theta, U)$. Consequently, different initializations of the algorithm may lead to different final clusterings. Care must be taken in the initialization of θ_j (see the practical hints that follow). If the initial values for, say, m_1, of θ_j lie away from the region where the data vectors lie, they may never be updated. As a consequence, k-means algorithm will proceed as if there were only $m - m_1$ θ_j's.
- Accurate estimation of the number of clusters (representatives) is crucial for the algorithm, since a poor estimate will prevent it from unraveling the clustering structure of X. More specifically, if a larger number of representatives is used, it is likely that at least one "physical" cluster will be split into two or more. On the other hand, if a smaller number of representatives is used, two or more physical clusters are likely to be represented by a single representative, which in general will lie in a sparse region (with respect to the number of data points) between those clusters.
- The algorithm is sensitive to the presence of outliers (that is, points that lie away from almost all data vectors in X) and "noisy" data vectors. Such points are the result of a noisy process unrelated to the clustering structure of X. Since both outliers and noisy points are necessarily assigned to a cluster, they influence the respective mean representatives.
- k-means is suitable for real-valued data and, in principle, should *not* be used with discrete-valued data.

Practical Hints

- Assuming that m is fixed, and to increase our chances of obtaining a reliable clustering, we may run k-means several times, each time using different initial values for the representatives, and select the best possible clustering (according to J). Three simple methods for choosing initial values for θ_j's are (a) random initialization, (b) random selection of m data vectors from X as the initial estimates of θ_j's, and (c) utilization of the clustering output of a simpler (e.g., sequential) algorithm as input.
- Two simple ways to estimate m are:
  - Use the methodology described for the BSAS algorithm.
  - For each value of m, in a suitably chosen range $[m_{min}, m_{max}]$, run the k-means algorithm n_{run} times (each time using different initial values) and determine the clustering (among the n_{run} produced) that minimizes the cost function J. Let J_m be the value of J for the latter clustering. Plot J_m versus m and search for a significant local change (it appears as a significant "knee"). If such a knee occurs, its position indicates the desired number of clusters. Otherwise, it is an indication that there is no clustering structure (that contains compact clusters) in the data set.
- Two simple ways to deal with outliers are (a) to determine the points that lie at "large" distances from most of the data vectors in X and discard them, or (b) to run k-means and identify the clusters with very few elements. An alternative is to use algorithms that are less sensitive to outliers (this is the case with the PAM algorithm, discussed later).

Example 7.5.1. Generate and plot a data set, X_3, that consists of $N = 400$ 2-dimensional points. These points form four equally sized groups. Each group contains vectors that stem from Gaussian distributions with means $m_1 = [0, 0]^T$, $m_2 = [10, 0]$, $m_3 = [0, 9]$, and $m_4 = [9, 8]^T$, respectively, and respective covariance matrices

$$S_1 = I, \quad S_2 = \begin{bmatrix} 1 & 0.2 \\ 0.2 & 1.5 \end{bmatrix}, \quad S_3 = \begin{bmatrix} 1 & 0.4 \\ 0.4 & 1.1 \end{bmatrix}, \quad S_4 = \begin{bmatrix} 0.3 & 0.2 \\ 0.2 & 0.5 \end{bmatrix}$$

where I denotes the 2×2 identity matrix. Then do the following:

1. Apply the k-means algorithm on X_3 for $m = 4$. Using the *rand* built-in MATLAB function, initialize the parameter vectors θ_j's. Compare the final estimates of θ_j's with the mean values of the Gaussians, m_j's. Plot the parameter vectors θ_j's and the points of X_3. Use different colors for vectors of different clusters.
2. Repeat step 1 for $m = 3$.
3. Repeat step 1 for $m = 5$.
4. Repeat step 1, now with the θ_j initialized as follows: $\theta_1(0) = [-2.0, -2.0]^T$, $\theta_2(0) = [-2.1, -2.1]^T$, $\theta_3(0) = [-2.0, -2.2]^T$, $\theta_4(0) = [-2.1, -2.2]^T$.
5. Repeat step 1, now with θ_1, θ_2, and θ_3 initialized randomly as before and $\theta_4(0)$ set equal to $[20, 20]^T$.
6. Comment on the results.

Solution. To generate and plot X_3, work as in Example 7.4.2, but with different Gaussian means. The plot shows that X_3 contains four clearly separated compact clusters.

Proceed as follows:

Step 1. To apply the k-means algorithm for $m = 4$ and random initialization of θ_j's, type

```
m=4;
[l,N]=size(X3);
rand('seed',0)
theta_ini=rand(l,m);
[theta,bel,J]=k_means(X3,theta_ini);
```

To plot X_3, using different colors for points from different clusters, and θ_j's (Figure 7.4(a)), type

```
figure(1), hold on
figure(1), plot(X3(1,bel==1),X3(2,bel==1),'r.',...
X3(1,bel==2),X3(2,bel==2),'g*',X3(1,bel==3),X3(2,bel==3),'bo',...
X3(1,bel==4),X3(2,bel==4),'cx',X3(1,bel==5),X3(2,bel==5),'md',...
X3(1,bel==6),X3(2,bel==6),'yp',X3(1,bel==7),X3(2,bel==7),'ks')
figure(1), plot(theta(1,:),theta(2,:),'k+')
figure(1), axis equal
```

Step 2. Work as in step 1 for $m = 3$ (Figure 7.4(b)).

Step 3. Work as in step 1 for $m = 5$ (Figure 7.4(c)).

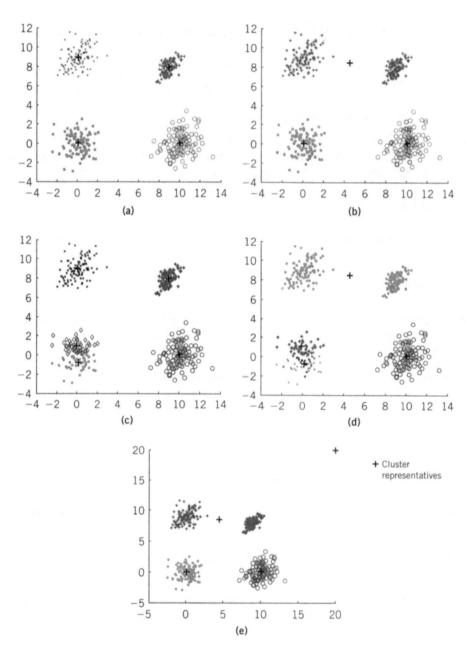

FIGURE 7.4

Clustering results obtained by the k-means algorithm in Example 7.5.1. Points from different clusters are indicated by different symbols and/or shading.

Step 4. Work as in step 1; for the initialization of θ_j's (see Figure 7.4(d)), type

```
theta_ini=[-2 -2; -2.1 -2.1; -2 -2.2; -2.1 -2.2]';
```

Step 5. Work as in step 1; for the initialization of θ_j's (see Figure 7.4(e)), type

```
theta_ini=rand(1,m);
theta_ini(:,m)=[20 20]';
```

Step 6. From the results obtained in step 1, observe that *k*-means has correctly identified the clusters underlying X_3. Moreover, the estimated θ_j's are in close agreement with the m_j's. In all other cases, however, *k*-means fails to identify the clustering structure of X_3. Specifically, in steps 2 and 3 it *imposes* clustering structures on X_3 with three and five clusters, respectively, although the true number of underlying clusters is four. In step 4, the bad initialization of θ_j's leads to a poor-quality clustering. Finally, in step 5, we have another bad initialization, where now a parameter vector (θ_4) is initialized away from the region where the vectors of X_3 lie. Consequently, it is never updated and the *k*-means proceeds as if $m = 3$. ∎

Exercise 7.5.1
Consider the data set X_2 generated in Exercise 7.4.1. Apply the *k*-means algorithm for $m = 2, 3$ and random initialization of θ_j's, and draw conclusions.

Hint
Observe that, although X_2 contains no clusters, the application of *k*-means imposes a clustering structure on it, as was the case in Example 7.5.1.

Table 7.1 Values of the Gaussian Means and Values of θ_j's for Data Sets in Examples 7.5.1 and 7.5.2

	Means (m_j's)	θ_j's (Example 7.5.1)	θ_j's (Example 7.5.2)
$j = 1$	0	0.073	0.308
	0	0.026	0.282
$j = 2$	9	8.955	8.778
	8	7.949	7.878
$j = 3$	10	10.035	9.700
	0	0.058	0.214
$j = 4$	0	0.075	0.290
	9	8.954	8.875

Example 7.5.2. Generate and plot a data set X_4, which consists of $N = 500$ 2-dimensional points. The first 400 are generated as in Example 7.5.1; the remaining 100 are generated from the uniform distribution in the region $[-2, 12] \times [-2, 12]$.

1. Apply the k-means algorithm on X_4 for $m = 4$. Initialize θ_j as in step 1 of Example 7.5.1.
2. Compare the estimates obtained for θ_j's with those obtained in step 1 of Example 7.5.1.

Solution. To generate the first 400 points of X_4, work as in Example 7.5.1. To generate the remaining 100, type

```
noise=rand(2,100)*14-2;
X4=[X4 noise];
```

Plot the data set, typing

```
figure(1), plot(X4(1,:),X4(2,:),'.b')
figure(1), axis equal
```

Clearly, the data points of X_4 form the four clusters, as it was the case with data set X_3 in Example 7.5.1. However, now they are in the presence of noise.

Step 1. To apply the k-means algorithm for $m = 4$, work as in step 1 of Example 7.5.1.

Step 2. Table 7.1 on the previous page shows the values of the Gaussian means as well as the estimates of θ_j's obtained here and in step 1 of Example 7.5.1. Clearly, the presence of noise degrades the quality of the θ_j's estimates obtained. ■

Example 7.5.3

1. Generate a data set X_5 consisting of 515 2-dimensional data points. The first 500 stem from the normal distribution with mean $m_1 = [0, 0]^T$; the remaining 15 stem from the normal distribution with mean $m_2 = [5, 5]^T$. The covariance matrices of the distributions are $S_1 = 1.5I$ and $S_2 = I$, respectively, where I is the 2×2 identity matrix.
2. Apply the k-means algorithm on X_5 for $m = 2$ and draw conclusions.

Solution. Take the following steps:

Step 1. To generate the data set X_5, type

```
randn('seed',0)
m=[0 0; 5 5];
S(:,:,1)=1.5*eye(2);
S(:,:,2)=eye(2);

n_points=[500 15];

X5=[];
```

```
for i=1:2
    X5=[X5; mvnrnd(m(i,:),S(:,:,i),n_points(i))];
end
X5=X5';
```

Plot the data set, typing

```
figure(1), plot(X5(1,:),X5(2,:),'.b')
figure(1), axis equal
```

The data set consists of two well-separated clusters of significantly unequal size.

Step 2. To apply the *k*-means algorithm and plot the results, work as in step 1 in Example 7.5.1. From the results obtained, we can see that the algorithm fails to identify successfully the two clusters. Specifically, it ends up with two clusters the first one of which is (roughly speaking) one half of the true "large" cluster underlying X_5; the second one contains the remaining points of the true "large" cluster as well as the points of the true "small" cluster. ■

Example 7.5.4

1. Generate and plot a data set X_6 consisting of *variously shaped non-overlapping clusters* in the 2-dimensional space. The first cluster consists of 600 points lying around the circle centered at (0, 0) and having radius equal to 6. The second cluster consists of 200 points lying around the ellipse centered at (0, 0) and having parameters $a = 3$ and $b = 1$. The third cluster consists of 200 points lying around the line segment with endpoints (8, −7) and (8, 7). The fourth cluster consists of 100 points lying around the semicircle centered at (13, 0) and having radius equal to 3 and y coordinates that are all negative.
2. Apply the *k*-means algorithm to data set X_6 and plot the clustering results. Draw conclusions.

Solution. Take the following steps:

Step 1. To generate the first cluster of points of the data set X_6, type

```
rand('seed',0)
n_points=[600 200 200 100]; %Points per cluster
noise=.5;
X6=[];
%Construction of the 1st cluster (circle, center (0,0), R=6)
R=6;
mini=-R;
maxi=R;
step=(maxi-mini)/(fix(n_points(1)/2)-1);
for x=mini:step:maxi
```

```
    y1=sqrt(R^2-x^2)+noise*(rand-.5);
    y2=-sqrt(R^2-x^2)+noise*(rand-.5);
    X6=[X6; x y1; x y2];
end
```

To generate the second cluster, type

```
%Construction of the 2nd cluster (ellipse, centered at (0,0), a=3,b=1))
a=3;
b=1;
mini=-a;
maxi=a;
step=(maxi-mini)/(fix(n_points(2)/2)-1);
for x=mini:step:maxi
    y1=b*sqrt(1-x^2/a^2)+noise*(rand-.5);
    y2=-b*sqrt(1-x^2/a^2)+noise*(rand-.5);
    X6=[X6; x y1; x y2];
end
```

To generate the third cluster, type

```
% Construction of the 3rd cluster (line segment, endpoints (8,-7), (8,7))
mini=-7;
maxi=7;
step=(maxi-mini)/(n_points(3)-1);
x_coord=8;
for y=mini:step:maxi
    X6=[X6; x_coord+noise*(rand-.5) y+noise*(rand-.5)];
end
```

Finally, to generate the fourth cluster, type

```
%Construction of the 4th cluster (semicircle, center (13,0), R=3;, y<0)
R=3;
x_center=13;
mini=x_center-R;
maxi=x_center+R;
step=(maxi-mini)/(n_points(4)-1);
for x=mini:step:maxi
    y=-sqrt(R^2-(x-x_center)^2)+noise*(rand-.5);
```

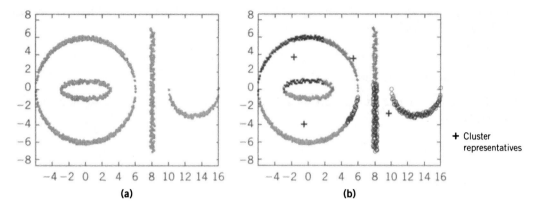

FIGURE 7.5

(a) Data set generated in Example 7.5.4. (b) Clustering result obtained by k-means. Different symbols and/or shades of gray indicate points from different clusters.

```
        X6=[X6; x y];
end
X6=X6';
```

Plot the data set (see Figure 7.5(a)), typing

```
figure(5), plot(X6(1,:),X6(2,:),'.b')
figure(5), axis equal
```

Step 2. Apply k-means on X_6 and plot the results, work as in step 1 of Example 7.5.1 (see Figure 7.5(b)). It is clear that, in principle, k-means is unable to handle cases where noncompact clusters underlie the data set. If there is an indication that such a clustering underlies in the data set, other clustering algorithms should be utilized, as will be discussed later on. ■

The next example demonstrates how k-means can estimate the number of clusters, m, and, based on that, estimate the clustering that best fits the data. Of course, it is assumed that only compact clusters are involved.

Example 7.5.5

1. Consider (and plot) the data set X_3 that was generated in Example 7.5.1. For each (integer) value of m in the range $[m_{min}, m_{max}]$, run the k-means algorithm n_{runs} times and from the n_{runs}-produced clusterings keep the one with the minimum value, J_m, of J. Plot J_m versus m. If the resulting graph exhibits a significant "knee," its position indicates the number of clusters that are likely to underlie X_3. Otherwise, we have an indication that X_3 likely possesses no clustering structure. Use $m_{min} = 2$, $m_{max} = 10$, and $n_{runs} = 10$.

2. Repeat step 1 for data sets X_4, X_1, and X_2, which were considered in Examples 7.5.2 and 7.4.2 and in Exercise 7.5.1, respectively.

3. Draw conclusions.

Solution. Take the following steps:

Step 1. To generate the data set X_3, work as in Example 7.5.1. To perform the procedure described before, type

```
[1,N]=size(X3);
nruns=10;
m_min=2;
m_max=10;
J_m=[];
for m=m_min:m_max
      J_temp_min=inf;
      for t=1:nruns
            rand('seed',100*t)
            theta_ini=rand(1,m);
            [theta,bel,J]=k_means(X3,theta_ini);
            if(J_temp_min>J)
                  J_temp_min=J;
            end
      end
      J_m=[J_m J_temp_min];
end
m=m_min:m_max;
figure(1), plot(m,J_m)
```

Step 2. Repeat step 1 for each of the three cases.

Step 3. The plots of J_m versus m for each case are shown in Figure 7.6. From the figure, it follows that for data set X_3 there exists a sharp knee at $m = 4$. This is an indication that the number of clusters underlying X_3 is four. A similar sharp knee is obtained at $m = 4$ for X_4, which is a noisy version of X_3. In the plot for X_1, where the clusters are not so clearly separated, a less-sharpened knee is encountered at $m = 4$. In all these cases, the methodology provides indications of the number of clusters underlying the data sets. However, in the plot of X_2, no significant knee is encountered, which is indicative of the fact that no clustering structure exists. ■

Partitioning Around Medoids Algorithm

The partitioning around medoids (PAM) algorithm resembles the k-means algorithm. The main difference is that the cluster representatives are restricted to be points of the data set X. For example, such a

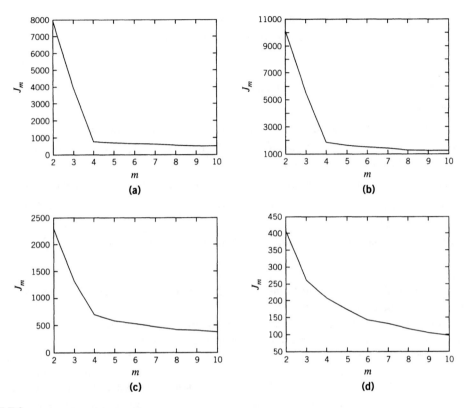

FIGURE 7.6

Plot of J_m versus m for the data sets in Example 7.5.5: (a) X_3 (sharp knee), (b) X_4 (sharp knee), (c) X_1 (less sharp knee), and (d) X_2 (no significant knee).

constraint may be imposed when the vectors of X have elements that take values from a discrete set, that is, from any subset of the set of integers [Theo 09, Section 11.2.2]. Once more, the number of (compact) clusters underlying the data set is assumed to be known. The set Θ of the vectors in X that best describe the clustering structure (also known as *medoids*) are determined via the minimization of a cost function $J(\Theta)$. This is defined as the summation, over all data vectors, of the distance between each data vector and its closest medoid.

The algorithm is iterative. It starts by assigning m randomly chosen vectors of X in Θ and then computing the corresponding value of J, $J(\Theta)$. At each iteration, all sets $\Theta_{ij} = (\Theta - \{x_i\}) \cup \{x_j\}, x_i \in \Theta$, and $x_j \in X - \Theta$ are considered. In words, Θ_{ij} results if x_i is removed from Θ and x_j is inserted. For each Θ_{ij}, the corresponding value of the cost function J, $J(\Theta_{ij})$, is computed, and the one (say Θ_{qr}) whose $J(\Theta_{qr})$ is minimum is selected. If $J(\Theta_{qr}) < J(\Theta)$, then Θ_{qr} replaces Θ and the procedure is repeated. Otherwise, the algorithm terminates. The ith cluster, C_i, formed by the algorithm is identified by those vectors that lie closer to the ith medoid (of the finally produced Θ) compared to the other medoids.

To apply the PAM algorithm on a data set, X, type

$$[bel, cost, w, a, cost] = k\_medoids(X, m, sed)$$

where

X is an $l \times N$ matrix whose columns contain the data vectors,

m is the number of clusters,

sed is a scalar integer used as the seed for the built-in MATLAB function *rand*,

bel is an N-dimensional vector whose ith element contains the label of the cluster where the ith data vector is assigned after the convergence of the algorithm,

$cost$ is the value of $J(\Theta)$ that corresponds to the (final) clustering generated by the algorithm,

w is an $l \times m$ matrix with columns that are the cluster representatives (medoids) obtained after the convergence of the algorithm,

a is an m-dimensional vector containing the indices of the data vectors used as medoids.

Remarks
- Like k-means, PAM imposes a clustering structure on the data set X, even though the data vectors in X do not exhibit a clustering structure.
- The algorithm is well suited to real-valued as well as discrete-valued data.
- PAM is less sensitive to the presence of noise compared to k-means.
- PAM is appropriate for small data sets. However, it is not efficient for large data sets since the computational cost per iteration is significant [Theo 09, Section 14.5.2]. To deal with this problem, other algorithms with the same philosophy, such as CLARA and CLARANS, that are less computationally intensive, have been developed. However, they cannot guarantee the convergence to a local minimum of the cost function $J(\Theta)$ [Theo 09, Section 14.5.2].

Example 7.5.6
1. Generate and plot the data set X_7, which consists of $N = 216$ 2-dimensional vectors. The first 100 stem from the Gaussian distribution with mean $m_1 = [0, 0]^T$; the next 100 stem from the Gaussian distribution with mean $m_2 = [13, 13]^T$. The other two groups of eight points stem from the Gaussian distributions with means $m_3 = [0, -40]^T$ and $m_4 = [-30, -30]^T$, respectively. The covariance matrices for all the Gaussians are equal to the 2×2 identity matrix. Obviously, the last two groups of points may be considered outliers.
2. Apply the k-means and the PAM algorithms on X_7, for $m = 2$. Plot the clustering in each case and comment on the results.

Solution. Take the following steps:

Step 1. To generate and plot X_7, type

```
randn('seed',0)
m=[0 0; 13 13; 0 -40; -30 -30]'; %means
[l,n_cl]=size(m);
```

```
S=eye(2); %covariance matrix
n_points=[100 100 8 8]; %points per distribution
X7=[];
for i=1:n_cl
    X7=[X7; mvnrnd(m(:,i)',S,n_points(i))];
end
X7=X7';
figure(1), plot(X7(1,:),X7(2,:),'.b')
```

Step 2. To apply the *k*-means algorithm on X_7, type

```
m=2;
[l,N]=size(X7);
rand('seed',0)
theta_ini=rand(l,m);
[l,m]=size(theta_ini);
[theta,bel,J]=k_means(X7,theta_ini);
```

Plot the data vectors, using different colors for points that stem from different clusters, working as in step 1 of Example 7.5.1 (see Figure 7.7(a)).

To apply the PAM algorithm on X_7, type

```
[l,N]=size(X7);
m=2;  %Number of clusters
sed=0;  %Seed for the rand function
[bel,cost,w,a]=k_medoids(X7,m,sed)
```

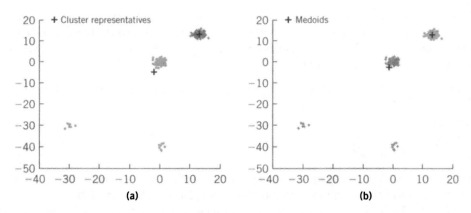

FIGURE 7.7

Clusterings generated by (a) *k*-means and (b) PAM when applied on the data set X_7, considered in Example 7.5.6.

Plot the clustering results, working as in step 1 of Example 7.5.1 (see Figure 7.7(b)).

The representative of the first cluster (C_1) computed by k-means is $\theta_1 = [-1.974, \ -4.789]^T$; the corresponding medoid computed by PAM is $[-1.3414, \ -2.6695]^T$. The second estimate is much closer than the first one to $[0, \ 0]^T$ (the actual mean of the main volume of the data vectors in cluster C_1). This is seen in Figure 7.7(b), which shows that the medoid that corresponds to the first cluster, C_1, remains close to C_1's main volume of data. This is because *the medoids are restricted to belong to X_7*. In other words, the medoid of C_1 is not allowed to move in the "empty region" between the first 100 points and the two groups of outliers. This restriction does not hold for k-means (see Figure 7.7(a)). As a consequence, in this case, the representative of C_1 is influenced by the outliers and thus is not a good representative of the main volume of the data vectors of C_1. ∎

Exercise 7.5.2
Repeat Example 7.5.1 for the PAM algorithm.

Exercise 7.5.3
Repeat Example 7.5.5 for the PAM algorithm.

Generalized Mixture Decomposition Algorithmic Scheme

This algorithm (GMDAS) relies on a probabilistic framework. Once more, the number of (compact) clusters, m, is assumed to be known. Specifically, the probability density function (pdf) $p(x)$ that describes the data set X is modeled by a weighted mixture of m Gaussian distributions, $p(x|j)$, $j = 1, \dots, m$, each associated with a cluster:

$$p(x) = \sum_{j=1}^{m} P_j p(x|j)$$

where $p(x|j)$ models the jth cluster. Each $p(x|j)$ is specified by its mean m_j and its covariance matrix S_j.

The aim of GMDAS is to adjust the parameters m_j and S_j of each $p(x|j)$, as well as the mixing parameters P_j (known also as *a priori probabilities*). To achieve this, it works iteratively. Some initial estimates of $m_j(0)$, $S_j(0)$, $P_j(0)$ are adopted for m_j, S_j, P_j, respectively, $j = 1, \dots, m$. Then, at each iteration, the algorithm updates, in order

- the a posteriori probabilities, $P(j|x_i)$ that x_i stems from the distribution that models the cluster C_j, $j = 1, \dots, m$, $i = 1, \dots, N$.
- the means m_j.
- the covariance matrices S_j.
- the a priori probabilities P_j.

GMDAS terminates when no significant change in the values of the parameters m_j, S_j, and P_j, $j = 1, \dots, m$, is encountered between two successive iterations [Theo 09, Section 14.2].

Note that the GMDAS does not specify explicitly a clustering on X. Instead, it gives (in addition to the estimates of the parameters of the Gaussian distributions) the a posteriori probabilities $P(j|x_i)$, $j = 1, \dots, m$, $i = 1, \dots, N$. However, if a specific clustering is required, we can define C_q as the cluster containing all x_i's for which $P(q|x_i)$ is maximum among all $P(j|x_i)$'s, $j = 1, \dots, m$.

To apply the GMDAS on a data set X, type

$$[ap, cp, mv, mc, iter, diffvec] = GMDAS(X, mv\_ini, mc\_ini, e, maxiter, sed)$$

where

X is an $l \times N$ matrix that contains the data vectors in its columns,

mv_ini is an $l \times m$ matrix whose columns contain the initial estimates of the means of the distributions,

mc_ini is an $l \times l \times m$ matrix whose $l \times l$ 2-dimensional "slices" are the initial estimates of the covariance matrices of the distributions,

e is the threshold involved in the terminating condition of the algorithm,[4]

$maxiter$ is the maximum number of iterations the algorithm is allowed to run,

sed is the seed used for the initialization of the built-in MATLAB function $rand$,

ap is an m-dimensional vector that contains the final estimates of the a priori probabilities,

cp is an $N \times m$ matrix with a (i, j) element that is the probability that the ith vector stems from the distribution that models the jth cluster,

mv and mc contain the final estimates of the means and the covariance matrices, respectively, and share a structure with mv_ini and mc_ini, respectively,

$iter$ is the number of iterations performed by the algorithm,

$diffvec$ is a vector with a tth coordinate that contains the sum of the absolute differences of the elements of the mv's, mc's, and the a priori probabilities between the tth and the $(t-1)$th iteration.

Remarks
- Like the k-means and PAM algorithms, GMDAS imposes a clustering structure on X, even if such a structure is not justified.
- The algorithm minimizes a suitably defined function and guarantees convergence to a local minimum of it.
- The algorithm is sensitive to outliers, because of the requirement that $\sum_{j=1}^{m} P(j|x_i) = 1$ for all x_i's.
- GMDAS is computationally demanding since, at each iteration, it requires the inversion of m covariance matrices. Two ways to deal with this problem are (a) to assume that the covariance matrices of all distributions are all equal and/or (b) to assume that each covariance matrix is diagonal.

Exercise 7.5.4
Repeat Example 7.5.1 using the GMDAS algorithm.

Hint
To obtain a (hard) clustering based on the returned a posteriori probabilities in the $N \times m$ matrix, cp, type

```
[qw,bel]=max(cp');
```

where bel contains the cluster labels of the data vectors.

---

[4]The algorithm terminates when the sum of the absolute differences of the mv's, mc's, and the a priori probabilities between two successive iterations is smaller than e.

Exercise 7.5.5

Repeat Example 7.5.5 using the GMDAS algorithm.

Hint

See the hint in the previous exercise to obtain a hard clustering from the a posteriori probabilities.

7.5.2 Nonhard Clustering Algorithms

In contrast to the previously examined algorithms, the algorithms in this category assume that each data vector may belong to (or may be compatible with) more than one cluster up to a certain number.

Fuzzy c-Means Algorithm

In the fuzzy c-means (FCM) algorithm each (compact) cluster is represented by a parameter vector θ_j, $j = 1, \ldots, m$. Also, it is assumed that a vector x_i of the data set X does *not necessarily* belong exclusively to a single cluster C_j. Rather, it may belong simultaneously to more than one cluster up to some degree. The variable u_{ij} quantifies the "grade of membership" of x_i in cluster C_j, and it is required that $u_{ij} \in [0, 1]$ and $\sum_{j=1}^{m} u_{ij} = 1$ for all x_i. Once more, the number of clusters, m, is assumed to be known.

The aim of FCM is to move each of the m available l-dimensional parameter vector (representative) θ_j, $j = 1, \ldots, m$, toward regions in the data space that are dense in data points. Finally, the algorithm involves an additional parameter q (>1) called the *fuzzifier*.

FCM is one of the most popular algorithms. It is iterative, starting with some initial estimates, $\theta_1(0), \ldots, \theta_m(0)$, for $\theta_1, \ldots, \theta_m$, respectively, and at each iteration t:

- The grade of membership, $u_{ij}(t-1)$, of the data vector x_i in cluster C_j, $i = 1, \ldots, N$, $j = 1, \ldots, m$, is computed, taking into account the (squared Euclidean) distances of x_i from all θ_j's, $j = 1, \ldots, m$.
- The representatives θ_j's are updated as the weighted means of all data vectors (each data vector x_i is weighted by $u_{ij}^q(t-1)$).

The algorithm terminates when the difference in the values of θ_j's between two successive iterations is small enough. It returns the values of the parameter vectors (representatives) θ_j's and the u_{ij}'s, $i = 1, \ldots, N, j = 1, \ldots, m$. If a hard clustering is required, we can define C_j as the cluster containing all x_i for which $u_{ij} > u_{ik}$, $k \neq j$.

To apply the FCM algorithm, type

$$[theta, U, obj\_fun] = fuzzy\_c\_means(X, m, q)$$

where

    X contains the data vectors in its columns,

    m is the number of clusters,

    q is the fuzzifier,

    theta contains the cluster representatives in its columns,

    U is an $N \times m$ matrix containing in its ith row the grade of membership of x_i in the m clusters,

    obj_fun is a vector whose tth coordinate is the value of the cost function, J, for the clustering produced at the tth iteration.

Remarks

- Like all previously presented cost function optimization algorithms, FCM imposes a clustering structure on X, even if this is not physically justified.
- FCM stems from the minimization of the cost function

$$J(\theta, U) = \sum_{i=1}^{N} \sum_{j=1}^{m} u_{ij}^q \|x_i - \theta_j\|^2$$

  where $\theta = [\theta_1^T, \dots, \theta_m^T]^T$, subject to the constraints $u_{ij} \in [0, 1]$ and $\sum_{j=1}^{m} u_{ij} = 1$. That is, $J(\theta, U)$ is a weighted sum of the distances of all x_i's from all θ_j's.
- The involvement of q is critical in fuzzy clustering. Typical values of q are in the range $[1.5, 3]$ [Theo 09, Section 14.3].
- The algorithm is sensitive in the presence of outliers because of the requirement that $\sum_{j=1}^{m} u_{ij} = 1$ for all x_i.
- Other fuzzy clustering algorithms where hypercurves of the second degree or hyperplanes are used as representatives have also been proposed. These are mainly useful in image processing applications [Theo 09, Section 14.3.2].

Exercise 7.5.6

Repeat Example 7.5.1, using FCM with $q = 2$.

Exercise 7.5.7

Repeat Example 7.5.3, using FCM with $q = 2$.

Exercise 7.5.8

Repeat Example 7.5.5, using FCM with $q = 2$.

The next exercise shows the influence of the fuzzifier parameter q in the resulting clustering.

Exercise 7.5.9

Apply the FCM on the data set X_3 generated in Example 7.5.1 for $q = 2$, $q = 10$, and $q = 25$. Define and plot the three corresponding hard clusterings, as discussed previously. Compare the u_{ij} parameters and the θ_j's for the three cases and draw conclusions.

Hint

For low values of q (e.g., $q = 2$), each data vector turns out to belong almost exclusively to a single cluster [Theo 09, Section 14.3]. That is, for each x_i, only a single u_{ij} has a very high value (above 90%) among $u_{i1}, \dots, u_{im}$. However, as q increases, the u_{ij}'s for each data vector x_i tend to become equal to $\frac{1}{m} = 0.25$. Especially in the case where $q = 25$, this leads to a clustering that does not correspond to the true underlying clustering structure of X_3.

The next example shows the effect of outliers on the performance of the FCM.

Example 7.5.7. Apply the FCM algorithm on the data set X_7 generated in Example 7.5.6. Produce a hard clustering, as previously discussed, and plot the results. Comment on the grade of memberships of the data points in the two obtained clusters. Compare the resulting representatives with those obtained from the application of k-means and PAM on X_7.

Solution. To apply the FCM algorithm on X_7, type

```
[theta,U,obj_fun] = fuzzy_c_means(X7,m,q)
```

To obtain a hard clustering using U, type

```
[qw,bel]=max(U');
```

where *bel* contains the cluster labels of the data vectors.

Plot the clustering results, using different symbols and colors for vectors that belong to different clusters, as in step 1 of Example 7.5.1 (see Figure 7.8).

Observation of the grade of memberships reveals that

- For the first 100 points, the grade of memberships in cluster C_1 is significantly higher ($>89.4\%$) than that in cluster C_2 ($<10.6\%$) (see Figure 7.8).
- For the next 100 points, the grade of memberships in cluster C_2 is significantly higher ($>97.2\%$) than that in cluster C_1 ($<2.8\%$).
- For the last 16 points (outliers), the grade of memberships in clusters C_1 and C_2 are significant ($>66.62\%$ for C_1 and $>30.10\%$ for C_2), so their effect on the computation of both θ_1 and θ_2 is not negligible.

Comparing the results shown in Figure 7.8 with those in Figure 7.7, we observe that the estimates of θ_2 (the representative of the upper right cluster) are better for k-means and PAM than for FCM (this is because the outliers have no effect on the estimation of θ_2 in k-means and PAM, which is not the case in FCM), and that the estimates of θ_1 (the representative of the other cluster) are better in PAM and FCM than in k-means, in the sense that in PAM and FCM θ_1 remains close to the main volume of the data set.

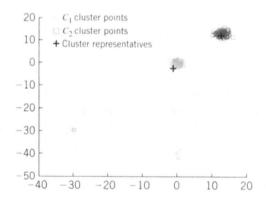

FIGURE 7.8

Clustering obtained by FCM on data set X_7 in Example 7.5.7. The three lower left groups of points are from cluster C_1; the upper right group of points constitute cluster C_2.

This happens because in FCM the outliers contribute to the estimation of θ_1 by (at least) 30%, while in k-means they contribute by 100% (since in the hard clustering case a vector belongs exclusively (100%) to a single cluster). ■

Possibilistic c-Means Algorithm

This algorithm (known as PCM) is also appropriate for unraveling compact clusters. The framework here is similar to the one used in FCM: Each data vector x_i is associated with a cluster C_j via a scalar u_{ij}. However, the constraint that all u_{ij}'s for a given x_i sum up to 1 is removed (it is only required that they lie in the interval $[0, 1]$). As a consequence, the u_{ij}'s (for a given x_i) are not interrelated anymore and they cannot be interpreted as "grade of membership" of vector x_i in cluster C_j, since this term implies that the summation of u_{ij}'s for each x_i should be constant. Rather, u_{ij} is interpreted as the "degree of compatibility" between x_i and C_j. The degree of compatibility between x_i and C_j is independent of that between x_i and the remaining clusters.

As with FCM, a parameter q (> 1) is involved in PCM. However it does not act as a fuzzifier as it was the case in FCM. Also, in contrast to FCM, PCM is less sensitive in knowing the "exact" number of clusters. Rather, an overestimated value of m can be used (see also the remarks given below). A set of parameters $\eta_j, j = 1, \ldots, m$, each one corresponding to a cluster, is also required (loosely speaking, they are estimates of the "size" of the cluster [Theo 09, Section 14.4]). Like k-means and FCM, PCM's goal is to move the θ_j's to regions of space that are dense in data points.

PCM is iterative. It starts with some initial estimates, $\theta_1(0), \ldots, \theta_m(0)$, for $\theta_1, \ldots, \theta_m$, respectively, and at each iteration,

- The "degree of compatibility", $u_{ij}(t-1)$, of the data vector x_i to cluster $C_j, i = 1, \ldots, N, j = 1, \ldots, m$, is computed, taking into account the (squared Euclidean) distance of x_i from θ_j and the parameter η_j.
- The representatives, θ_j's, are updated, as in FCM, as the weighted means of all data vectors (each data vector x_i is weighted by $u_{ij}^q(t-1)$).

The algorithm terminates when the difference in the values of θ_j's between two successive iterations is small enough. It returns the values of the parameter vectors (representatives) θ_j's and the "compatibility coefficients" u_{ij}'s, $i = 1, \ldots, N, j = 1, \ldots, m$.

To apply PCM on a data set X, type

$$[U, theta] = possibi(X, m, eta, q, sed, init\_proc, e\_thres)$$

where

X contains the data vectors in its columns,

m is the number of clusters,

eta is an m-dimensional array whose jth coordinate is the η_j parameter for the cluster C_j,

q is the "q" parameter of the algorithm,

sed is a scalar integer used as the seed for the built-in MATLAB function *rand*,

init_proc is an integer taking values 1, 2, or 3, with 1 corresponding to the *rand_init* initialization procedure, which chooses randomly m vectors from the smallest hyper-rectangular that contains all vectors of X and its sides are parallel to the axes; 2 corresponding to *rand_data_init*, which chooses randomly m among the N vectors of X; and 3 corresponding to *distant_init*, which chooses the m vectors of X that are "most distant" from each other. (The latter procedure achieves, in general, better initialization at the cost of increased computations),

e_thres is the threshold involved in the terminating condition of the algorithm,

U is an $N \times m$ matrix with the (i, j) element that denotes the "degree of compatibility" of the ith data vector with the jth cluster (after the convergence of the algorithm),

theta is an $l \times m$ matrix, each column of which corresponds to a cluster representative (after the convergence of the algorithm).

Remarks

- In contrast to the previous algorithms discussed in this section, PCM does not impose a clustering structure on X. This means that when the number of representatives it uses is higher than the "true" number of clusters, after convergence some θ_j's will (almost) coincide, and if the algorithm starts from a proper initialization point, then hopefully all clusters (dense regions) will be represented by one θ_j while some of them may be represented by two or more (almost) identical θ_j's. On the other hand, when the number of representatives, m, is less than the true number of clusters, say k, then after convergence the algorithm will potentially recover m out of k clusters. As a consequence, the case where a representative lies in a sparse region between clusters, is not encountered.
- Like the previous algorithms, PCM results from the minimization of a suitably defined cost function. Alternative PCM schemes have also been proposed [Theo 09, Section 14.4].
- PCM is sensitive to the initial θ_j values and the estimates of η_j's. One way to estimate the η_j values, under the assumption that X does not contain many outliers, is to run the FCM algorithm and, after its convergence, estimate each η_j as a (weighted) average of the dissimilarities between x_i's and θ_j's, as the latter is computed by FCM. Then, the estimates of θ_j's produced by FCM may be used to initialize PCM [Theo 09, Section 14.4].

Exercise 7.5.10

1. Apply the PCM algorithm on the data set X_3 generated in Example 7.5.1 for $m = 4$, $m = 6$, and $m = 3$. Use $q = 2$ and $\eta_j = 4$, $j = 1, \ldots, m$, and initialize the θ_j's using the m vectors of X that are "most distant" from each other (use the *distant_init* procedure). Compare the estimated θ_j values with the true ones and comment on the results.
2. Repeat step 1, using the *rand_init* and *rand_data_init* MATLAB functions for the initialization of θ_j's for $m = 4$.
3. Draw conclusions.

Note that in the case where the true number of clusters is overestimated (in our case for $m = 6$), the PCM successfully estimates the four θ_j's that correspond to the (true) four underlying clusters in X_3 (some of the estimates coincide). In the opposite case, PCM successfully estimates three out of the true four θ_j's. Finally, poor initialization of the PCM may lead to poor clustering results.

Exercise 7.5.11

Apply PCM on the data set X_5 generated in Example 7.5.3 for $m = 2$, $q = 2$. Use the *distant_init* procedure for the θ_j initialization and set $\eta_j = 4$, $j = 1, \ldots, m$.

Hint

Note that the PCM fails to identify the second (small) cluster.

7.6 MISCELLANEOUS CLUSTERING ALGORITHMS

In this section, we consider algorithms that produce a single clustering and do not fall into either the sequential or the cost function optimization category.

Competitive Leaky Learning Algorithm

Competitive leaky learning (LLA) is an algorithm suitable for unraveling compact clusters. Once again, the number of clusters, m, that underlie the data set X, is assumed to be known. The aim of LLA is to move m l-dimensional parameter vectors, w_j's, $j = 1, \ldots, m$,[5] to regions that are "dense" in points of X. Each parameter vector represents one "dense" region (cluster). The strategy is that of *competition* among w_j's.

The LLA algorithm is iterative. It starts with some initial estimates $w_1(0), \ldots, w_m(0)$, for $w_1, \ldots, w_m$, respectively. At each iteration, t, a vector x is presented to the algorithm and the $w_j(t-1)$ that is closer to x than any other $w_k(t-1), k = 1, \ldots, m$ ($k \neq j$) is identified. $w_j(t-1)$ is the *winner* in the competition on x, and $w_j(t)$ is computed as

$$w_j(t) = w_j(t-1) + \eta_w(x - w_j(t-1)) \tag{7.2}$$

The remaining $w_k(t)$'s (*losers*) are computed as

$$w_k(t) = w_k(t-1) + \eta_l(x - w_k(t-1)), \quad k \neq j \tag{7.3}$$

with $\eta_w \gg \eta_l$. The $C_j(t)$ cluster, of the clustering formed at the tth iteration, contains all $x \in X$ for which $w_j(t)$ is closer compared to any other representative, $j = 1, \ldots, m$.

Care is taken to ensure that, in one *epoch*, which consists of N successive iterations, all data vectors will be considered by LLA once. Convergence is achieved when the values of w_j's remain almost unaltered between two successive epochs or the maximum number of epochs has been reached. The outputs are the estimated values of w_j's and the corresponding clustering where each cluster C_j consists of all vectors x of X that lie closer to w_j than any other representative.

To apply LLA on a data set X, type

$$[w, bel, epoch] = LLA(X, w\_ini, m, eta\_vec, sed, max\_epoch, e\_thres, init\_proc)$$

where

    X contains the data vectors in its columns,

    w_ini contains the initial estimates of the representatives in its columns,

    m is the number of representatives (utilized only when w_ini is empty),

    eta_vec is a two-dimensional vector containing the η_w and η_l parameters of the algorithm,

    sed is the "seed" for the built-in MATLAB function *rand*,

    max_epoch is the maximum number of epochs the algorithm is allowed to run,

---

[5]We use w_j instead of θ_j to comply with the notation usually adopted for the competitive schemes.

e_thres is a (scalar) parameter used in the termination condition,

init_proc is defined as in PCM,

w contains the final estimates of the representatives in its columns,

bel is an N-dimensional vector whose ith element contains the index of the representative that lies closest to x_i,

epoch is the number of epochs performed by the algorithm in order to converge.

Remarks

- The learning-rate parameters η_w and η_l are chosen in the range [0, 1] with $\eta_w \gg \eta_l$.
- Geometrically speaking, all representatives move toward the data vector x currently considered by the algorithm. However, the losers move at a much slower rate than the winner, as implied by the choice of η_w and η_l.
- LLA "imposes" a clustering structure on X, as is the case with most of the algorithms that have been discussed.
- LLA is not overly sensitive to the initialization of the w_j's because, even if a w_j initially lies away from the region where the data vectors lie, it will gradually move to that region given Eq. (7.3). Therefore, it is likely to win at a given x at some iteration.
- For $\eta_l = 0$, the *basic competitive learning scheme* is obtained. In this case, only the winner is updated (i.e., moves toward the data vector x at hand), while the values of the other representatives remain unaltered. This makes the algorithm sensitive to poor initialization since if a w_j initially lies away from the region where the data vectors lie, it is likely to lose in all competitions for the vectors of X. In this case, there is no way it can move close to the region where the data lie and so it has not the ability to represent a cluster physically formed in X (such a w_j is also called a *dead* representative).
- Other competitive learning algorithms have been proposed in the literature. In close affinity with them is the *self-organizing map* (SOM) scheme. However, in SOMs the representatives w_j's are interrelated [Theo 09, Section 15.3].

Exercise 7.6.1

1. Apply LLA on the data set X_3 generated in Example 7.5.1, for $m = 4$, $m = 3$, and $m = 6$. Use $\eta_w = 0.1$ and $\eta_l = 0.0001$, *max_epoch* = 100, and *e_thres* = 0.0001. Use the *distant_init* MATLAB function for the w_j initialization. In each case, plot the data points (all with the same color) as well as the w_j's (final estimates).
2. Repeat step 1 for $m = 4$, where now $\eta_l = 0.01$.

   Note that, in the case where the number of representatives is underestimated or overestimated, the resulting clustering does not correspond to the actual clustering structure of the points in X_3. In addition, if η_l is not much smaller than η_w, the algorithm gives poor results, even if m is equal to the true number of clusters.

Exercise 7.6.2

Apply LLA on the data set X_5 generated in Example 7.5.3, for $m = 2$, adopting the parameter values used in Exercise 7.6.1.

Hint

Note that it succeeds in identifying the two clusters even though they have significantly different sizes, in contrast to, say, k-means and FCM.

Exercise 7.6.3

Apply LLA on the data set X_3 generated in Example 7.5.1, for $m = 4$, where now the w_j's are initialized as $w_1(0) = [5.5, 4.5]^T$, $w_2(0) = [4.5, 5.5]^T$, $w_3 = [5, 5]^T$, and $w_4 = [50, 50]^T$. Use $\eta_w = 0.1$ and (a) $\eta_l = 0.0001$ and (b) $\eta_l = 0$ (basic competitive learning scheme).

Note that for $\eta_l = 0.0001$, all representatives represent clusters in X_3, although the representative w_4 has been initialized away from the region where the points of X_3 lie. For $\eta_l = 0$, however, w_4 does not change.

Valley-Seeking Clustering Algorithm

According to this method (known as VS), the clusters are considered as peaks of the pdf, $p(x)$, that describes X, separated by valleys. In contrast to the algorithms considered so far, no representatives (parameter vectors) are used here. Instead, clustering is based on the *local region*, $V(x)$, around each data vector $x \in X$. The latter is defined as the set of vectors in X (excluding x) that lie at a distance less than a from x, where a is a user-defined parameter. As a distance measure, the squared Euclidean may be used (other distances may be used as well). VS also requires an (overestimated) value of the number of clusters, m.

The algorithm is iterative, starting with an initial assignment of the vectors of X to the m clusters; at each epoch (N successive iterations) all data vectors are presented once. During the tth epoch and for each x_i in X, $i = 1, \ldots, N$, the region $V(x_i)$ is determined and the cluster where most of the data vectors in $V(x_i)$ belong is identified and stored. After all data vectors have been presented (during the tth epoch), reclustering takes place and each x_i is now assigned to the cluster that has the largest number of points in $V(x_i)$. The algorithm terminates when no reclustering occurs between two successive epochs.

To apply the VS algorithm on a data set X, type

$$[bel, iter] = valley\_seeking(X, a, bel\_ini, max\_iter)$$

where

X contains the data vectors in its columns,

a is the parameter that specifies the size of the neighborhood $V(x)$ of a data point x,

bel_ini is an N-dimensional vector whose ith coordinate contains the label of the cluster where the x_i vector is initially assigned,

max_iter is the maximum allowable number of iterations,

bel is an N-dimensional vector having the same structure as bel_ini, described earlier and contains the cluster labels of x_i's after convergence,

$iter$ is the number of iterations performed until convergence is achieved.

Remarks

- In certain cases, VS may recover noncompact clusters.
- The algorithm is sensitive to the choice of a. One way to face this sensitivity is to run the algorithm for several values of a and carefully interpret the results.
- The algorithm is sensitive to the initial assignment of the data vectors to clusters. Poor initialization leads to poor clustering results. One solution is to run another algorithm (e.g., a sequential algorithm) and use the resulting clustering as the initial one for VS.
- VS is a *mode-seeking* algorithm. That is, if more than the actual number of clusters in X are used initially, then in principle, after convergence, some of them will become empty. This implies that VS does not impose a clustering structure on X. In this sense, it resembles PCM.

Exercise 7.6.4

Consider the data set X_3 generated in Example 7.5.1. Adopt the squared Euclidean distance and apply the VS algorithm on it for $a = 1^2, 1.5^2, 2^2, \ldots, 8^2$. For the definition of the initial clustering
(a) use $m = 7$ clusters with random initialization,
and
(b) the output of the BSAS algorithm with $\Theta = 2.5$. For each case, plot the clustering result and draw conclusions.

Hint

To generate a random initial clustering, type

```
m=7;
rand('seed',0)
bel_ini= fix(m*rand(1,N))+1;
```

To generate initial clustering using the BSAS algorithm, type

```
theta=2.5;
q=N;
order=[];
[bel_ini, m]=BSAS(X3,theta,q,order);
```

To apply VS on X_3 and to plot the clustering results, type

```
max_iter=50;
for it=1:.5:8
    a=it^2;
    [bel,iter]=valley_seeking(X3,a,bel_ini,max_iter);
    % Plotting of the points of the clusters
    figure(11), close
    figure(11), plot(X3(1,bel==1),X3(2,bel==1),'r.',....
    X3(1,bel==2),X3(2,bel==2),'g*',X3(1,bel==3),X3(2,bel==3),'bo',....
    X3(1,bel==4),X3(2,bel==4),'cx',X3(1,bel==5),X3(2,bel==5),'md',....
    X3(1,bel==6),X3(2,bel==6),'yp',X3(1,bel==7),X3(2,bel==7),'ks')
end
```

VS with random initialization fails to identify the clustering structure of X_3; the opposite holds true when the initialization stems from BSAS. This happens because, in the case where Θ is "small," BSAS tends to generate several small compact clusters with no significant overlap. The application of VS on such a clustering will potentially merge the small neighboring clusters that are parts of a larger physical cluster. In contrast, with random initialization, the initial clustering is likely to have several largely overlapping clusters, which are more difficult to handle (in this case, each $V(x_i)$ is likely to contain points from all clusters).

Note that not all values of a are appropriate for unraveling the true clustering structure of X_3.

Exercise 7.6.5

Repeat Exercise 7.6.4 for the data set X_5 generated in Example 7.5.3.

Hint

Note that VS succeeds in identifying the two clusters of significantly different size.

Example 7.6.1

1. Generate and plot the data set X_8, which contains 650 2-dimensional data vectors. The first 300 lie around the semicircle with radius $r = 6$, which is centered at $(-15, 0)$, and they have their second coordinate positive. The next 200 lie around the line segment with endpoints $(10, -7)$ and $(10, 7)$. The next 100 lie around the semicircle with radius $r = 3$, which is centered at $(21, 0)$, and have their second coordinate negative. Finally, the last 50 points belong to the spiral of Archimedes and are defined as $(x, y) = (a_{sp}\theta\cos(\theta), a_{sp}\theta\sin(\theta))$, where $a_{sp} = 0.2$ (a user-defined parameter) and $\theta = \pi, \pi + s, \pi + 2s, \ldots, 6\pi$, where $s = 5\pi/49$.

2. Adopt the squared Euclidean distance and apply the VS algorithm on X_8 for $a = 1^2, 1.5^2, 2^2, \ldots, 8^2$. For the definition of the initial clustering, use the output of the BSAS algorithm with $\Theta = 2.5$. Draw your conclusions.

3. Consider the result of VS if the semicircle in X_8, which corresponds to the third group of points, was centered at $(12, 0)$.

Solution. Take the following steps:

Step 1. To generate the first group of points in X_8, type

```
rand('seed',0)
n_points=[300 200 100 50]; %No of points in the first 3 clusters
noise=.5;
X8=[];
%Construction of the 1st cluster (circle, center (-15,0), R=6)
R=6;
x_center1=-15;
y_center1=0;
mini=x_center1-R;
maxi=x_center1+R;
step=(maxi-mini)/(n_points(1)-1);
for x=mini:step:maxi
    y1=y_center1 + sqrt(R^2-(x-x_center1)^2)+noise*(rand-.5);
    X8=[X8; x y1];
end
```

To generate the second group, type

```
%Construction of the 2nd cluster (line segment, endpoints (10,-7), (10,7))
mini=-7;
maxi=7;
step=(maxi-mini)/(n_points(2)-1);
```

```
x_coord=10;
for y=mini:step:maxi
    X8=[X8; x_coord+noise*(rand-.5) y+noise*(rand-.5)];
end
```

To generate the third group, type

```
%Construction of the 3rd cluster (semicircle, center (21,0), R=3;, y<0)
R=3;
x_center=21;
y_center=0;
mini=x_center-R;
maxi=x_center+R;
step=(maxi-mini)/(n_points(3)-1);

for x=mini:step:maxi
    y=y_center - sqrt(R^2-(x-x_center)^2)+noise*(rand-.5);
    X8=[X8; x y];
end
```

Finally, to generate the fourth group, type

```
% Construction of the fourth cluster (archimidis spiral)
asp=0.2;
step=(5*pi)/(n_points(4)-1);
count=0;
x_tot=[];
y_tot=[];
for theta=pi:step:6*pi
    count=count+1;
    r=asp*theta;
    x_tot=[x_tot; r*cos(theta)];
    y_tot=[y_tot; r*sin(theta)];
end
X8=[X8; x_tot y_tot];
```

Step 2. For the values of a in the range $[4^2, 6^2]$, VS succeeds in identifying the clusters of X_8 (see Figure 7.9(a)).

Step 3. For the alternative scenario (Figure 7.9(b)), VS fails to do so (identifying the two rightmost clusters as a single cluster). Thus, we conclude that VS can deal with clusters of arbitrary shape only under the assumption that they are well separated from each other. ∎

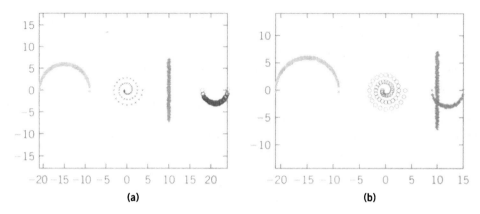

FIGURE 7.9

Clusterings produced by the VS algorithm in Example 7.6.1: (a) step 2 (four clusters); (b) step 3 (three clusters). Points from different clusters are denoted by different symbols/shades of gray.

Spectral Clustering

Spectral clustering algorithms utilize graph theory concepts and certain optimization criteria that stem from matrix theory.[6] More specifically, the algorithms of this kind construct a weighted graph, G, where (a) each vertex, v_i, corresponds to a point, x_i, of the data set X, and subsequently (b) associate a weight w_{ij} with the edge e_{ij} that connects the two vertices, v_i and v_j. The weight w_{ij} is an indication of the "distance" between the corresponding data points x_i and x_j. The aim is to cut the graph into m disconnected components via the optimization of a criterion. These components identify the clusters underlying X. In the sequel, we consider the 2-cluster case (that is, $m = 2$); the criterion to be optimized is the so-called *normalized cut*, or *Ncut* [Theo 09, Section 15.2.4].

Before describing the algorithm, some definitions are in order. Among the various ways of defining the weights of the graph, a common one is

$$w_{ij} = \begin{cases} \exp\left(-\frac{||x_i - x_j||^2}{2\sigma^2}\right), & \text{if } ||x_i - x_j|| < e \\ 0, & \text{otherwise} \end{cases} \tag{7.4}$$

where e and σ^2 are user-defined parameters and $|| \cdot ||$ denotes the Euclidean distance.

In words, given a data point x_i, for all points x_j that lie from x_i a distance greater than e, we assign $w_{ij} = 0$. For the x_j points whose distance from x_i is less than e, the weight w_{ij} decreases as the distance between x_i and x_j increases. Thus, the weights encode information related to the mutual distances among the points of X.

Once the weighted graph has been formed, the goal is to divide (cut) it into two parts, say A and B, so that the points in A and B have the *least similarity* compared to any other bipartitioning. Similarity

---

[6]Other algorithms that use graph theory alone (without using matrix theory criteria) can be found in [Theo 09, Section 15.2].

in this case is quantified in terms of the distance-related weights. According to the normalized cut criterion, separation of the two parts of the graph (clusters) takes place so that the edges connecting the two parts have minimum sum of weights (indicating clusters separated as much as possible according to the criterion used). The normalized cut criterion also considers the "volume" of the clusters and takes care to avoid forming small isolated clusters.

The respective optimization turns out to be NP-hard. This is alleviated by slightly reformulating the problem, which then becomes an eigenvalue-eigenvector problem of the so-called Laplacian matrix of the graph. The Laplacian matrix is directly related to the weights associated with the graph; that is, it encodes the distance information among the points to be clustered [Theo 09, Section 15.2.4].

To apply the described algorithm on a data set, X, type

$$bel = spectral\_Ncut2(X, e, sigma2)$$

where

X contains the data vectors in its columns,

e is the parameter that defines the size of the neighborhood around each vector,

$sigma2$ is a user-defined parameter that controls the width of the Gaussian function in Eq. (7.4),

bel is an N-dimensional vector whose ith element contains the label of the cluster to which the ith data vector is assigned.

Remarks
- Spectral clustering algorithms impose a clustering structure on X.
- In principle, spectral clustering algorithms are able to recover clusters of various shapes.
- Other spectral clustering algorithms that stem from the optimization of criteria such as the so-called *ratiocut* have been proposed [Theo 09, Section 15.2.4]. A discussion on the quality of the clusterings that result from the spectral clustering method can be found in [Guat 98].
- In the case where more than two clusters are expected, the previous scheme can be used hierarchically. That is, at each step each resulting cluster is further partitioned into two clusters [Shi 00]. A different approach can be found in [Luxb 07].

Exercise 7.6.6
Consider the data set X_2 from Exercise 7.4.1 and apply the previous algorithm using $e = 2$ and $sigma2 = 2$. Draw conclusions.

Hint
Note that the algorithm imposes a clustering structure on X_2, although X_2 does not possess a clustering structure.

Exercise 7.6.7
1. Generate and plot the data set X_9, which consists of 200 2-dimensional vectors. The first 100 stem from the Gaussian distribution with mean $[0, 0]^T$; the remaining points stem from the Gaussian distribution with mean $[5, 5]^T$. Both distributions share the identity covariance matrix.
2. Apply the previous spectral clustering algorithm on X_9 using $e = 2$ and $sigma2 = 2$. Draw conclusions.

Hint
Note that the algorithm correctly identifies the clusters in X_9.

Example 7.6.2. Do the following:

1. Generate and plot the data set X_{10} consisting of 400 data points lying around two circles. Specifically, the first 200 points lie around the circle with radius $r_1 = 3$, which is centered at $(0,0)$; the remaining points lie around the circle with radius $r_2 = 6$, which is centered at $(1,1)$.
2. Apply the spectral clustering algorithm on X_{10} for $e = 1.5$ and $sigma2 = 2$ and plot the results.
3. Repeat this for $e = 3$. Comment on the results.

Solution. Take the following steps:

Step 1. To generate the data set X_{10}, type

```
rand('seed',0)
R1=3; %Radius of the 1st circle
R2=6; %Radius of the 2nd circle
center=[0 0; 1 1]'; % Centers of the circles (in columns)
n_points=[200 200]; %Number of points per cluster
step1=2*R1/(n_points(1)/2-1);
step2=2*R2/(n_points(2)/2-1);
%Points around the first circle
X10=[];
for x=-R1+center(1,1):step1:R1+center(1,1)
    y=sqrt(R1^2-(x-center(1,1))^2);
    X10=[X10; x center(2,1)+y+rand-.5; x center(2,1)-y+rand-.5];
end
%Points around the second circle
for x=-R2+center(1,2):step2:R2+center(1,2)
    y=sqrt(R2^2-(x-center(1,2))^2);
    X10=[X10; x center(2,2)+y+rand-.5; x center(2,2)-y+rand-.5];
end
```

Plot the data set by typing

```
X10=X10';
[l,N]=size(X10)
figure(1), plot(X10(1,:),X10(2,:),'k.')
figure(1), axis equal
```

Step 2. To apply the spectral clustering algorithm, type

```
e=1.5;     %Thershold for the distance in the definition of W
sigma2=2; %The sigma^2 in the exponential in the definition of W
bel=spectral_Ncut2(X10,e,sigma2);
```

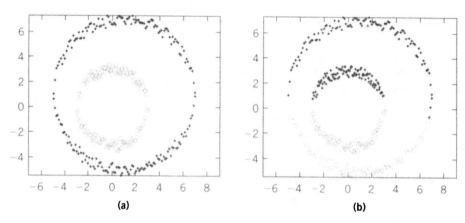

FIGURE 7.10

Clustering resulting from application of the spectral clustering algorithm on data set X_{10} in Example 7.6.2 when (a) $e = 1.5$ and (b) $e = 3$. Points assigned in the same cluster are denoted by the same symbol. Observe the sensitivity in the choice of parameters.

Plot the clustering results (see Figure 7.10(a)), typing

```
figure(2),plot(X10(1,bel==0),X10(2,bel==0),'ro',...
X10(1,bel==1),X10(2,bel==1),'b*')
figure(2), axis equal
```

Step 3. Work as in step 2, setting *e* equal to 3 (Figure 7.10(b)). Comparing Figures 7.10(a) and 7.10(b), note the influence of the parameter values on the quality of the resulting clustering. Provide a physical explanation for that. ■

Exercise 7.6.8
Repeat Example 7.6.2 for the case where the second circle is centered at (3,3), for various values of *e* and *sigma*2. Comment on the results.

Hint
Note that, in this case, the algorithm fails to identify the two (overlapping) clusters.

7.7 HIERARCHICAL CLUSTERING ALGORITHMS

In contrast to the clustering algorithms discussed so far, which return a *single* clustering, the algorithms in this section return a *hierarchy* of N *nested* clusterings, where N is the number of data points in X. A clustering $\Re$, consisting of k clusters, is said to be *nested* in the clustering $\Re'$, containing $r\ (< k)$ clusters, if each cluster in $\Re$ is a subset of a cluster in $\Re'$. For example, the clustering $\Re_1 = \{\{x_1, x_2\}, \{x_3\}, \{x_4, x_5\}\}$ is nested in the clustering $\Re_2 = \{\{x_1, x_2, x_3\}, \{x_4, x_5\}\}$, but $\Re_1$ is not nested in $\Re_3 = \{\{x_1, x_3\}, \{x_2\}, \{x_4, x_5\}\}$ or in $\Re_4 = \{\{x_1, x_3, x_4\}, \{x_2, x_5\}\}$.

The two main categories of hierarchical clustering algorithms are:

- *Agglomerative.* Here the initial clustering $\Re_0$ consists of N clusters, each containing a single element of X. The clustering $\Re_1$, produced at the next step, contains $N - 1$ clusters and $\Re_0$ is nested in it. Finally, the $\Re_{N-1}$ clustering is obtained, which contains a single cluster (the whole data set X).
- *Divisive.* Here the reverse path is followed. The initial cluster $\Re_0$ consists of a single cluster (the whole data set X). In the next step the clustering $\Re_1$ is produced, which consists of two clusters and is nested in $\Re_0$. Finally, the $\Re_{N-1}$ clustering is obtained, which consists of N clusters, each containing a single element of X.

In the sequel, we consider only the agglomerative clustering algorithms. Specifically, (a) the generalized agglomerative algorithmic scheme and (b) specific algorithms that stem from it are discussed.

7.7.1 Generalized Agglomerative Scheme

This scheme (known as GAS) starts with the clustering $\Re_0$, which consists of N clusters, each containing a single data vector. The clustering $\Re_t$ (at the tth level of the clustering hierarchy) consists of (a) the cluster formed by the merging of the two "most similar" ("less distant") clusters of the $\Re_{t-1}$ clustering, and (b) all the remaining clusters of the $\Re_{t-1}$ clustering. The resulting clustering, $\Re_t$, now contains $N - t$ clusters (note that $\Re_{t-1}$ contains $N - t + 1$ clusters). The algorithm continues until the $\Re_{N-1}$ clustering is produced, where all points belong to a single cluster. It returns the hierarchy of clusterings.

Remarks
- If two points come together in a single cluster at clustering $\Re_t$ (tth level of the clustering hierarchy), they will remain in the same cluster for all subsequent clusterings (i.e., for $\Re_{t+1}, \ldots, \Re_{N-1}$).
- The number of operations required by GAS is $O(N^3)$.

An important issue related to GAS is the definition of a measure of proximity between clusters. In the sequel, we discuss a recursive definition of the distance (denoted by $d(\cdot)$) between two clusters— specifically, the distance between any pair of clusters in the $\Re_t$ clustering is defined in terms of the distances between the pairs of clusters in $\Re_{t-1}$. This gives rise to some of the most widely used agglomerative hierarchical algorithms.

Let $d(x_i, x_j)$ denotes the distance between two data vectors. By definition, the distance between two single-element clusters is defined as the distance between their elements: $d(\{x_i\}, \{x_j\}) \equiv d(x_i, x_j)$. Consider two clusters C_q, C_s at the $\Re_t$ clustering, $t > 0$ (tth level of hierarchy):

- If both C_q and C_s are included in the $\Re_{t-1}$ clustering (level $t - 1$), their distance remains unaltered in $\Re_t$.
- If C_q is the result of the merging of the clusters C_i and C_j in the $\Re_{t-1}$ clustering, and C_s is another cluster different from C_i and C_j in $\Re_{t-1}$, then $d(C_q, C_s)$ is defined as

$$d(C_q, C_s) = a_i d(C_i, C_s) + a_j d(C_j, C_s) + b d(C_i, C_j) + c|d(C_i, C_s) - d(C_j, C_s)| \qquad (7.5)$$

Different choices of the parameters a_i, a_j, b, and c give rise to different distance measures between clusters and consequently lead to different clustering algorithms. Two of these follow.

7.7.2 Specific Agglomerative Clustering Algorithms

Single-link: It results from GAS if in Eq. (7.5) we set $a_i = a_j = 0.5$, $b = 0$, and $c = -0.5$. In this case Eq. (7.5) becomes

$$d(C_q, C_s) = \min\{d(C_i, C_s), d(C_j, C_s)\} \tag{7.6}$$

It turns out that Eq. (7.6) can also be written as

$$d(C_q, C_s) = \min_{x \in C_q, y \in C_s} d(x, y) \tag{7.7}$$

Complete-link: It results from GAS if in Eq. (7.5) we set $a_i = a_j = 0.5$, $b = 0$, and $c = 0.5$. In this case Eq. (7.5) becomes

$$d(C_q, C_s) = \max\{d(C_i, C_s), d(C_j, C_s)\} \tag{7.8}$$

It turns out that Eq. (7.8) can also be written as

$$d(C_q, C_s) = \max_{x \in C_q, y \in C_s} d(x, y) \tag{7.9}$$

Example 7.7.1. Consider the data set $X_{11} = \{x_1, x_2, x_3, x_4, x_5, x_6\}$ and let

$$D = \begin{bmatrix} 0 & 1 & 4 & 20 & 22 & 23 \\ 1 & 0 & 3 & 22 & 24 & 25 \\ 4 & 3 & 0 & 23 & 25 & 26 \\ 20 & 22 & 23 & 0 & 3.5 & 3.6 \\ 22 & 24 & 25 & 3.5 & 0 & 3.6 \\ 23 & 25 & 26 & 3.6 & 3.7 & 0 \end{bmatrix}$$

be the 6×6 matrix whose (i, j) element, d_{ij}, is the distance between the data vectors x_i and x_j (see Figure 7.11).
1. Apply, step by step, the single-link algorithm on X_{11}.
2. Repeat step 1 for the complete link algorithm.

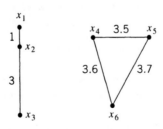

FIGURE 7.11

Data set considered in Example 7.7.1. The numbers (1, 3, 3.5, 3.6, 3.7) indicate respective distances. Large distance values are not shown.

Solution. Take the following steps:

Step 1. Single-link algorithm. Initially $\Re_0 = \{\{x_1\},\{x_2\},\{x_3\},\{x_4\},\{x_5\},\{x_6\}\}$ (level 0 of the clustering hierarchy). The two closest clusters in $\Re_0$ are $\{x_1\}$ and $\{x_2\}$, with $d(\{x_1\},\{x_2\}) = 1$. These are merged to form the next clustering, $\Re_1 = \{\{x_1,x_2\},\{x_3\},\{x_4\},\{x_5\},\{x_6\}\}$ (level 1). The closest clusters in $\Re_1$ are $\{x_1,x_2\}$ and $\{x_3\}$ since, taking into account Eq. (7.7), $d(\{x_1,x_2\},\{x_3\}) = \min(d(\{x_1\},\{x_3\}),d(\{x_2\},\{x_3\})) = 3$ is the minimum distance between any pair of clusters in $\Re_1$. Thus, $\Re_2 = \{\{x_1,x_2,x_3\},\{x_4\},\{x_5\},\{x_6\}\}$ (level 2).

The closest clusters in $\Re_2$ are $\{x_4\}$ and $\{x_5\}$ since $d(\{x_4\},\{x_5\}) = 3.5$ is the minimum distance between any pair of clusters in $\Re_2$. Thus, $\Re_3 = \{\{x_1,x_2,x_3\},\{x_4,x_5\},\{x_6\}\}$ (level 3). Similarly, the closest clusters in $\Re_3$ are $\{x_4,x_5\}$ and $\{x_6\}$, since $d(\{x_4,x_5\},\{x_6\}) = \min(d(\{x_4\},\{x_6\}),d(\{x_5\},\{x_6\})) = 3.6$ is the minimum distance among any pair of clusters in $\Re_3$, and so $\Re_4 = \{\{x_1,x_2,x_3\},\{x_4,x_5,x_6\}\}$ (level 4).

Finally, the two clusters in $\Re_4$ are joined to form the final clustering, $\Re_5 = \{\{x_1,x_2,x_3,x_4,x_5,x_6\}\}$ (level 5). Note that $d(\{x_1,x_2,x_3\},\{x_4,x_5,x_6\}) = \min_{i=1,2,3,j=4,5,6} d(x_i,x_j) = 20$.

Step 2. Complete-link algorithm. Initially $\Re_0 = \{\{x_1\},\{x_2\},\{x_3\},\{x_4\},\{x_5\},\{x_6\}\}$ (level 0 of the clustering hierarchy). The two closest clusters in $\Re_0$ are $\{x_1\}$ and $\{x_2\}$, with $d(\{x_1\},\{x_2\}) = 1$, which are merged to form the next clustering, $\Re_1 = \{\{x_1,x_2\},\{x_3\},\{x_4\},\{x_5\},\{x_6\}\}$ (level 1).

The closest clusters in $\Re_1$ are $\{x_4\}$ and $\{x_5\}$ since $d(\{x_4\},\{x_5\}) = 3.5$, which is the minimum distance among all cluster pairs in $\Re_1$ (according to Eq. (7.9), $d(\{x_1,x_2\},\{x_3\}) = \max(d(\{x_1\},\{x_3\}), d(\{x_2\},\{x_3\})) = 4$). Thus, $\Re_2 = \{\{x_1,x_2\},\{x_3\},\{x_4,x_5\},\{x_6\}\}$ (level 2).

The closest clusters in $\Re_2$ are $\{x_4,x_5\}$ and $\{x_6\}$ since $d(\{x_4,x_5\},\{x_6\}) = \max(d(\{x_4\},\{x_6\}), d(\{x_5\},\{x_6\})) = 3.7$ is the minimum distance between any pair of clusters in $\Re_2$. Thus, $\Re_3 = \{\{x_1,x_2\},\{x_3\},\{x_4,x_5,x_6\}\}$ (level 3). Similarly, the closest clusters in $\Re_3$ are $\{x_1,x_2\}$ and $\{x_3\}$ since $d(\{x_1,x_2\},\{x_3\}) = max(d(\{x_1\},\{x_3\}), d(\{x_2\},\{x_3\})) = 4$ is the minimum distance between any pair of clusters in $\Re_3$. Thus, $\Re_4 = \{\{x_1,x_2,x_3\},\{x_4,x_5,x_6\}\}$ (level 4).

Finally, the two clusters in $\Re_4$ are joined to form the final clustering, $\Re_5 = \{\{x_1,x_2,x_3,x_4,x_5,x_6\}\}$ (level 5). Note that $d(\{x_1,x_2,x_3\},\{x_4,x_5,x_6\}) = \max_{i=1,2,3,j=4,5,6} d(x_i,x_j) = 26$. ∎

Dendrograms

An issue that often arises with hierarchical clustering algorithms concerns visualization of the hierarchies formed. One tool often used is the so-called *proximity dendrogram* (more specifically, *the dissimilarity (similarity) dendrogram* if a dissimilarity (similarity) distance measure between clusters has been adopted). This has a tree structure like the one shown in Figure 7.12, which shows the dissimilarity dendrogram of the clustering hierarchy after applying the single-link algorithm to the data set X_{11}.

At level 0 of the hierarchy, each data vector forms a single cluster. At level 1, $\{x_1\}$ and $\{x_2\}$ are merged into a single cluster, forming the clustering $\Re_1$; this is illustrated by joining them with the junction shown in the figure, which corresponds to dissimilarity level 1. We say that *the clustering $\Re_1$ is formed at dissimilarity level* 1. At the second level of the hierarchy, the clusters $\{x_1,x_2\}$ and $\{x_3\}$ are merged and a junction at dissimilarity level 3 is inserted. Thus, clustering $\Re_2$ is formed at dissimilarity level 3.

Continuing in this spirit, we can see how the remaining part of the dendrogram is constructed. $\Re_0$, $\Re_1$, $\Re_2$, $\Re_3$, $\Re_4$, $\Re_5$ are created at dissimilarity levels 0, 1, 3, 3.5, 3.6, 20, respectively.

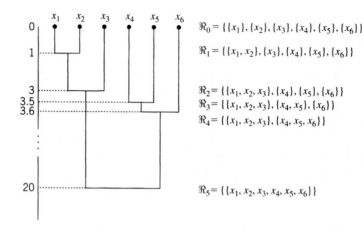

FIGURE 7.12

Dissimilarity dendrogram produced by the single-link algorithm when applied on data set X_{11} in Example 7.7.1.

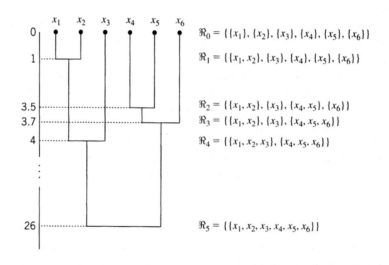

FIGURE 7.13

Dissimilarity dendrogram obtained by the complete-link algorithm when applied on data set X_{11} in Example 7.7.1.

Clearly, the proximity dendrogram is a useful tool in visualizing information concerning a clustering hierarchy. Its usefulness becomes more apparent in cases where the number of data points is large (Figure 7.13 shows the dissimilarity dendrogram formed by the complete link algorithm when applied on data set X_{11}).

To run the generalized agglomerative scheme (GAS), type

$$[bel, thres] = agglom(prox\_mat, code)$$

where

prox_mat is the $N \times N$ dissimilarity matrix for the N vectors of the data set X,

($prox\_mat(i,j)$ is the distance between vectors x_i and x_j),

code is an integer indicating the specific clustering algorithm to be used (1 stands for single link; 2 stands for complete link),

bel is an $N \times N$ matrix whose (i,j) element contains the cluster label for the jth vector in the ith clustering. (The first row of bel corresponds to the N-cluster clustering; the second row, to the $(N-1)$-cluster clustering; and the Nth row, to the single-cluster clustering),

thres is an N-dimensional vector containing the dissimilarity levels where each new clustering is formed.

Remarks

- The clusterings generated by the single-link algorithm are formed at lower dissimilarity levels, while those generated by the complete-link algorithm are formed at higher dissimilarity levels. This is due to the fact that the *min* and *max* operators are used to define their distance measures. All the other algorithms are compromises between these extreme cases.
- Algorithms such as *unweighted pair group method average* (UPGMA), *unweighted pair group method centroid* (UPGMC), *Ward*, or *minimum variance* all stem from Eq. (7.5) for different choices of parameters [Theo 09, Section 13.2.2].
- An important issue with hierarchical algorithms is that of *monotonicity*. We say that a hierarchy of clusterings generated by such algorithms exhibits the monotonicity property *if the dissimilarity level where the tth clustering of the hierarchy, $\Re_t$, is formed is greater than the dissimilarity levels of all clusterings formed at previous levels*. Monotonicity is a property of the clustering algorithm, not of the data set at hand. It can be shown that the single-link and complete-link algorithms exhibit the monotonicity property, while other agglomerative algorithms do not (e.g., UPGMC, described in [Theo 09, Section 13.2.2]).
- The single-link and complete-link algorithms, as well as a number of others, may be derived from a graph theory framework [Theo 09, Section 13.2.5].
- In cases where there are ties (i.e., more than one pair of clusters share the same minimum distance at the tth level of the clustering hierarchy), one pair is arbitrarily selected to be merged. This choice affects, in general, the clustering hierarchy formed by the complete-link and all other clustering algorithms that stem from Eq. (7.5) except the single-link algorithm.

7.7.3 Choosing the Best Clustering

When a clustering hierarchy is available, an important issue is the choice of the specific clustering that best represents the underlying clustering structure of the data set X. Several methods have been proposed for this. A simple one is to search the hierarchy for clusters that have a large *lifetime*. The lifetime of a cluster is defined as the absolute difference between the proximity level at which the cluster is formed and the proximity level at which it is absorbed into a larger cluster. In the dendrogram of Figure 7.12 for example, the clusters $\{x_1,x_2,x_3\}$ and $\{x_4,x_5,x_6\}$ have large lifetimes, which indicates that the clustering that best represents the corresponding data set is $\{\{x_1,x_2,x_3\},\{x_4,x_5,x_6\}\}$. Similar comments hold for the dendrogram in Figure 7.13.

Two other methods are proposed in [Bobe 93] and also discussed in [Theo 09]. In the sequel, we consider an extended version of one of them. According to this method, where the most representative clustering of X in the hierarchy contains clusters that exhibit "low dissimilarity" among its members. The "degree of dissimilarity" in a cluster C is measured in terms of the quantity

$$h(C) = max_{x,y \in C} d(x,y)^7$$

where $d(x,y)$ is the dissimilarity between the vectors x and y. In addition, a threshold of dissimilarity, θ, is employed. The criterion for choosing the clustering in the hierarchy that best describes the underlying clustering structure of X may be stated as

"Choose the $\Re_t$ clustering if there exists a cluster C in the $\Re_{t+1}$ clustering with $h(C) > \theta$."

The parameter θ may be defined as

$$\theta = \mu + \lambda\sigma$$

where μ and σ are the mean and the standard deviation of the dissimilarities between the data points of X and λ is a user-defined parameter. Clearly, the choice of λ is crucial. To avoid the risk of relying on a single value of λ, we may work as follows. Let λ scan a range of values and obtain, for each such value, the clustering $\Re_t$ that satisfies the previous criterion. Then, excluding the cases where $\Re_0$ and $\Re_{N-1}$ have been selected, compute the fraction of the number of times each clustering has been selected and, finally, consider the clustering selected most of the times as the likeliest to represent the data set under study.

However, note that, along with the most frequently selected clustering, the next few frequently selected clusterings may fit the data well (especially if they have been selected a significant number of times). After all, this is the main benefit of hierarchical clustering—it suggests more than one clustering that fit the data reasonably well. This may prove useful in providing a more complete "picture" of the clustering structure of X.

To apply the previously described technique, type

$$[lambda, cut\_point\_tot, hist\_cut] = dendrogram\_cut(bel, prox\_mat)$$

where

prox_mat and *bel* are defined as in the *agglom* function,

lambda is a vector of the values of the λ parameter, for which a clustering (other than $\Re_0$ and $\Re_N$) is obtained,

cut_point_tot is a vector containing the index of the selected clustering for a given value of λ,

---

[7]Other measures may be used.

hist_cut is a vector whose *t*th component contains the number of times the *t*th clustering has been selected (excluding 1-cluster and *N*-cluster clusterings).

This function also plots the corresponding histogram.

Example 7.7.2. Generate and plot the data set X_{12}, using the prescription followed in Example 7.5.1. Here each of the four clusters consists of 10 points. Then

1. Compute the matrix containing the (squared Euclidean) distances between any pair of vectors of X_{12} and a vector that accumulates the upper diagonal elements row-wise.
2. Apply the single-link and complete-link algorithms on X_{12} and draw the corresponding (dissimilarity) dendrograms.
3. Determine the clusterings that best fit the clustering structure of X_{12}. Comment on the results.

Solution. To generate the data set X_{12}, type

```
randn('seed',0)
m=[0 0; 10 0; 0 9; 9 8];
[n_clust,l]=size(m);
S(:,:,1)=eye(2);
S(:,:,2)=[1.0 .2; .2 1.5];
S(:,:,3)=[1.0 .4; .4 1.1];
S(:,:,4)=[.3 .2; .2 .5];
n_points=10*ones(1,4);
X12=[];
for i=1:n_clust
    X12=[X12; mvnrnd(m(i,:),S(:,:,i),n_points(i))];
end
X12=X12';
[l,N]=size(X12);
```

Plot X_{12} (see Figure 7.14(a)), typing

```
figure(3),plot(X12(1,:),X12(2,:),'.b')
```

Then proceed as follows.

Step 1. To compute the distance matrix for the data vectors of X_{12}, type

```
for i=1:N
    for j=i+1:N
        dista(i,j)=dist(X12(:,i),X12(:,j));
        dista(j,i)=dista(i,j);
    end
end
```

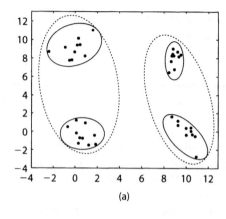

(a)

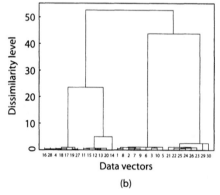

(b)

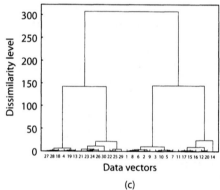

(c)

FIGURE 7.14

(a) The data set X_{12}, considered in Example 7.7.2. (b)–(c) The dissimilarity dendrograms obtained by the single-link and complete-link algorithms, respectively, when they are applied on X_{12}. The horizontal axis contains the labels of the data vectors.

To stack the computed distances to a data vector, type

```
dist_vec=[];
for i=1:N-1
    dist_vec=[dist_vec dista(i,i+1:N)];
end
```

Step 2. To apply the single link algorithm on X_{12} and draw the corresponding dissimilarity dendrogram (see Figure 7.14(b)), type

```
Z=linkage(dist_vec,'single');
[bel,thres]=agglom(dista,1);
figure(10), dendrogram(Z)
```

The function *linkage* is a built-in MATLAB function, which performs agglomerative clustering and returns its results to a different (more compact but less comprehensible) format, compared to the form adopted in the *agglom* function. In addition, the function *dendrogram* is also a built-in MATLAB function, which takes as input the output of the *linkage* and draws the corresponding dendrogram. Work similarly with the complete link, where now the second argument in the function *agglom* will be equal to 2 and the second argument of the function *linkage* will be equal to *'complete'* (see also Figure 7.14(c)).

Step 3. To determine the clusterings of the hierarchy generated by the single-link algorithm that best fit the underlying structure of X_{12}, type

```
[lambda,cut_point_tot,hist_cut] = dendrogram_cut(bel,dista);
```

This function forms a histogram with the frequency of selection of each cluster (see Figure 7.15(a)). Note that the first bar corresponds to the 2-cluster clustering case. The corresponding histogram for the complete-link algorithm is shown in Figure 7.15(b).

From Figures 7.14(b) and (c), it follows that the clusterings in the hierarchy generated by the complete-link algorithm are formed at higher dissimilarity levels compared to those of the clusterings generated by the single-link algorithm. Despite that and other minor differences, both dendrograms suggest that the 2-cluster and 4-cluster clusterings best fit the clustering structure of X_{12}. This is verified by the histograms in Figure 7.15 and is in line with our intuition (see Figure 7.14(a)). ■

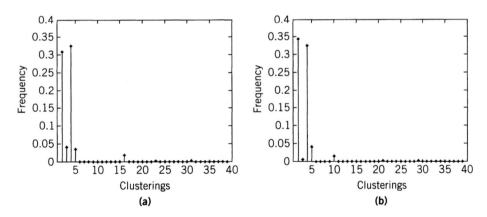

(a)   (b)

FIGURE 7.15

Choice of the clusterings that best fit the clustering structure of X_{12}. (a)–(b) The histograms showing the frequency selection of the clusterings of the hierarchy produced by the single-link and the complete-link algorithms, respectively, when they are applied on the data set X_{12} (the clusterings $\Re_0$ and $\Re_{N-1}$ have been excluded).

Exercise 7.7.1

Generate and plot the data set X_{13}, using the prescription followed in Example 7.6.1, here with the four clusters consisting of 30, 20, 10, and 51 points, respectively. Repeat Example 7.7.2 for X_{13}. Draw conclusions.

Note that the single- and complete-link algorithms can in principle detect clusters of various shapes provided that they are well separated.

Appendix

This appendix lists the functions (m-files) developed by the authors and used in the examples in this book. Functions used that are part of MATLAB's commercial distribution have been omitted; the reader is referred to the respective MATLAB manuals.

In the following list, functions are ordered alphabetically by chapter. For further function details, including descriptions of input and output arguments, refer to MATLAB's help utility. Also see the complete source code of the listed m-files, provided as part of the software on the companion website.

Chapter 1

bayes_classifier Bayesian classification rule for c classes, modeled by Gaussian distributions (also used in Chapter 2).

comp_gauss_dens_val Computes the value of a Gaussian distribution at a specific point (also used in Chapter 2).

compute_error Computes the error of a classifier based on a data set (also used in Chapter 4).

em_alg_function EM algorithm for estimating the parameters of a mixture of normal distributions, with diagonal covariance matrices.

EM_pdf_est EM estimation of the pdfs of c classes. It is assumed that the pdf of each class is a mixture of Gaussians and that the respective covariance matrices are diagonal.

euclidean_classifier Euclidean classifier for the case of c classes.

Gaussian_ML_estimate Maximum Likelihood parameters estimation of a multivariate Gaussian distribution.

generate_gauss_classes Generates a set of points that stem from c classes, given the corresponding a priori class probabilities and assuming that each class is modeled by a Gaussian distribution (also used in Chapter 2).

k_nn_classifier k-nearest neighbor classifier for c classes (also used in Chapter 4).

knn_density_estimate k-nn-based approximation of a pdf at a given point.

mahalanobis_classifier Mahalanobis classifier for c classes.

mixt_model Generates a set of data vectors that stem from a mixture of normal distributions (also used in Chapter 2).

mixt_value Computes the value of a pdf that is given as a mixture of normal distributions, at a given point.

mixture_Bayes Bayesian classification rule for c classes, whose pdf's are mixtures of normal distributions.

Parzen_gauss_kernel Parzen approximation of a pdf using a Gaussian kernel.

plot_data Plotting utility, capable of visualizing 2-dimensional data sets that consist of, at most, 7 classes.

Auxiliary functions gauss.

Chapter 2

base_clas_coord Implements a specific weak classifier.

*base_clas_coord*_out Computes the output of the weak classifier implemented by the base_clas_coord function.

boost_clas_coord Generation of a "strong" classifier, using the Adaboost algorithm, that utilizes weak classifiers generated by the base_clas_coord function.

boost_clas_coord_out Computes the output of a "strong" classifier B as a weighted sum of the outputs of the weak classifiers.

CalcKernel Computes the value of a kernel function between two points.

kernel_perce Implements the kernel perceptron algorithm.

NN_evaluation Returns the classification error of a neural network based on a data set.

NN_training Returns a trained multilayer perceptron.

perce Realizes the perceptron learning rule, in a batch mode.

perce_online Realizes the online perceptron learning rule.

plot_kernel_perce_reg Plots the decision boundary that is generated by the kernel perceptron algorithm.

plot_NN_reg Plots the decision boundary that is formed by a neural network.

SMO2 Generates a SVM classifier using either Platt's algorithm or one of its two modifications proposed by Keerthi.

SSErr Generates the linear classifier that optimizes the sum of error squares criterion.

svcplot_book Support Vector Machine plotting utility. It plots the decision regions, the decision surfaces and the margin obtained by a SVM classifier.

Chapter 3

cut_cylinder_3D Generates a cut cylinder in the 3-dimensional space.

im_point Performs the projection of a vector on the subspace spanned by the first m principal components, that result after performing kernel PCA on a data set.

K_fun Computes the value of a kernel function (polynomial or exponential) for two vectors.

kernel_PCA Performs kernel PCA based on a given set of data vectors.

lapl_eig Performs Laplacian eigenmap based on a given data set.

pca_fun Performs Principal Component Analysis (PCA) based on a data set.

plot_orig_trans_kPCA Plots, in different figures, (a) the data points and the classifier in the original (2-dimensional) data space and (b) the projections of the data points and the classifier in the space spanned by the two most significant principal components, as they are computed using the kernel PCA method.

scatter_mat Computes the within scatter matrix, the between scatter matrix and the mixture scatter matrix for a *c*-class classification problem, based on a given data set.

spiral_3D Creates a 3-dimensional Archimedes spiral.

svd_fun Performs Singular Value Decomposition (SVD) of a matrix.

Chapter 4

compositeFeaturesRanking Scalar feature ranking that takes into account the cross-correlation coefficient.

divergence Computes the divergence between two classes.

divergenceBhata Computes the Bhattacharyya distance between two classes.

exhaustiveSearch Exhaustive search for the best feature combination, depending on the adopted class separability measure.

Fisher Computes Fisher's discriminant ratio of a scalar feature in a 2-class problem.

normalizeMnmx Performs MinMax normalization in a given interval [*l r*].

normalizeSoftmax Performs Softmax normalization in the interval [0 1].

normalizeStd Performs data normalization to zero mean and standard deviation equal to 1.

plotData Plotting utility for class data.

plotHist Plots the histograms of two classes for the same feature.

ROC Plots the ROC curve and computes the area under the curve.

ScalarFeatureSelection Ranking Features are treated individually and are ranked according to the adopted class separability criterion.

ScatterMatrices Class separability measure, which is computed using the within-class and mixture scatter matrices.

SequentialBackward Selection Feature vector selection by means of the Sequential Backward Selection technique.

SequentialForward FloatingSelection Feature vector selection by means of the Sequential Forward Floating Selection technique.

SequentialForward Selection Feature vector selection by means of the Sequential Forward Selection technique.

simpleOutlierRemoval Removes outliers from a normally distributed data set by means of the thresholding method.

Chapter 5

BackTracking Performs backtracking on a matrix of node predecessors and returns the best path. This function is also used in Chapter 6.

DTWItakura Computes the Dynamic Time Warping cost between two feature sequences, based on the standard Itakura local constraints.

DTWItakuraEndp Similar to *DTWItakura*, with the addition that endpoints constraints are allowed in the test sequence.

DTWSakoe Computes the Dynamic Time Warping cost between two feature sequences, based on the Sakoe-Chiba local constraints.

DTWSakoeEndp Similar to *DTWSakoe*, with the addition that endpoints constraints are allowed in the test sequence.

editDistance Computes the Edit (Levenstein) distance between two sequences of characters.

Auxiliary functions stEnergy, stZeroCrossingRate, IsoDigitRec.

Chapter 6

BWDoHMMsc Computes the recognition probability of an HMM, given a sequence of discrete observations, by means of the scaled version of the Baum-Welch (any-path) method.

BWDoHMMst Same as *BWDoHMMSc*, except that no scaling is employed.

MultSeqTrainDoHMMBWsc Baum-Welch training (scaled version) of a Discrete Observation HMM, given multiple training sequences.

MultSeqTrain DoHMMVITsc Viterbi training (scaled version) of a Discrete Observation HMM, given multiple training sequences.

MultSeqTrainCoHMMBWsc Baum-Welch training (scaled version) of a Continuous Observation HMM, given multiple training sequences.

VitCoHMMsc Computes the scaled Viterbi score of an HMM, given a sequence of l-dimensional vectors of continuous observations, under the assumption that the pdf of each state is a Gaussian mixture.

VitCoHMMst Same as *VitCoHMMsc* except that no scaling is employed.

VitDoHMMsc Computes the scaled Viterbi score of a Discrete Observation HMM, given a sequence of observations.

VitDoHMMst Same as *VitDoHMMsc*, except that no scaling is employed.

Chapter 7

agglom Generalized Agglomerative Scheme (GAS) for data clustering. It runs, on demand, either the single-link or the complete-link algorithm.

BSAS Basic Sequential Algorithmic Scheme (BSAS algorithm) for data clustering.

CL_step Performs a step of the complete-link algorithm.

dendrogram_cut Determines the clusterings of a hierarchy that best fit the underlying clustering structure of the data set at hand.

fuzzy_c_means FCM algorithm for data clustering.

GMDAS Generalized Mixture Decomposition Algorithmic Scheme (GMDAS algorithm) for data clustering.

k_means k-means clustering algorithm.

k_medoids k-medoids clustering algorithm.

LLA Competitive leaky learning algorithm for data clustering.

possibi Possibilistic clustering algorithm, adopting the squared Euclidean distance.

SL_step Performs a step of the single-link algorithm.

spectral_Ncut2 Spectral clustering based on the normalized cut criterion.

valley_seeking Valley-seeking algorithm for data clustering.

Auxiliary functions cost_comput, distan, distant_init, rand_data_init, rand_init, reassign.

References

[Bobe 93] Boberg J., Salakoski T., "General formulation and evaluation of agglomerative clustering methods with metric and non-metric distances," *Pattern Recognition*, Vol. 26(9):1395–1406, 1993.

[Guat 98] Guattery S., Miller G.L., "On the quality of spectral separators," *SIAM Journal of Matrix Analysis and Applications*, Vol. 19(3):701–719, 1998.

[Keer 01] Keerthi S.S., Shevade S.K., Bhattacharyya C., Murthy K.R.K., "Improvements to Platt's SMO Algorithm for SVM Classifier Design," *Neural Computation*, Vol. 13(3):637–649, 2001.

[Luxb 07] Luxburg U., "A tutorial on Spectral Clustering," *Statistics and Computing*, Vol. 17(4): 395–416, 2007.

[Meas 08] Mease D., Wyner A. "Evidence contrary to the statistical view of boosting," *Journal of Machine Learning Research*, Vol. 9:131–156, 2008.

[Petr 06] Petrou M., Sevilla P.G., *Image Processing: Dealing with Texture*, John Wiley & Sons, 2006.

[Shi 00] Shi J., Malik J., "Normalized cuts and edge segmentation," *IEEE Transactions on Pattern Analysis and Machine Intelligence*, Vol. 22(8):888–905, 2000.

[Theo 09] Theodoridis S., Koutroumbas K. *Pattern Recognition*, 4th ed., Academic Press, 2009.

Index

Lightning Source UK Ltd.
Milton Keynes UK
UKOW03f0228130615

253385UK00023B/924/P

Community Ecology